Jesus and Pocahontas

Jesus and Pocahontas

Gospel, Mission, and National Myth

HOWARD A. SNYDER
Foreword by Randy Woodley

CASCADE *Books* • Eugene, Oregon

Cascade Books
An Imprint of Wipf and Stock Publishers
199 W. 8th Ave., Suite 3
Eugene, OR 97401

www.wipfandstock.com

ISBN 13: 978-1-4982-0288-6

Cataloguing-in-Publication Data

Snyder, Howard A.
    Jesus and Pocahontas : gospel, mission, and national myth / Howard A. Snyder.

    xx + 264 p. ; 23 cm. Includes bibliographical references and index.

    ISBN 13: 978-1-4982-0288-6

    1. Pocahontas, d. 1617. 2. Indians of North America—Missions—History. 3. Culture conflict—United States—History. I. Title.

E99.P85 S72 2015

Manufactured in the U.S.A.   05/13/2015

Unless otherwise indicated, all biblical quotations are from the New Revised Standard Version (NRSV).

Contents

Foreword

When Howard Snyder first asked me to look at the manuscript for this book, I must admit my initial reaction to the title was not exactly enthusiastic. To be completely honest, I have never taken Pocahontas's conversion seriously, thinking, like many people, that her conversion merely serves to support the myth of American imperial expansion and the assimilation of Native Americans into a society based upon white normalcy.

Then I started reading. I soon learned that there is room for an alternative view of this old American story, seen from a broader perspective, that takes the history of Jamestown and Pocahontas, Christian mission, and the American nationalistic myth into serious account. The view presented by Howard Snyder in *Jesus and Pocahontas: Gospel, Mission, and Myth* has never been told. It is fresh, scholarly, integrative, and deeply respectful to both early Jamestown and early American Indian accounts. Professor Snyder's telling is a fair and balanced view of an often mistold story.

In *Jesus and Pocahontas,* Howard Snyder presents us with a realistic look at the myth that Americans have built in order to support one particular ethnocentric American reality. As an indigenous scholar, I am always happy to read a more factual and balanced history than the ones that support the current American myth of presumed progress and civilization. In his research Snyder has revealed a much more complex story than commonly found in a simple Pilgrim versus Indian theme as popularized by past novels and Disney. The characters surrounding the Jamestown story are multilayered and complex, as are the rationales for their predictable, and sometimes surprisingly unpredictable, behaviors.

In this journey to discover Jamestown and the Powhatan Confederacy anew, the reader is exposed to real people, not caricatures who fit the story. In the book we find indigenous peoples who welcome the settlers and those indigene who are hostile to the newcomers. The story reveals Euro-Americans and whole groups of American settler Europeans whose loyalties, including the rationale for their actions, fall more closely aligned with the natives than their fellow Europeans. The story of Jamestown in *Jesus and Pocahontas* challenges us all to reexamine not only the myth itself, but to look at where the myth has taken us in terms of social, historical, theological, and missional concerns. After reading *Jesus and Pocahontas*, I believe much of the current thought of those wishing to follow the teachings of Christ, especially from a missional perspective, will need serious adjustment.

Despite the sparse record, Howard's insightful analysis of Pocahontas's conversion and her own Christian experience is fascinating, imaginative, and plausible. This insight alone makes the book worth the read but its uses go far beyond this one theme. In his own words, "Jamestown and the story of Pocahontas is a case study in how the gospel of Jesus Christ time and again gets twisted over the course of Christian history and missionary endeavor. The Pocahontas story casts a long shadow." Indeed, as an indigenous follower of Jesus I have felt the weight of that shadow. Snyder's retelling of the story seeks to reimagine another, Christ-honoring myth based upon what so many of us have missed in the actual story.

I do not pass out compliments lightly to non-Indian writers who deal with Native American history and culture. In such writings I have seen the worst of paternalism and superiority time and again. But happily, I am very impressed with Howard's work. I think he has a keen understanding of both the indigenous and European historical contexts, of mission, and of the nationalistic American myth. This book really speaks to the church and the nation, offering the possibility of a changed world view.

I feel honored that my esteemed former professor asked me to comment on this project. After reading this book I have not been disappointed in the least. I encourage you to give the Pocahontas story another read from Howard Snyder's perspective. I think you will agree, he has begun a new and important conversation; a conversation in which I wish to participate!

—Randy S. Woodley

Randy Woodley is a distinguished professor of faith and culture and director of indigenous and intercultural studies at George Fox University, Portland, Oregon. A Keetoowah Cherokee, he has ministered among First Nations people for over twenty-five years and is the cofounder of Eagle's Wings Ministry. His books include *Living in Color: Embracing God's Passion for Ethnic Diversity* and *Shalom and the Community of Creation: An Indigenous Vision*.

Personal Note

If you ever get the chance, visit historic Jamestown, Virginia. It's just a few miles from Colonial Williamsburg, and it takes you back to the earliest successful British colony in America, years before the Pilgrims.

Jamestown Island is a national historic site and a place of ongoing archeological research. Nearby is Jamestowne Settlement, a remarkable re-creation of the original settlers' experience, including full-size replicas of the three small ships, *Susan Constant, Godspeed,* and *Discovery,* that brought the first hundred adventurers to Virginia in 1607. The park includes a recreated Powhatan Indian village, a life-size replica of the original Jamestown fort, and an extensive museum explaining the history and prehistory of the Indians, the Africans, and the English who make up the origins of what we know today as the United States of America.

So plan to spend a whole day.

On the beautiful fall day my wife and I visited, workers at the original Jamestown site, on the island, were just finishing their day's work digging up the foundations of the 1608 chapel. Archeologists have discovered the outlines of the original 1607 stockade fort built to defend the colonists from the Indians.

Here also is the entreating bronze statue of Pocahontas, and on a high pedestal overlooking the broad James River a large statue of John Smith, mislabeled "Governor of Virginia 1608."

After seeing these, you can then take the free car ferry across the two-mile expanse of the James River. Look back and see the original Jamestown site, with its Smith statue, the tower of the remains of a later church building, and a tall obelisk commemorating the site, reminding one of the Washington Monument in the nation's capital.

Except for the buildings, you see Jamestown Island much as the British would have seen in from their ships in the spring of 1607.

On the sunny November day Jan and I crossed on the ferry, we chat-
ted at the rail with a journalist who covers the Jamestown area. A geologist
friend of his, he said, is studying the original Jamestown water supply. He's
discovered that the shallow shaft wells the colonists drilled were actually
drawing water mainly from the stagnant swamp on the north side of the
island, rather than good water from the river which flows by the south side.
This water was foul and probably accounted for a good many of the early
colonists' deaths.

The story told in the following pages begins in Jamestown but expands
to the world.

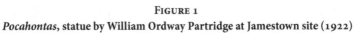

FIGURE 1
Pocahontas, **statue by William Ordway Partridge at Jamestown site (1922)**

Permissions

Permission to quote from Edward Wright Haile, ed., *Jamestown Narratives: Eyewitness Accounts of the Virginia Colony, The First Decade: 1607–1617* (Champlain, VA: RoundHouse, 1998) has generously been granted by RoundHouse.

Quotations from Robert S. Tilton, *Pocahontas: The Evolution of an American Narrative* (New York: Cambridge University Press, 1994) are reprinted with the permission of Cambridge University Press.

Quotations from the book *The Long Death* are reprinted with the permission of Scribner Publishing Group, a division of Simon & Schuster, Inc., from *The Long Death* by Ralph K. Andrist. Copyright © 1964 by Ralph K. Andrist. Copyright renewed © 1992 by Ralph K. Andrist. All rights reserved.

Excerpts from POCAHONTAS AND THE POWHATAN DILEMMA by Camilla Townsend. Copyright © 2004 by Camilla Townsend. Reprinted by permission of Farrar, Strauss and Giroux, LLC.

Fever
Words and Music by John Davenport and Eddie Cooley. Copyright (c) 1956 by Fort Knox Music Inc. and Trio Music Company. Copyright Renewed. All Rights for Trio Music Company Controlled and Administered by BUG Music, Inc., a BMG Chrysalis company. International Copyright Secured All Rights Reserved. Used by Permission. Reprinted by Permission of Hal Leonard Corporation.

Introduction

Nearly every American knows the story of Pocahontas. Yet in most versions Pocahontas's Christian baptism gets only a sentence, if that.

Pocahontas's conversion was probably the most important event in her short life. This book reveals things about that conversion—how she met Jesus—never previously reported. In so doing, it reveals a lot about gospel, culture, and the mythologies of nationhood—all contemporary issues.

This is a true story, and it's a love story. It is also a wrenching tragedy in ways still hard to grasp four centuries after Pocahontas's death. It involves intrigue, deception, sex, violence—but also faith, love, and mission.

Pocahontas was about ten when English colonists waded ashore in Tsenacomoco, now called Virginia, in 1607. Once they'd seen her, the early settlers never forgot her. They were fascinated by this precocious native child who in turn was just as curious about them. Seven years later she would marry one of them—John Rolfe—becoming the firstfruits of what English Christians hoped would be a great gospel harvest and the key to British control of North America.

But Pocahontas's story raises hosts of questions.

Was her conversion to the Christian faith *real*? Did she truly fall in love with Jesus?

Was Pocahontas actually an "Indian princess," as the British thought?

Were Pocahontas and John Rolfe truly in love?

How could it be that Pocahontas's husband triggered the great tobacco boom?

And what about famous Captain John Smith? Did he and Pocahontas really have "a very mad affair," as Peggy Lee sang in the 1950s hit "Fever"?[1]

---

1. See Price, *Love and Hate*, 5. Peggy Lee released the song in 1956. Pocahontas sings of Captain Smith: "He gives me fever with his kisses, fever when he holds me tight. . . ."

More importantly: what does all this have to do with gospel, mission, and nationhood today?

FACT OR FICTION

Pocahontas was born near the end of England's Elizabethan era. This remarkable period is well captured by historian Samuel Eliot Morison: "Under Elizabeth I (1558–1603), England embarked on a course of expansion, spiritual and material, such as few nations have ever experienced. It was the age of Sir Philip Sidney and Shakespeare, of Sir Humfrey Gilbert and Sir Walter Raleigh, of highest skill in matters maritime, and supreme achievements in poetry, prose, and music. In England during that happy era, the scholar, the divine, and the man of action were often one and the same." Although "every attempt at colonization in Elizabeth's reign failed," things were about to change dramatically.[2]

This also was the age of Pocahontas. Her story takes us quickly to the heart of the myth of America's romantic, benign, and pious beginnings. The true story shakes national foundations. It is also an instructive case study in evangelism, mission, and gospel encounters with culture.

In popular imagination, Pocahontas often gets lifted out of her real Jamestown home and merged into the Plymouth Rock story. Psychologically, Pocahontas blends into the pretty tableau of Pilgrims and Indians at the first Thanksgiving.[3] I remember grade school—strutting turkeys, orange pumpkins, dressed-up Pilgrims that we drew or made of construction paper.

Jamestown and Plymouth were both founded in the early 1600s. Commercial Jamestown embodied the American spirit just as much as did pious Plymouth. Together, these colonies capture the dynamics and contradictions of American culture and highlight perennial issues of church and mission.

The myth of Plymouth has to be corrected by the truth of Jamestown. The Jamestown story, the Pocahontas story, is a lot more complex than it first looks.

Here are the facts. Jamestown came first, then Plymouth. Investors in England and about a hundred "adventurers" founded Virginia's Jamestown colony in 1607. The Pilgrims, also numbering about a hundred, landed at

2. Morison, *Oxford History*, 43.
3. See McKenzie, *First Thanksgiving*.

Plymouth Rock in Massachusetts more than a decade later—in December of 1620. Captain John Smith had actually visited the site seven years earlier and named it Plymouth, after England's port city. He pronounced it "an excellent good harbour, good land, [with] no want of any thing but industrious people."[4]

Pocahontas was a real person—an American Indian with her own family and culture. She was born about 1596, professed Christian faith in 1614, and married John Rolfe soon afterwards (a second marriage for both). She was born about the time young Will Shakespeare was writing *Romeo and Juliet* and *A Midsummer Night's Dream*. Pocahontas died in 1617, within a year of Shakespeare's own death, and could have met him in England.

Dying young, Pocahontas left just one son. Yet today thousands of Americans claim the blood of Pocahontas runs warm in their veins. Pocahontas's son Thomas "left descendants now numbering in the thousands, such that the first and finest among the planter aristocracy, including some residents of the White House trace their line back to Pocahontas and thus to her famous father, Chief Powhatan, notes Edward Wright Haile.[5] As David Price puts it, Pocahontas would become "the ancestral mother of Virginia's elite," with such Virginia aristocrats in her family tree as John Randolph.[6] Thomas Jefferson, though not a descendant, was pleased that both his daughters married men who were.[7]

Pocahontas was an Indian of the Powhatan federation. I call her and her people "Indians" simply because this is the way the story has been told from the beginning. "Indians" is inaccurate, of course; these are Native Americans, or First Americans, or First Nations peoples—designations that are more culturally apt. But within the understanding of the time, the story is about settlers and Indians—as it still is in popular mythology and in most of the considerable literature and film about Pocahontas.[8]

---

4. Price, *Love and Hate*, 171.

5. Haile, ed., *Jamestown Narratives*, editorial comment, 794. Estimates of the number of Pocahontas's descendants in the US vary widely due (in some cases) to uncertain genealogies. Descendants number at least in the thousands; some sources put the number at over one hundred thousand. See Tilton, *Pocahontas*, 2; Brown et al., *Pocahontas' Descendants*. There is also a compact disc, "Pocahontas Descendant Genealogy Resource CD."

6. Price, *Love and Hate*, 242.

7. Tilton, *Pocahontas*, 11.

8. I have written or commented on Native Americans in some of my previous books: Snyder, *Populist Saints, Concept and Commitment, "Live While you Preach,"* and *Signs of the Spirit*.

But Pocahontas was not her real name. It was a childhood nickname. Her real name was secret and—as we shall see—important to her true identity. Much of the story covered here is in fact about the potency of names and naming.

Names, and sensitivity to them, are important. In 2013 a *Washington Post* editorial called on the Washington Redskins football team to change its name because it's "a racial slur of Native Americans so offensive that it should no longer be tolerated."[9] Since then a number of others have joined the call or raised questions about similar uses of Indian tribal names[10]— bringing to public attention what has long been a simmering issue.[11]

How did "Redskins" become the name of a professional football team based just a couple days' journey from the spot where Pocahontas was kidnapped by white men many years earlier? Why has no one objected till now?

WHY POCAHONTAS NOW

Four things prompt this fresh look at Pocahontas and her relationship with Jesus and with American national myths.

First, today we know much more about Pocahontas. New research has been done, new books written. Ironically, we know more about her than the Jamestown settlers did.

Second, culture's role in the Christian faith is an increasingly pressing issue. Culture is key in both the Pocahontas and Jesus stories. Of course "culture" means something quite different today than it did in the 1600s. Still, the Christian faith—all religious faith, in fact—is deeply rooted in culture.

Inevitably faith is in bed with culture. In this book we trace the roles culture played and then reflect on it more deeply in the last chapters.

Today the interplay between religion, culture, politics, and economics is increasingly obvious, globally and locally. For Christians, the culture question grows more pressing—not just in "foreign" missions, but "at home" as the church finds burgeoning cultural diversity all around. The

9. "*Washington Post* Demands Change."

10. Katzenstein, "Time to sideline Washington's race-based team name?"; Huetteman, "Lawmakers Press N.F.L. on Name of Redskins"; Huetteman, "Senator Urges Redskins Change."

11. King and Springwood, eds., *Team Spirits.*

Pocahontas story is one of the most instructive and well documented—yet neglected—case studies in Christianity and culture in all history. It is a case study in Christian missions. The 2010 book *Remembering Jamestown: Hard Questions about Christian Mission* recognized this, but said next to nothing about Jamestown.[12]

Pocahontas is especially instructive for North Americans (including Canadians) because her story is so deeply embedded in our cultural genes. This means the story has global import as well.

Third, the true story of Pocahontas and her relationship with Jesus turns out to be much more fascinating and prophetic than the popular myth. It has all the elements of a good tale—romance, mystery, subplots, faith; ignorance and arrogance; betrayal and murder; greed and cruelty; love and kindness; shattered hopes and heartbreaking disappointments; harrowing, improbable rescues; even cannibalism (by the British, not the natives).

Amazement at what was, and ache for what might have been.

Fourth, this is a story for now. The United States has never fully faced its violent origins. The conquest of native peoples and lands was neither a minor subplot nor a necessary evil. The Pocahontas story is a strategic conquest story. It initiated three hundred years of relentless "ethnic cleansing as the American Empire expanded westward," as Professor Dan Hawk of Ashland Theological Seminary recently wrote.[13] The conquest theme was sanitized as a mythic civilizing crusade, as we shall see. Hawk notes that "conquest narratives as narratives of origin *unify* and *identify*, and they do so through the rendering of oppositions."[14]

At the very beginning of the American narrative Pocahontas becomes the "indigenous helper" who is co-opted in the service of conquest and national myth. By purportedly saving John Smith and then marrying John Rolfe and adopting his faith, Pocahontas fulfills a key mythic function. "The popular account shapes the story to the contours of the Myth, so that Pocahontas occupies a place in American imagination, literature, and cinema second to no other Native American," notes Hawk.[15]

So there is much to learn here, and it comes in the form of a strange story that happens to be true.

12. Yong and Zikmund, eds., *Remembering Jamestown.*

13. Hawk, "Indigenous Helpers," 112.

14. Ibid.

15. Ibid., 121.

We focus especially on Pocahontas "the first Native Christian"—so the British claimed. In all the writing and myths about Pocahontas, no one seems to have asked: in what sense did Pocahontas become a true follower of Jesus Christ? What happened to her spiritually? How much did she understand of Jesus and the good news he offered and enacted?

Instead, what developed was the Pocahontas myth. Yet, as Camilla Townsend insists:

> Pocahontas . . . was a real person. She was not always a myth. Long before she became an icon, she was a child who walked and played beneath the towering trees of the Virginia woods, and then an adult woman who learned to love—and to hate—English men. Myths can lend meaning to our days, and they can inspire wonderful movies. They are also deadly to our understanding. They diminish the influence of facts, and a historical figure's ability to make us think; they diminish our ability to see with fresh eyes. What has the myth of Pocahontas kept hidden? And if the real woman could speak, what might she tell us about our country's inception?[16]

OVERVIEW

This book moves generally from narrative to analysis. First we introduce Pocahontas and her world. Next we see how Jamestown survived—but nearly didn't—then see the key role of John Smith, and learn whether Pocahontas really rescued him (Chapters 1–6).

We focus next on how Pocahontas met Jesus—the crux of the book. This is also the story of John Rolfe and Anglican missionary Alexander Whitaker. We explore the key role of the Church of England catechism in Pocahontas's conversion (Chapters 7–9).

We deal then with the tragedy of Pocahontas. This includes her fateful voyage to England, her life as a London celebrity, and her tragic death (Chapters 10–11).

Chapters 12 through 15 reflect on the meaning of the story and the questions of gospel, mission, and national mythmaking. We trace what became of the Pocahontas story in the four hundred years since her death, up to and including Disney and the dreamy 2006 movie *The New World*,

16. Townsend, *Pocahontas*, ix–x.

starring young Q'orianka Kilcher as Pocahontas. Gazing at the many faces and uses of Pocahontas we may want to ask, "Did Pocahontas die for our sins?"

Chapter 16 summarizes the "long, bitter trail" from Pocahontas's time to our own, identifying recurring patterns.

Finally, we glimpse Pocahontas in heaven; hear her speak. This leads to a discussion of the "so what" questions—the urgencies that are still with us (Chapters 17–20).

The book thus becomes a case study in mission practice and theory, interlaced with dynamics of culture and national mythology, with this added plus: unlike mission studies that deal with today's events, in this case *we know the rest of the story.* We know much about what the early settlers thought and said and how things turned out.

With one big exception. We know almost nothing of what Pocahontas herself actually thought. We have nothing written from her own hand (true also of Jesus) and very few records of conversations. We wish we knew what was going on in Pocahontas's mind and emotions!

But we do find some intriguing clues and some clear hints.

Here then is the real Pocahontas story you won't find anywhere else.

Rayna Green, curator of the American Indian Program for the National Museum of American History at the Smithsonian Institution in Washington, DC, wrote in 1975: "Perhaps if we explore the meaning of Native American lives outside the boundaries of the stories, songs, and pictures given us in tradition, we will find a more humane truth."[17]

---

17. Green, R., "Pocahontas Perplex," 715.

Chapter One

Little Princess Pocahontas?

Pocahontas met Jesus sometime in 1613. She was seventeen.

Pocahontas may have heard about Jesus occasionally from the Jamestown settlers, for as a child she often visited the colony.

The big problem, of course, is that Pocahontas did not meet Jesus *alone*. It wasn't an encounter like Jesus' talk with the Samaritan woman at the well (John 4).

When Pocahontas met Jesus, he was surrounded by hosts: British colonists and clergy; imported British culture; British ships and guns; and above all, the British church-state arrangement. To be British meant to be Christian, and to be *really* Christian meant to be British.

When Pocahontas met Jesus, she was a captive hostage.

Yet Pocahontas became a Christian, a convert, and this changed history.

Pocahontas understood that her conversion to Christianity and her marriage to John Rolfe was a package deal. We don't know fully what was on her mind, but we find some hints.

Current Pocahontas stories largely ignore her conversion. If they mention it at all they treat it cynically or as a minor incident, or deplore it as British cultural imposition. Here we try to understand her faith on its own terms—as much as possible the way Pocahontas herself (and her Indian and English compatriots) did.

Pocahontas lived in Tsenacomoco, meaning "densely inhabited land." The English called it Virginia. In the early 1600s this beautiful, bountiful land was soon caught up in the vast European project of colonization, as Central and South America had been earlier. The French founded Quebec City in 1608. The Spanish had already established St. Augustine, Florida, in 1565.

Even as early as the time of Christopher Columbus, however, England was thinking about far-off colonies. In 1496 King Henry VII granted Letters Patent to the Italian explorer John Cabot (Giovanni Caboto) to sail across the Atlantic and "conquer, occupy, and possess" for England any lands he found that were "unknown to Christians" and to spread Christianity among the natives. Cabot did in fact reach North America in 1497 (an area that is now the eastern coast of Canada) and successfully returned, though no colony was established.[1]

The first British settlement in the New World to survive would be Jamestown, founded 110 years after Cabot's voyage.

Our story begins in 1596, about ten years before Jamestown, the probable year of Pocahontas's birth.

REAL INDIAN PRINCESS?

Pocahontas was indeed a chief's daughter and a favored child. Her father was Wahunsenacawh (spelled various ways by the English), better known as Chief Powhatan. Much more than a local chieftain, Powhatan was the *mamanatowick* or paramount chief of the large Algonquian-speaking Powhatan Nation of 20 or so tribes stretching inland from the Chesapeake Bay for about 150 miles.

Powhatan himself was born in the Indian town of Powhatan, about seventy miles inland along the James (or Powhatan) River, near present-day Richmond. He had inherited the overall chieftainship of six tribes (the Powhatan, Arrohateck, Appamattuck, Pamunkey, Mattaponi, and Youghtanund). Subsequently "through peaceful alliance and intermarriage, as well as war and the forced resettlement of survivors, he had brought other tribes into submission," as Camilla Townsend notes. Previously merely "the Powhatan tribe's chief, he now took the political name 'Powhatan' as his own, giving it as well to all the tribes who were tributary to him."[2]

1. Little, *Story of Bristol*, 22–23.
2. Townsend, *Pocahontas*, 12, 13. Cf. Rountree, *Pocahontas*, 28, 39 (spellings as given

Pocahontas herself, the high chief's daughter, was born about ten years before English settlers came ashore at the small river island they named Jamestown. The man in charge was Captain Christopher Newport, but the settlers included Captain John Smith, destined to play a key role in the Virginia saga.[3]

Pocahontas was probably born at or near Werowocomoco, her childhood town. Like all Powhatan Indian children, she was given two names. In a village ceremony she was named Amonute, but she also had a secret name, later to be revealed as Matoaka. But she soon won the nickname Pocahontas, "Little Mischief."[4]

All eyewitness accounts agree that Pocahontas was naturally high-spirited and precocious—the nickname Pocahontas suggests as much. Some of the English translated "Pocahontas" as "Little Wanton," meaning "unruly" or "free of restraint." She was a bird flitting here and there, delighting those around her, like little Pippa in Robert Browning's *Pippa Passes.*[5]

Chief Powhatan had many wives and children, but this lively girl "got and kept his attention . . . by sheer force of personality," as Helen Rountree puts it. "Children could get lost" in a major chief's large extended family, "unless a child had the personality of a Pocahontas."[6] Rountree adds, "She was trying to get her busy father's attention, amidst a welter of stepmothers and half siblings, and her father was a formidable man that 'at the least frown their greatest will tremble.' So she became a court jester, making him laugh in spite of himself, and at himself, until he protested that she was a cruel, bawdy, undisciplined little girl. The teasing nickname he gave her stuck. It would be wonderful to know what names she had been calling him."[7]

---

in Rountree). Rountree notes that Powhatan "inherited six district chiefdoms, each with its weroance who ruled over a lesser weroance in each satellite town; any or all of these people could have been cousins of his" (*Pocahontas*, 39). Townsend, *Pocahontas*: "the noble families of most of the chieftainships were related by marriage" (12).

3. As noted elsewhere, Pocahontas's exact birth year is unknown, but most sources place it around 1596. See Custalow and Daniel, *True Story,* 11. This matches John Smith's assertion that Pocahontas was "a child of ten years old" when she was sent by Powhatan, with an escort, to request the release of some Indian captives in Jamestown's early days (Haile, *Jamestown Narratives,* 181).

4. Rountree, *Pocahontas,* 37–38, 166–67; Townsend, *Pocahontas,* 13–14.

5. As the chief's daughter she would however have been well supervised, note Custalow and Daniel (*True Story,* 9).

6. Rountree, *Pocahontas,* 25, 35.

7. Ibid., 38. The quote within the quotation is from Strachey, "History of Travel," 617.

Most of Chief Powhatan's many wives and children were the fruit of political arrangements—a key means of consolidating his large Indian federation. In this sense Pocahontas was not as special as the English thought. It would be no surprise however if Powhatan's favorite daughter at any one time would be his youngest—especially if she had the butterfly personality of a Pocahontas.

Of Pocahontas's mother little is known. She appears to have been from a neighboring tribe that Powhatan had perhaps conquered. Her marriage to Powhatan would have been mainly political. She would have had little social status beyond being one of the paramount chief's many wives. In her own tribe she had significant social status, perhaps a chief's daughter.

Englishmen who visited Powhatan reported that he usually had about a dozen wives around him. Townsend notes, "For his political purposes, Powhatan needed many children by many different women."[8] Multiple wives were also important as providers of hospitality, since "a leader or chief was expected to provide for everyone, especially guests and dignitaries."[9]

After giving birth, a wife usually returned with the baby to her native town. The child would later come to take his or her place in the king's household. In order to "ensure their loyalty to their father and his people," Townsend writes, his children "had to be raised with him. So after a child was weaned and no longer in need of constant care, at about the age of four or five, it came back to live with Powhatan's family"—common practice among many Native American peoples.[10]

This was Pocahontas's experience. She probably lived with her mother in her native village until she was around six, then became part of Powhatan's large extended family at Werowocomoco.

Pocahontas thus "lived in the heartland of her father's chieftainship, surrounded by his personal army of at least forty warriors."[11] She would have slept in a typical Powhatan house made of reed mats stretched over oval arches made of saplings. Some of the English described these dwellings as being in the shape of a bread loaf, or an oven.[12]

---

8. Townsend, *Pocahontas*, 16.

9. Randy Woodley, email to author, January 30, 2014.

10. Townsend, *Pocahontas*, 16.

11. Ibid., 12.

12. Such houses have been recreated at the historic Jamestown Settlement near the original Jamestown site.

LITTLE MISS MISCHIEF

Like other Indian children, in warm weather Pocahontas would have run around naked. At puberty she would have worn a deerskin apron in her town but donned a breechclout and leggings when going into the woods in order to protect the skin. Women and men dressed the same, for both worked to sustain the village.[13]

Although called "Mischief" or "Little Playful One," Pocahontas had work to do as part of the chief's household. She helped plant corn, gather wild fruits and nuts, and tend fires. "Every morning the women divided into groups and set out on their self-appointed tasks."[14] Much time was spent planting, tending, and later harvesting beans, squash, corn, and various fruits grown in small garden patches. The Powhatan tribes had developed a kind of ecologically balanced organic farming, "intermingling the seeds [of various crops] so that the different species provided one another with what they needed—shade, varied nutrients, or trellises for climbing vines"[15]—the kind of thing being rediscovered today.

Nursing mothers took their babies with them to the fields, hanging their cradleboards on nearby tree branches while working, but stopping to tend the little ones as needed.[16]

Work varied by the season. Sometimes it involved gathering a kind of poisonous wild tuber (Tuckahoe) while paddling along the river in dugout canoes or wading knee-deep along the shore. The Indians had learned how to safely process these tubers and turn them into flour for bread. Work could also mean cooking meals or making mats for sitting or sleeping or decorating or insulating the walls of houses. Or work might mean tanning the skins of animals killed by the men on their hunting forays.[17]

This was Pocahontas's life for her first dozen years. When winter came, Pocahontas and the other girls and women would have "put on their fur mantles and stayed in the village, weaving baskets and mats, tanning and softening hides, sewing and embroidering."[18]

13. Rountree, *Pocahontas,* 36–37.

14. Townsend, *Pocahontas,* 17.

15. Ibid.

16. Cf. ibid., 18.

17. Ibid., 19.

18. Ibid., 24.

Growing up in an Indian village was itself an education. "There were eleven hundred edible species in the area, and Pocahontas was expected to learn them all from the older women," Townsend notes.[19]

With darkness came dancing, singing, and storytelling. "If it was only an ordinary evening," Townsend writes, "Pocahontas might have sat in the flickering light of the torches and the central fire, hands busy twisting silk grass fibers into cordage," a task common to the young girls. "At her age Pocahontas listened to the older people tell stories" but never interrupted or asked questions. She could ask the older women later.[20]

About the time Pocahontas came to live in Powhatan's household, a younger favored wife of Powhatan, Winganuske, gave birth to a daughter who in time herself became "a great darling of the king's."[21] Several years later, around the time of Pocahontas's marriage, Governor Thomas Dale took special interest in this younger version of Pocahontas; Dale arrived in Jamestown in 1611 and became Virginia colony's autocratic ruler.[22]

The Powhatan were matrilineal: "Men ruled, unless there was no male heir, but power passed through women. A chief was succeeded not by his son but by his younger brothers (his mother's other sons) and after them, in the next generation, by his sister's sons."[23] Because of this, Pocahontas was not really a "princess" in the European sense—don't think Princess Bride or Sleeping Beauty.

This native system had several advantages over the British system. It meant that girl children were as valued as boys—in some ways, even more so. It also meant, as Townsend notes, that "whole clans of brothers and sisters had an obvious shared interest in remaining united and maintaining their family's power."[24]

Chief Powhatan used the matrilineal system to expand his empire. By strategically marrying a woman from another tribe he effectively co-opted that tribe's matrilineal line and consolidated his expanding rule. "The Indians never explained this [matrilineal system] to the English, at least not in such a way that they could understand," notes Townsend.[25]

19. Ibid., 18.
20. Ibid., 20.
21. Strachey, "History," 620.
22. See chapter 9.
23. Townsend, *Pocahontas*, 15.
24. Ibid., 15.
25. Ibid.

What was Pocahontas's social status, then, as a young Indian woman? From the perspective of English society, Pocahontas was, in effect, royalty. Her social position was actually much higher than that of Captain John Smith, who played a crucial role in Pocahontas's life. Smith's parents were simple farmers, "putting him just one rung above peasanthood. Soldiering was to be his ticket out."[26] But in British eyes Pocahontas was a child of the king.

This was Pocahontas—lively, bright, mischievous, resourceful. We know little about her mother, but Pocahontas seems to have inherited her father's intelligence and wiliness. So we need to understand more about Chief Powhatan and the Powhatan people.

26. Price, *Love and Hate*, 5.

Chapter Two

Her Daddy's Empire

Pocahontas wasn't just a poor little Indian moppet from a primitive native village, as the English at first saw her. Her home was the heart of an empire. Her father, Chief Powhatan, headed a large Indian federation. And Chief Powhatan was not happy to have the English (or earlier, the Spanish) come to give him competition.

The Powhatan empire, with a combined population estimated at 13,000 to 34,000, was more than a loose association of tribes. It was a regional domain under Chief Powhatan's headship, as we have seen.

Powhatan's domain was quite different, however, than the complex Iroquois Confederation that some have plausibly argued influenced American revolutionaries as they were looking for models in designing the US government.[1] In his *Notes on the State of Virginia,* published in 1787, Thomas Jefferson commented on the Powhatan Indians and on Chief Powhatan. Among the Indians, he wrote, matters "such as making war, concluding peace, or forming alliances with the neighbouring nations, are deliberated on and determined in a national council of the chiefs" and their warrior counselors, and "as their government seems to rest wholly on persuasion," they endeavour, by mutual concessions, to obtain unanimity."[2] Yet the Powhatan were themselves newcomers to the area—or had been, three

1. Price, *Love and Hate,* 251; Weatherford, *Indian Givers,* 133–50.

2. Jefferson, *Notes on the State of Virginia,* 203. See 92–107, 202–8 and many other references.

centuries earlier. They apparently were part of a larger Algonquin migration south from the St. Lawrence-Great Lakes area. As historian Philip Barbour put it, these northern tribes (in a pattern familiar to history the world over) probably "found other tribes in possession which they pushed back toward the hills; for they established an outpost on the James River, just below the site of modern Richmond, to act as a fort to protect their other villages toward the sea from hostile non-Algonkian tribes to the west." This fort became the Indian town of Powhatan, where Wahunsenacawh (or Wahunsonacock, or Wahunsenaca[3])—later himself known as Powhatan—was born around 1545.[4] Unknowingly, the British landed in the very heart of Powhatan's federation!

As all the early English accounts noted, "Powhatan's 'empire' had been a recent development and was, to some extent, still forming," writes Rountree.[5] The chief "had fought many wars to make himself the paramount chief, the *mamanatowick*, with power over about thirty subordinate chiefdoms and perhaps twenty thousand people."[6] An astute leader, Powhatan may have built his "empire" partly as a defensive move against the Europeans (Spanish, French, English) who were beginning to probe the North Atlantic coast. But the Powhatans also had to deal with enemy tribes around them, such as the Susquehannocks and the Monacans, who spoke languages foreign to them.[7]

At the time of the Jamestown settlement, Powhatan's base was the town of Werowocomoco ("King's House"), near the mouth of the York (or Pamunkey) River. This was about twenty miles north of Jamestown. Here Chief Powhatan had an impressive eighty-foot longhouse on a rise in the town.[8]

3. Custalow and Daniel, *True Story*, 5, 113. Chief Powhatan in fact had many names. The English knew him principally as Chief Powhatan.

4. Barbour, *Pocahontas*, 1–2.

5. Rountree, *Powhatan Indians*, 140.

6. Townsend, *Pocahontas*, 12.

7. Rountree, *Pocahontas*, 38–39; Townsend, *Pocahontas*, 13; Bailyn, *Barbarous Years*, 19–27. "Tribes or towns who were enemies, or at war at the time, had simply not settled on a peace agreement. Usually these would take several years and lots of negotiations took place, especially concerning free trade and economic issues" (Randy Woodley, email to author, January 30, 2014).

8. Price, *Love and Hate*, 47; Townsend, *Pocahontas*, 4; Haile, ed., *Jamestown Narratives*, 53, 207. Only in recent years has the town's site been definitely identified.

The name "Powhatan" thus meant three things. It referred to the large federation of Indian tribes in the area, to Chief Powhatan's birth town, and to the paramount chief himself.

By extension, "Powhatan" referred also to the river which the English named the James —one of the four major rivers that empty into Chesapeake Bay. The Indians called these (north to south) the Patawomeck (Potomac), the Rappahannock (name retained by the English), the Pamunkey (York), and the Powhatan (James). Both Jamestown and Werowocomoco were located just upriver from the mouth of Chesapeake Bay.

Chief Powhatan was already a mature, experienced political leader when the English arrived. He was a little past fifty when Pocahontas was born. He would live to about seventy-three, apparently surviving Pocahontas herself by only a few months.

Chief Powhatan was paramount ruler by the early 1600s, but he was no absolute monarch. "He was a brilliant strategist forging a new political unity out of groups that had lived separately for centuries," notes Townsend. "Those on the outskirts of his territory had least reason to fear his wrath and do his bidding. Even the Chickahominy [Indians], though surrounded by his followers, managed as a particularly large group to avoid having him name their werowances [chiefs]—though they made periodic tribute payments to help keep the peace."[9]

It took the English quite a while to figure out the intricacies of the various Indian groups and how they were related. "What the English did not realize" at first, notes David Price, "was that they were facing a tightly run, martially adept empire. Only gradually, over some months, would they come to understand the reach of Chief Powhatan's power."[10]

THE ENGLISH THREAT

Powhatan immediately saw the English as a threat. Wily and always wary, he devoted a good deal of attention to strategic intelligence gathering. He needed to know what the English were capable of and what they were up to.

The English invaders probed the mouth of Chesapeake Bay and soon came ashore on a low island in the James River (as they called it). They named their settlement Jamestown, after their king. The land actually belonged to the Paspahegh Indians, not the Powhatan, but most of the native

9. Townsend, *Pocahontas*, 14.

10. Price, *Love and Hate*, 40.

towns in the area were subject to Chief Powhatan. From the Paspahegh, Powhatan soon learned about the new arrivals.

The place where the British settled was technically a peninsula, but its neck of land was so narrow that it was virtually an island. Though it was currently uninhabited, the Paspahegh saw the land as part of their territory, their hunting ground.

The British went ashore at Jamestown on May 14, 1607. They quickly made a sort of barricade of tree limbs and began their settlement. Only later would they discover that as the summer wore on "a swamp would emerge that bred disease-bearing mosquitoes, and the water supply would turn brackish."[11]

THE ENGLISH SETTLEMENT AT JAMESTOWN

Jamestown lies about thirty miles upriver from where the James River empties into the mouth of Chesapeake Bay. The colonists—men and boys, no women—started going ashore at Jamestown a couple of weeks after their three ships, the *Susan Constant,* the *Godspeed,* and the *Discovery,* arrived at Chesapeake Bay.[12] The ships were under the overall command of Captain Christopher Newport (for whom Newport News, Virginia, at the mouth of the James River, would be named). Newport (1561–1618) was a weathered veteran of Atlantic crossings; earlier he had lost his right arm as a privateer in the West Indies.[13]

These were ships of the Virginia Company of London. The expedition was not an official project of the British crown. Though chartered by King James I, the Virginia Company of London was a for-profit venture, funded by what today are called venture capitalists. They hoped to make money on a high-risk investment. It was from the beginning an iffy business, and the company struggled to find enough investors.[14]

---

11. Ibid., 38; quotation from Townsend, *Pocahontas,* 48.

12. At 120 tons, the *Susan Constant* was the largest ship and carried 71 colonists. It returned to England within weeks of arriving in Virginia. The *Godspeed,* commanded by Captain Bartholomew Gosnold, carried 39 colonists, plus 13 sailors. The *Discovery,* at 20 tons, was the smallest; it was commanded by Captain John Ratcliffe. See Price, *Love and Hate,* 17–18. Full-size re-creations of these ships may be seen and boarded at the Historic Jamestown Settlement.

13. Price, *Love and Hate,* 18.

14. Vaughan, *American Genesis,* 98.

There were two kinds of investors, or "adventurers"—those who ventured their funds, and those many without funds who as settlers ventured their lives. The latter were at much greater risk. "God willing, theirs would be the first English colony to survive in the Americas. If it did, all the unsuccessful earlier efforts would be vindicated. And [the investors] would be rich," notes Townsend.[15]

The English of course knew from earlier European explorations that North America was already inhabited. They vastly underestimated the numbers of native Indians, however. Forested, with many rivers and streams, the land looked mostly empty and inviting.

In fact there had been a massive die-off of native populations in the Americas after the first European explorers unwittingly introduced smallpox, typhus, influenza, diphtheria, and other highly communicable diseases. Epidemics spread through native populations, racing on ahead of the Europeans, wiping out up to ninety percent of defenseless tribes. When European settlers later arrived they often found largely depopulated areas, sometimes even abandoned native cities.[16]

Fatal disease spread west with the expanding frontier—a deadly, slow-moving scourge that gradually crossed one tribal boundary after another. For example, in the 1780s a smallpox epidemic hit the Mandan people along the upper reaches of the Missouri River in what is now North Dakota. A second smallpox epidemic in the spring of 1837 wiped out most of the remaining Mandans and quickly spread to the Hidatsa, Assiniboin, Arikara, and other tribes. Worst hit, the Missouri River Mandans were reduced from about 1600 in 1834 to 130 three years later.[17]

"The great Mandan chief Four Bears," writes Russell Freedman, "watched in horror as his people wasted away and perished. He saw his wives and children suffer and die." Blaming the whites, Four Bears tried to mount an attack on nearby Fort Clark—but he couldn't find enough healthy warriors to gather a war party.[18]

In 1491, probably a million or more people lived in the Americas—more than in Europe. One careful study calculated that "in the first 130 years of contact about 95 percent of the people in the Americas died." The

15. Townsend, *Pocahontas*, 29.

16. Mann, *1491*, especially 100–104.

17. Freedman, *Indian Winter*, 73.

18. Ibid., 75.

Canadian geographer W. George Lovell called it "the greatest destruction of lives in human history."[19]

This massive die-off was part of a much larger story of ecology and ecological invasion which social historian Alfred W. Crosby calls the Columbian Exchange. In a pattern that has recurred throughout history, newcomers introduce diseases as well as plants and animals against which the invaded ecology has no natural defenses.[20]

The Jamestown settlers did not know this, of course. They soon found, however, that they had landed in a hornet's nest of several native tribes.

King James told the Virginia Company to treat the American "savages" civilly and charitably so as to draw them "to the true knowledge of God, and obedience to us."[21] (The mind-set and world view of the English adventurers is nicely captured here in one sentence.)

As officer in charge, Captain Christopher Newport had a specific mission: to ferry the settlers safely to Virginia, set up a colony, and return to London. There he would report on his efforts and organize more expeditions to reinforce the initial venture.

Before returning to England, Newport sailed further up the James River on a sort of reconnaissance mission. He hoped to find the source of the river—maybe a large lake, or even a rumored passage to the Pacific. This produced the first significant English contact with the native population. As Haile comments, "Here east and west are at a first encounter. The sides are wary but friendly."[22]

About noon on Thursday, May 21, 1607, Newport and a crew of twenty-three set off by boat from Jamestown. Expecting shallow waters, they used a *shallop*, a two-masted, shallow-bottomed barge, designed for river navigation and built by Newport's crew with lumber brought from England.

Newport and his men were impressed by the deep forests and the abundant wildlife, including "many turkeys."

Twenty miles upriver the English came upon a native village. They went ashore to establish contact. Captain Gabriel Archer, one of Newport's crew and its chronicler, reported that the Indians "entertained us with

19. Mann, *1491*, 101–3.

20. Crosby, *Columbian Exchange*; Crosby, *Ecological Imperialism*.

21. Quoted in Townsend, *Pocahontas*, 39 (English modernized).

22. Haile, ed., *Jamestown Narratives*, 101.

dances and much rejoicing."[23] The English discovered that these Indians were not Powhatan, and in fact viewed the Powhatan as enemies.

After spending the night on the shallop, Newport and his men continued further upriver. They encountered a large dugout canoe manned by eight Indians, or "savages" as the English called them. One of the English crew knew the Powhatan word *wingapoh*, meaning "good man," and the English called out to the natives and got them to paddle over to the shallop.

Using sign language, the English asked the Indians about the course of the river. Perhaps thinking these strangers were lost, one of the Indians began tracing out the river's course with his foot. Gabriel Archer gave the man paper and pen, showing how to use it, and the Indian "laid out the whole river from the [Chesapeake] Bay to the end of it, so far as passage was for boats"—that is, to the falls, much further upriver.[24]

Newport and his party eventually reached the falls of the James River at present-day Richmond. They were indeed impassable. The English explored the area for a few days, encountering more groups of Indians, and then returned to Jamestown on May 27, a week after departing.[25]

The English actually discovered several Indian towns up and down the river, both Powhatan and non-Powhatan. The explorers were treated courteously and sometimes entertained as honored guests. The natives were eager to trade, which seemed a good omen for the brand-new Jamestown settlement.[26] John Smith however, who was with the party, thought he sensed animosity among some of the Indians.[27]

JAMESTOWN ATTACKED

Arriving back in Jamestown, Newport was shocked to discover that a large Indian force had attacked the new settlement in his absence. (English

23. Archer, "A relation," 103. Archer and a few others wrote accounts of this important initial exploration.

24. Ibid., 103.

25. The English had in fact arrived at the eastern North American fall line, "the place where the hard rocks of the Appalachian Mountains give way to the plains" that slope gently to the Atlantic. The fall line cuts vertically through all the area's eastern-flowing rivers and thus prevented explorers from finding the fabled waterway to the Pacific. Numerous cities were later built along rivers at the fall line: Richmond, Baltimore, Philadelphia, and Washington, DC (Winchester, *Men Who United*, 169–70).

26. Archer, "A relation," 103–15.

27. Price, *Love and Hate*, 42.

estimates varied; John Smith says 400 Indians, while Gabriel Archer says two hundred.) The Indians attacked as the unsuspecting settlers were planting corn, their guns still packed away in crates.

The Indians "gave a very furious assault," Archer wrote. They "came up almost into the fort [and] shot through the tents" with their arrows before being driven back by guns from the nearby ships. Eleven English were injured. One man and a boy died, and an undetermined number of Indians were killed. The skirmish "endured hot about an hour," Archer said. He commented that the Indians in battle proved themselves to be "a very valiant people."[28]

Clearly this was a coordinated attack orchestrated by Chief Powhatan. The Indian force included warriors from several of the tribes of the lower James River that owed allegiance to Powhatan: Appomattocks, Weyanocks, Paspaheghs, Quioccohannocks, and Chisiaks.[29] The English now realized that the few Indians who occasionally made seemingly friendly visits to their settlement over the past week were actually "sizing up the colony's defenses and gauging the right time to strike."[30]

Powhatan wanted to wipe out the small group of invaders before they could get a foothold—snuff out the disease before it spread.[31] But the Indians hadn't counted on English guns and cannons.

Immediately the settlers began digging in. Captain Newport's seamen labored together with the colonists to enclose the settlement within a palisade. Each night Newport and his seamen retired to their ships, where they also took their meals.

The Indians attacked several more times, but now more cautiously. They came on "with more fear," Gabriel Archer wrote, remaining out of musket range. On Friday May 29 the Indians "finding one of our dogs they killed him" and shot some "40 arrows into and about the fort." On Sunday "they came lurking in the thickets and long grass." Discovering one of the settlers, Eustace Clovell, "straggling without the fort" the Indians "shot 6 arrows into him, wherewith he came running into the fort, crying Arm! Arm!— [the arrows] sticking still" in his body. "He lived 8 days and died."[32]

---

28. Archer, "A relation," 115. See also John Smith's account in Haile, ed., *Jamestown Narratives*, 147.

29. Townsend, *Pocahontas*, 49.

30. Price, *Love and Hate*, 43.

31. Archer, "A relation," 115–18.

32. Ibid., 116.

The Indians' intention was pretty clear, even if frustrated by English firepower. The little Jamestown settlement—still hardly more than an encampment—remained vulnerable and precarious, a tiny island in a hostile sea.

Captain Newport, however, was under orders to return to England. He and some forty seamen departed on June 22, after five weeks in the New World, leaving the settlers on their own. Fledgling Jamestown had about three months' provision and one of the original three English ships.

With Newport's departure, leadership of the colony fell mainly to Edward Maria Wingfield, a well-placed English gentleman and one of the original Virginia Company investors who had come as a colonist. He served as president of the small council that governed the Jamestown settlement.

Meanwhile, Chief Powhatan shifted tactics. One day the Jamestown folks saw two lone natives peaceably approaching their fort. Chief Powhatan had decided to try direct contact.

Powhatan's envoys told the settlers that the Indians now wished to be friends. The English could "sow and reap in peace." Other chiefs in the area were under Powhatan's authority and they would now treat the English as friends—"or else he would make wars upon them with us," as Edward Maria Wingfield wrote.[33]

But with Captain Newport gone, the Jamestown colony nearly fell apart. The inexperienced settlers fell to quarreling among themselves, unsure what to do. The Indians did not want them there and were not behaving as expected. Then many settlers fell ill and died from a parasite and from salt poisoning, either from overconsumption of sturgeon (as John Smith thought) or from the river water, brackish due to proximity to the ocean and its tidal flows.[34]

Smith wrote, "God being angry with us plagued us with such famine and sickness that the living were scarce able to bury the dead." Captain Bartholomew Gosnold, who had commanded one of the British ships, the *Godspeed*, was among the dead. Smith himself, a tough and seasoned character, also "tasted of the extremity" of the illness, he reported, but eventually "by God's assistance [he] recovered."[35] Nearly half of the original 105 settlers perished.

33. Wingfield, "Discourse," 184. Cf. Price, *Love and Hate*, 47.

34. Their water may have been polluted as well, because their shallow wells likely drew foul swamp water from the north side of the island rather than from the river itself.

35. Smith, "True Relation," 148.

Without normal British social structures and constraints, with settlers' deaths an almost daily occurrence, and with diminishing food supplies, the community fell into near chaos—in ironic contrast with the well-structured Powhatan society. Jamestown was now a tiny culture under great stress.

It might not have survived, had it not been for the kindness of some of the nearby Indians. John Smith reported that "it pleased God in our extremity to move the Indians to bring us corn [on the cob] to refresh us when we rather expected . . . they would destroy us."[36] By mid-September, Smith reports, "Our provision being now within twenty days spent, the Indians brought us great store both of corn and bread ready-made. And also there came such abundance of [migrating] fowls into the rivers as greatly refreshed our weak estates, whereupon many of our weak men were presently able" to venture out a ways from the fort. He adds, "As yet we had no houses to cover us, our tents were rotten, and our cabins worse than nought."[37]

And now winter was nigh. Building more substantial structures became urgent. Such was the division among the colonists however that little got done. There was much "malice, grudging, and muttering," Smith wrote; "most of our chiefest men [were] either sick or discontented," while the rest were "in such despair as they would rather starve and rot with idleness than be persuaded to do anything for their own relief."[38]

Meanwhile far away in England, oblivious to all this, investors were abuzz with the financial promise of the American colonies. Everyday Englishmen however were more fascinated by the growing stream of William Shakespeare's plays than by the drama unfolding across the sea.

36. Ibid., 148–49.
37. Ibid., 149.
38. Ibid., 148–49.

Chapter Three

Enter Pocahontas

Captain John Smith—former soldier, now an adventurer—was about twenty-seven when he landed at Jamestown in May of 1607 with the 143 other settlers, men and boys.[1]

Edward Haile calls Smith "one of history's extraordinary characters" and the "central figure in the establishment of the Jamestown colony."[2] Yet Smith himself was not in charge of the expedition that founded Jamestown. As noted, one-armed Captain Christopher Newport was. En route to America, Smith, "like the rest of the passengers, would have slept on a straw mattress on the decks or in a hammock."[3] He was merely one of the passengers, and a rather unruly one, at that. Only later, thanks to his skills and hardy health, would he become key to Jamestown's survival.

An adventurer at heart, Smith had invested the minimal nine pounds required to be part of the Virginia expedition. Due to his military and foreign travel experience, he was appointed one of the seven-member Virginia Company council to be set up in America.[4] Smith later ended up in charge mainly because he was the toughest and most resourceful and far-seeing of the colonists, especially in times of crisis. He was a survivor. In the

1. Several early accounts mention boys among the first Jamestown settlers, though generally no ages are given. Most were likely in the service of "gentlemen" in the group.

2. Haile, ed., *Jamestown Narratives*, 59.

3. Price, *Love and Hate*, 16.

4. Townsend, *Pocahontas*, 47.

twentieth century Hart Crane, in his long poem "The Bridge," aptly called Smith "all beard and certainty."[5]

Smith was called "Captain" because of his prior exploits as a mercenary in Europe. In his teens he ran off to become a soldier and was briefly a pirate in the Mediterranean. He eventually joined the army of Archduke Ferdinand of Austria in his war against Muslim Turks. Here Smith attained the rank of captain. He was captured and sold into slavery, but eventually escaped. Archduke Ferdinand gave him an honorary discharge. Ever after, he was known as *Captain* John Smith.[6]

He was a tough character, with extraordinary presence of mind. Smith's farm upbringing and his extensive travels and cross-cultural experiences toughened him physically and emotionally. He constantly scribbled notes, and so provides remarkably detailed accounts. His embellishments and exaggerations have frustrated later historians. Yet he was a keen observer. In the case of Jamestown we have multiple early accounts, so this provides some checks and balances.

The big critical exception, however, is Smith's earliest encounters with Pocahontas. Here we have only his word. This has led to uncertainty and sharp conflicts in interpretation. Yet much of our story—in fact, *much of the subsequent history of North America*—flows out of the relationship between this unusual Englishman and the young Powhatan lass known to history as Pocahontas.

It was a most unusual, lopsided, upside-down relationship—the reverse of what one might expect. John Smith was a peasant; Pocahontas a chief's daughter—but Smith was much older. And of course normal social status and social distinctions were all thrown into confusion in the strange and often confusing context of the small, struggling English settlement in Virginia and the poorly understood Powhatans whose unwelcome guests the white men were.

Unlike most of his compatriots, Smith truly tried to understand the Indians, asking questions and taking notes.[7]

---

5. Quoted in Wachutka, "Myth Making," lines 165–66.

6. Haile, ed., *Jamestown Narratives,* 59–60; Townsend, *Pocahontas,* 46–47.

7. Price, *Love and Hate,* 7.

FOOD FOR JAMESTOWN

By late fall in 1607, supplies at Jamestown were running alarmingly low. Captain Newport had not returned, and the Indians brought no more food. The settlers who survived illness were saved in part by the cooler fall weather and by huge flocks of migrating birds; even weakened settlers could kill some. With the village's store of grain nearly exhausted, the colonists watched anxiously for Newport's return. Frightened eyes scanned the horizon for first sight of the English ships' "great white wings," as the Indians called their sails.

Finally, John Smith took action. He set off by barge with a few others to try to trade for food with the Indians. Smith had become slightly acquainted with some of the Indians who came to check out the settlers' fort—out of curiosity, perhaps, but also as reconnaissance. At this point neither the Indians nor the English were quite sure what to make of the other. Was it safe to be friendly, or should they be wary and perhaps hostile?

Just upriver was the mouth of the smaller Chickahominy River, still unexplored, and Smith decided to check it out. He soon encountered Chickahominy Indians—an independent tribe not under Powhatan control. Smith found the Chickahominy willing to trade. He acquired a good quantity of Indian corn in exchange for beads and metal implements. Smith brought the supplies back to Jamestown and later returned twice for more. Naturally the Jamestown settlers came to see Smith as a key leader, even a savior.[8]

But then Smith and his band traveled too far. Venturing farther up the Chickahominy, they unwittingly entered Powhatan winter hunting grounds. Powhatan warriors captured Smith as he was onshore. Some of them killed two of his crew, John Robinson and Thomas Emry, as they lay resting in their canoe.[9]

Smith was actually captured by Opechancanough, an important Powhatan chief of the Powhatan confederation. A large and impressive man of about sixty, Opechancanough was a half-brother or cousin to Chief Powhatan, and something like an uncle to Pocahontas. Due to his matrilineal

---

8. Townsend, *Pocahontas*, 50–51. The fact that Indians were often at first willing to trade for corn, giving up a key resource, suggests that they were economically fairly prosperous and secure.

9. Rountree, *Pocahontas*, 67–69; Townsend, *Pocahontas*, 45, 51. Townsend maintains that Powhatan sent Opechancanough specifically to capture Smith, partly to gather intelligence from him.

family connections he was actually Powhatan's heir, and in fact succeeded him as paramount chief when Powhatan died in 1618.[10]

Opechancanough first took Smith to the Indians' temporary hunting village. Later—apparently when the Indians had completed their hunting in the area and were ready to move back downriver—Opechancanough took Smith to various Indian towns in succession over several days. "At each place I expected they would execute me," Smith said, "yet they used me with what kindness they could." The Indians were in fact rather fascinated with Smith and his equipment, such as his "compass dial." Smith explained its use and proceeded on "a discourse of the roundness of the earth, the course of the sun, moon, stars, and planets."[11] Smith had facility with languages and had already learned some Powhatan words. Day by day he picked up others, eventually becoming fairly fluent—in marked contrast to almost all the other English.

News of Smith's capture spread quickly through the network of Indian towns. "All the women and children" in each village "came forth to meet" the Indian party and their captive, who was always guarded by armed Indian bowmen.[12] Smith noted that the Indians lived in lodges made of mats stretched over curved poles or branches—shelters easily dismantled and carried to the Indians' next site.[13]

By now it was December and the weather had turned colder. Still Opechancanough and his party kept moving from town to town. At one Paspahegh town the local chief "took great delight in understanding the manner of our ships and sailing the seas, the earth and skies, and of our God," Smith wrote.[14]

Opechancanough led the party to the Indian town of Menapacute on the York (Pamunkey) River where another half-brother, Opitchapam, ruled the populous Pamunkey people. Here Smith counted about a hundred houses spread over a fairly wide plain—and the chief's residence on a "high

---

10. Cf. Rountree, *Pocahontas,* 27–29, 189; Townsend, *Pocahontas,* 24, 44–46. At this point it appears that Opechancanough was third in line in the succession; apparently the first (Opitchapam) and second predeceased Powhatan himself.

11. Smith, "True Relation," 157.

12. Ibid., 157–58.

13. Ibid., 159.

14. Ibid., 158.

sandy hill" in the town. "More abundance of fish and fowl and a pleasanter seat cannot be imagined," Smith wrote.[15]

Opechancanough now allowed Smith to send a written message to Jamestown via Indian couriers, assuring the English he was safe and well cared for. If the Jamestown settlers thought Smith had been killed by the Indians, Smith warned, they might come seeking revenge.

Not knowing English nor how to read, Opechancanough was unaware that Smith's note also warned Jamestown of a possible imminent Indian attack. Opechancanough was in fact frustrated in trying to get information about Smith, his people, and their intentions, due to the language barrier.

As Smith traveled from town to town with the Indians, he finally realized their final destination was Werowocomoco, Chief Powhatan's capital on the York (Pamunkey) River, twenty miles north of Jamestown.

SMITH AT POWHATAN'S CAPITAL

Opechancanough and his party arrived at Werowocomoco with their exotic captive on about December 30, 1607. Here Smith would finally meet Chief Powhatan himself, about whom he had heard so much.

Walking into Werowocomoco in the late afternoon, Opechancanough and his warriors led Smith through the town to Powhatan's house.

At Werowocomoco Smith was again treated as an honored guest—or so it seemed. Chief Powhatan understood that Smith was a strategic asset and a person of status among the English. It made sense to keep him alive, at least for the time being.

With his bushy beard, short stocky frame, light skin, and strange clothes and smell, Smith was a curiosity. Unsure of his captors' intent, Smith feared for his life. Maybe the Indians were fattening him to be the main course at a feast! (He later learned the Powhatan weren't cannibals.)

Though wary of the English, Powhatan and Opechancanough were also "intensely curious" about them, and especially about Smith.[16] Price notes that Opechancanough "was far more skeptical of English intentions, and more eager to be rid of these foreigners, than was his older brother," Chief Powhatan. Opechancanough "held a more coldly realistic view of the long-term threat from the English."[17]

15. Ibid., 159.

16. Rountree, *Pocahontas*, 68.

17. Price, *Love and Hate*, 63.

JOHN SMITH MEETS POWHATAN

When Smith arrived bound at Werowocomoco, little Pocahontas was probably among the children and women who ran out to see him.[18] "There is no knowing what she first thought of the short, stocky man past his youth, with an unkempt beard, bound as a captive. . . . In clothing, coloring, and physical type he looked different from any person she had ever seen," notes Townsend.[19]

Powhatan's dwelling was the largest house in the town. His longhouse had an elaborate entrance; Henry Spelman, who lived among the Powhatan for two years and learned their language, wrote that kings' houses were "both broader and longer than the rest, having many dark windings and turnings before any come where the king is."[20]

When Smith was led into Chief Powhatan's royal chamber (an area perhaps twenty feet wide and thirty to forty feet long[21]), he was amazed by what he saw. There was Powhatan, seated like royalty, ready to receive this foreigner who was rapidly becoming famous among them. Townsend describes the scene: Powhatan "was reclining in state on a low platform, with long chains of white beads and pearls around his neck, dressed in a gorgeous fur robe decorated with the extraordinary black-ringed tails of *aroughcun* [raccoons], an animal no Englishman had ever seen before. He was symbolically surrounded by his subject tribes in the persons of his wives—though the political point was lost on Smith, who later referred to them only as 'wenches.' After some moments of silence, Powhatan made an elaborate speech."[22]

Chief Powhatan was following tribal protocol for receiving a dignitary. The initial period of silence was intentional, enhancing the sense of awe and of the chief's authority. Possibly it was accompanied by the smoking of a pipe of tobacco by the chief and passed as well to Smith, before food was served.[23]

In his own account a few months later, Smith wrote:

18. Townsend, *Pocahontas*, 46.

19. Ibid., 46. Barbour describes the Smith-Powhatan encounter in some detail in *Pocahontas*, 23–26.

20. Spelman, "Relation of Virginia," 487.

21. Cf. Rountree, *Pocahontas*, 78.

22. Townsend, *Pocahontas*, 51–52. It may not literally be true that no Englishman had seen a raccoon before.

23. Rountree, *Pocahontas*, 76.

[Chief Powhatan was] proudly lying upon a bedstead a foot high, upon ten or twelve mats, richly hung with many chains of great pearls about his neck, and covered with a great covering of [raccoon skins]; at his head sat a woman, at his feet another, on each side sitting upon a mat upon the ground were ranged his chief man on each side [of] the fire, ten in rank, and behind them as many young women [i.e., more of Powhatan's wives] each a great chain of white beads over their shoulders, their heads painted in red, and [Chief Powhatan] with such a grave and majestical countenance as drave me into admiration to see such state in a naked savage.[24]

Present in addition to Powhatan's "loveliest wives" would likely have been his immediate heirs: his three brothers and two sisters (this being a matrilineal society), some priests and councilors, and some of the tribal chiefs who were subject to Powhatan.[25]

"Establishing his own high status and power was [Powhatan's] (and his subjects') major concern in this first and very formal meal taken with the outlander," as Rountree notes. "A chief of Powhatan's importance would want his guest to be aware that many of the decorative, nubile ladies he saw were his host's wives."[26]

As platters of food were carried in, Smith saw he was to be the guest at an elaborate feast.

Where was Pocahontas? The eleven-year-old was probably busy with the other women and girls (her stepmothers and half-sisters, mainly) preparing food and doing chores. Her father's audience with Smith was not a children's event, though during the feasting some of the women and children probably passed in and out, serving food.[27]

At some point Pocahontas met and briefly interacted with Smith. Later history suggests that from the beginning Pocahontas felt sympathy and perhaps affection for the stranger. They were probably out of doors "when the two sat and tried to converse through the language barrier."[28]

---

24. Smith, "True Relation," 160–61.

25. Rountree, *Pocahontas,* 78.

26. Ibid., 78.

27. Rountree writes, "Eleven-year-old girls (and boys, for that matter) were not very important on diplomatic occasions, and no historical account mentions any children at any formal Powhatan reception that preceded a feast. . . . The foreigner was going to remain in town for several days, so Pocahontas and her half siblings would have plenty of chances to meet him later on" (Rountree, *Pocahontas,* 77).

28. Ibid., 78.

Perky and inquisitive as she was, she was curious about him. Mutual affection and fascination started to form a bond; this was not the invention of later romanticizers.

DID POCAHONTAS RESCUE JOHN SMITH?

What happened shortly after the feast has sparked hot controversy for 400 years. The traditional story: Chief Powhatan set about to execute Smith but was thwarted by his compassionate daughter, who rushed forward and threw herself on Smith to save him. Others argue that this presumed harrowing encounter was actually an adoption ceremony through which Powhatan established his authority over Smith as a way of neutralizing the English threat. Smith would now be honor-bound to respect the Indians' rights, and in fact be an adopted member of the tribe—and thus loyal to Powhatan. As Randy Woodley points out, "Everyone in Indian country must have a status of relationship to be clear on proper protocol expectations. Making Smith a relative of Pocahontas would have actually forbade any romantic encounter in the future as marriage between clan members and relatives was strictly taboo."[29]

The former story is more dramatic and romantic, and ever popular. Many scholars, however, think the latter is historically more plausible. The issue is, did Pocahontas rescue John Smith from death by clubbing, as Smith later told the tale, or did Powhatan in some sense "adopt" Smith in order to pacify the English invaders? Or was the story an invention of Smith's fertile mind?

This is how John Smith first reported the story about fifteen years later, describing himself in the third person:

> Having feasted him after their best barbarous manner they could, a long consultation was held, but the conclusion was two great stones were brought before Powhatan. Then as many as could laid hands on him [Smith], dragged him to them, and thereon laid his head; and being ready with their clubs to beat out his brains, Pocahontas, the king's dearest daughter, when no entreaty could prevail, got his head in her arms and laid her own upon his to save him from death; whereat the emperor was contented he should live

---

29. Randy Woodley, email to author, January 30, 2014.

to make him hatchets, and [for] her bells, beads, and copper, for
they thought him as [capable] of all occupations as themselves.[30]

Interestingly, one of the most dramatic retellings of this story was by John
Marshall, the first US Chief Justice of the Supreme Court, in his 1804 five-
volume *Life of George Washington*: "There [John Smith] was doomed to be
put to death, by laying his head upon a stone, and beating out his brains
with clubs. He was led to the place of execution, and his head bowed down
for the purpose of death, when Pocahontas, the king's darling daughter,
then about thirteen years of age, whose entreaties for his life had been inef-
fectual, rushed between him and his executioner, and folding his head in
her arms, and laying hers upon it, arrested the fatal blow. Her father was
then prevailed on to spare his life."[31]

Anthropologist Helen Rountree is counted among the skeptics of the
rescue story. Her explanation: Smith was in fact never "in any danger";
Powhatan did not yet know the English adventurers' intentions, and Smith
was a significant "potential source of information" (which is certainly true).
Although Smith had been taken captive, his "position, on the evening of
December 30, 1607, was that of a representative of his country." Rountree
believes the "logical conclusion . . . is that Pocahontas did not rescue John
Smith. Even if she had been inside the house at the time, he would not have
needed rescuing from anything other than overeating."[32]

Historian Camilla Townsend in her 2004 study similarly dismissed
the rescue story as Smith's self-serving invention. Smith had in fact reported similar unverifiable adventures in other parts of the world. In his travel
narratives Smith "never failed to mention that at each critical juncture a
beautiful young woman had fallen in love with him and interceded on his
behalf." Rountree similarly points out that if Smith is to be believed, he "had
a knack for getting into drastic situations and then being rescued by high-
ranking females. He claimed it happened [to] him not only in Virginia but
also in Turkey and the Russian steppes."[33]

30. Smith, "General History: The Third Book," 239. The date was apparently December 30 or 31, 1607, though some scholars who interpret the event as an adoption ceremony place it later. In his many writings, Smith told this story a total of eight times, and
it never seems to have been contradicted or questioned by any of the Native Americans
who were present. See Lemay, *Did Pocahontas Save*, 58–63.

31. Marshall, *Life of George Washington*, 1:42.

32. Rountree, *Pocahontas*, 79–80, 82.

33. Townsend, *Pocahontas*, 52–53; Rountree, *Pocahontas*, 80. Townsend quotes examples from Smith's writings. Barbour concludes that "The ceremony of which Smith

So did Pocahontas's dramatic rescue of John Smith in December 1607 really happen? It still remains an open question. Though the event may seem highly unlikely, it *could* have occurred. Even the Virginia anthropologist Helen Rountree does not positively rule it out, speaking rather of "the rescue that *may* not have happened."[34]

Price argues that the rescue occurred just as Smith described it, pointing out that Smith hardly comes off as a hero. "To be taken prisoner . . . and then to be saved by a young native girl was hardly an admirable achievement." Price sees no "reason to doubt that Pocahontas was just who she appeared to be that day: a girl acting compassionately toward the pitiable stranger in front of her."[35]

Smith himself later wrote that Pocahontas's "compassionate pitiful [pitying] heart . . . gave me much cause to respect her" and that she was in fact instrumental in saving Jamestown.[36]

The veracity of the story hinges finally on the credibility of Smith's reports. Smith was a careful observer and narrator, and if he sometimes exaggerated, his reports generally accord with other reliable documents, where available.

Having weighed the evidence on both sides, I conclude that the rescue may have happened pretty much as Smith describes—adding however some qualifications based on issues of cultural understanding. The simplicity and naïveté of Smith's language argues for it. That the story is improbable is certainly no argument against it; many of the most significant real happenings in history were improbable! That's partly why they are so important. It could indeed have been an adoption enactment however, misunderstood by Smith.

Haile's comment is apt: "For my part, I see in this man, who entitles a chapter 'What happened,' a simplicity and directness bespeaking a fundamental honesty, a vainglory that charms more than it deceives."[37] It is

---

had been the object was almost certainly a combination of mock execution and salvation, in token of adoption into Powhatan's tribe" (Barbour, *Pocahontas*, 24).

34. Rountree, *Pocahontas,* 76 (emphasis added); see 76–82.

35. Price, *Love and Hate,* 242, 245. Price discusses the question at some length and finds the historian Lemay convincing (*Did Pocahontas Save*). Regarding Smith's somewhat varying accounts, Haile comments, "Why did Smith keep putting served wine in new bottles? To sell books, for he lived on nothing else unless the charity of his friends" (Haile, ed., editorial comment, *Jamestown Narratives,* 216).

36. Quoted in Price, *Love and Hate,* 5.

37. Haile, introducing Smith's "General History: The Third Book," in Haile, ed.,

also well to remember that Smith, though no scholar, was a prolific author, and the rescue story occupies only a few pages of the thousands that he published.

However one assesses the great rescue account, the rest of the story is clear enough. Chief Powhatan's main concern was to find out more about the English. What were they up to? Native encounters with occasional Spanish incursions in the previous century gave good reason to be wary.

Powhatan asked Smith directly about English intentions. Smith was devious. Rather than saying that the English intended to stay permanently, establish a commercial colony, and bring the Indians under their control, Smith invented a tale. He claimed the English had been attacked at sea by Spanish ships, and then a storm had driven them into Chesapeake Bay. The Jamestown settlement was temporary, he implied; the English were repairing one of their damaged ships and waiting for Captain Newport to return (true) and take them all back to England (false).

Why then, Powhatan asked, had the English gone exploring further upriver? Smith invented another tale: A child of his "father" (King James I) had been killed by inland Indians, probably the Monacans (enemies of the Powhatans), and the English were seeking to avenge the death.

This claim led to an extended discussion, probably dimly understood on both sides, between Powhatan and Smith about North American and European geography.[38]

Chief Powhatan could see that the English were powerful, with their ships ("floating islands"), guns, and potentially large numbers. Perhaps they could be valuable allies against his inland Indian enemies—his main concern at the moment—and perhaps also against further Spanish incursions.

An alliance with the English as a defense against the Spanish actually made some sense.[39] One hundred-fifty years later French alliances with northern and inland Indian tribes became the basis for the so-called French and Indian War (1754–1763).

Powhatan was still wary and suspicious, however. He did not fully trust either the English or Smith's explanations. As Rountree puts it, "Powhatan concluded that the Strangers were worth gathering in as allies against

---

Jamestown Narratives, 217. Haile adds that Smith "had a reputation for being difficult and he earned it. After many books he died in poverty. . . . [He was] a fascinating character, one larger than anybody but Powhatan" (ibid.).

38. Rountree, *Pocahontas,* 82–83; Price, *Love and Hate,* 66–67.

39. Custalow and Daniel, *True Story,* 17.

his inland enemies. However, they were also well worth keeping a close watch upon."[40]

So Powhatan offered a deal. He would give the English the town of Capahowasick, just downriver from his capital on the York (Pamunkey) River and twenty miles or so from the Jamestown site, in exchange for good relations with the English. Smith really had no authority to negotiate, but of course he was the only Englishman present. Smith says Powhatan wanted the English to give up the idea of a more inland site further up the James River "and to live with him upon his river," at Capahowasick (where of course Powhatan could keep an eye on them). Powhatan "promised to give me corn, venison, or what I wanted to feed us; hatchets and copper we should make for him, and none should disturb us. This request I promised to perform."[41] Powhatan also wanted Smith to send him "two great guns and a grindstone" as part of the deal.[42]

Powhatan thought, or perhaps pretended, that Smith agreed to this deal and thus had made a solemn covenant according to Indian practice and culture. (This becomes important later in Smith's relationship with Pocahontas.) Smith probably took the deal more as an initial arrangement of coexistence. Rountree says, "It is unlikely that [Smith] realized to what extent the alliance was taken seriously by Powhatan," whom Smith did not fully trust; and in any case Powhatan's intention "was to assimilate the Strangers, not vice versa." Smith probably also didn't realize "the extent to which the alliance was a personal one, between two leaders, in Powhatan's mind," and thus of lasting significance.[43] In keeping with Powhatan culture, the chief now considered Smith his "son." Though both men were wary of the other, from Powhatan's point of view they had entered into a personal honor-bound covenant.

During his brief time at Werowocomoco following his rescue, Smith interacted some with the Powhatan people, including Pocahontas. Rountree writes,

> Time probably had to be made to satisfy the curiosity of the townspeople about the exotic visitor. Most had never seen a European before. He would have appeared unearthly pale to them, and they probably wondered if he was white all over. His face was

40. Rountree, *Pocahontas*, 83.

41. Smith, "True Relation," 162.

42. Smith, "General History: The Third Book," 240.

43. Rountree, *Pocahontas*, 83.

hairier than any native man's could ever be. His clothing was most peculiar and decidedly impractical for the life a 'real man' led. His body odor must have been awful, for it is unlikely that he would have been forced to bathe in the icy York River, as the townspeople did each morning. But his value as a curiosity was inestimable, and he must have been surrounded by a welter of people when he was not visiting with Powhatan.

It would have been during these more relaxed times that Pocahontas made [Smith's] acquaintance. And as she had charmed her father, so she seems ultimately to have made more of an impression upon [Smith] than anyone else in the town. How much of that impression stemmed from their first meeting at Werowocomoco is impossible to say.[44]

RETURN TO JAMESTOWN

With an escort of Indians, Smith started back to Jamestown on January 1, 1608. Chief Powhatan sent Smith back to Jamestown thinking that he had converted Smith "and the country he came from into allies of his own. Sealing the alliance may or may not have been done in some colorful way," such as the more elaborate account Smith gave later, in 1624.[45]

Opposite motives were at work. The English wanted the Indians to be part of the British Empire. Chief Powhatan wanted to make the British "part of the Powhatan nation."[46]

Leaving Werowocomoco on New Year's Day, 1608, Smith and several Powhatan warriors traveled back to Jamestown. The party was led by Rawhunt, Chief Powhatan's "most trusted messenger."[47] This was normally a one-day walk through the woods, south from the York to the James River. But Smith's Indian escort took their time. The group stayed overnight at an Indian hunting lodge.

The delay may have been intentional. Captain Newport and his supply ships (the "First Supply," as it was called) were about to arrive in Jamestown, and some of Powhatan's scouts may have spotted the white sails on the horizon. A day's delay enabled Smith's Indian escort to arrive in Jamestown on

44. Ibid., 83. Rountree invents the name "Chawnzmit" for Smith, suggesting that this is probably how "Smith" would have sounded to the Powhatans (6).

45. Ibid., 84.

46. Custalow and Daniel, *True Story*, 65.

47. Price, *Love and Hate*, 70.

January 2, the same day Newport arrived—giving them crucial intelligence to report to Powhatan. Indians from villages along the James River, probably curious, "lined the riverside . . . watching the watercraft with their 'wings' spread and speculating about what the ships had brought this time."[48]

Smith and his Indian escort finally walked into Jamestown early on January 2. Now safely returned, John Smith sent some gifts back to Chief Powhatan, though not the big guns Powhatan requested. Smith cleverly showed the Indians a couple of two-ton cannons, too heavy to carry, fearfully demonstrating one by firing it into an ice-covered tree.

The Indian escort returned to Chief Powhatan with the gifts Smith had sent and with details of Captain Newport's arrival—including the news that still more Englishmen and supplies had disembarked. Newport brought with him about sixty new colonists and enough provisions to see the colony through the winter.[49]

48. Rountree, *Pocahontas*, 85.

49. Price, *Love and Hate*, 71.

Chapter Four

John Smith, Powhatan, Pocahontas

Smith was back home, but not out of trouble. He found the Jamestown colonists very upset with him. They blamed him for the deaths of John Robinson and Thomas Emry, the two members of Smith's party who had been slain by the Indians when the group went exploring upriver a month earlier. Some even accused Smith of "scheming to inherit Powhatan's kingdom by marrying his daughter," notes Price—evidence they had learned of the Pocahontas story. Price comments however that "Smith's attitude toward Pocahontas was platonic from all appearances, and there was no reason to suspect otherwise. In any case, he knew he would not have stood to inherit the role of *mamanatowick,* or emperor, by marrying Pocahontas," given the Powhatan matrilineal system.[1]

Smith himself noted, "Great blame and imputation was laid upon me by them for the loss to our two men which the Indians slew."[2] At least one of the Jamestown settlers wanted Smith hanged.

Smith was saved by the timely arrival of Captain Christopher Newport later in the day in the ship *John and Francis.* Newport "personally put a stop to such criminal nonsense."[3]

---

1. Price, *Love and Hate,* 121.

2. Smith, "True Relation," 164.

3. Barbour, *Pocahontas,* 27. This scene is depicted but misinterpreted in the movie *The New World* (2010), discussed later.

Newport found the Jamestown colony shrunk from its original 105 men and boys to only about 40.[4] Many of the survivors were determined to abandon the colony altogether and return to England. Jamestown was on the verge of collapse. It was barely rescued by Newport's arrival and by Smith's determination and common sense. With the newcomers, Jamestown now had about 100 settlers, plus Newport's crew. The supplies Newport brought meant "we were victualed for twelve weeks," Smith noted.[5]

Several days later, one of the new settlers accidentally set his lodgings ablaze. This sparked a fire that destroyed most of the village. The wooden buildings were "but thatched with reeds," Smith noted; as a result "our fort was burned and the most of our apparel, lodging, and private provision" gone. It was still the cold of winter. "Many of our old men [who were] diseased and [many] of our new [arrivals perished]" in the "extreme frost," Smith wrote. "Good Master Hunt our preacher lost all his library and all he had but the clothes on his back, yet none never heard him repine at his loss."[6]

Newport's crew helped the settlers rebuild the fort and lodgings—a tough job in mid-winter. Some of the newly arrived provisions were destroyed in the fire, though some were safe aboard the *John and Francis*—intended to provision the ship's return voyage to England on April 10. The colonists struggled to survive. Due to "the extremity of the bitter cold frost," the scarcity of provisions, and dissension among the colonists, "more than half of us died . . . in that piercing winter," Smith recorded.[7]

Surprisingly, rescue came from the Powhatan Indians themselves. Honoring his new alliance with Smith, Chief Powhatan sent provisions—deer, bread, raccoon skins, and other supplies. More arrived every few days, brought by groups of Indians. Some trade now began between the settlers and the Indians. The colonists lacked food, but they had metal hatchets, copper, and other things the Indians coveted.

---

4. A second supply ship, also carrying more colonists, was sailing with Newport's ship, but got blown off course in a storm and ended up in the West Indies. See chapter 4.

5. Smith, "True Relation," 173.

6. Ibid.; Smith, "General History: The Third Book," 246–47.

7. Smith, "General History: The Third Book," 247.

POWHATAN AGAIN ENTERTAINS JOHN SMITH

In his interactions with Chief Powhatan during his captivity at Werowo-comoco, Smith had spoken of his "father"—a powerful chieftain and "lord of all the waters." Smith was actually referring to Captain Christopher Newport, who outranked Smith.[8] About a month after Newport's return to Jamestown, Powhatan sent word that he wanted to meet this distinguished "father." Consequently Smith and Newport, together with a contingent of about forty armed men, sailed down the James to Chesapeake Bay and up the York River to Werowocomoco. Unsure of Powhatan's intentions, they were wary of a possible trap.

Smith and twenty armed men went ashore near Werowocomoco but promptly got lost in the woods. The Indians found them and conducted them to the town. There "forty or fifty great platters of fine bread" signaled they were welcome guests. Newport and the rest of the men remained with the ships.

Powhatan again received Smith with great pomp. Smith describes the event:

> [W]ith loud tunes [the Indians] all made signs of great joy. This proud savage, having his finest women and the principal of his chief men assembled [and seated] in ranks as before, [Powhatan himself sat] as upon a throne at the upper end of the house with such a majesty as I cannot express nor yet have often seen either in pagan or Christian. With a kind countenance he bade me welcome and caused a place to be made by himself to sit. I presented him a suit of red cloth, a white greyhound, and a hat. As jewels he esteemed them, and with a great oration made by three of his nobles (if there be any amongst savages), kindly accepted them with a public confirmation of a perpetual league of friendship.
>
> After that he commanded the Queen of Apamatuc, a comely young savage, to give me water, a turkey cock, and bread to eat. Being thus feasted, he began his discourse.[9]

Chief Powhatan of course wanted to know where Smith's "father" was, whom he said "I much desire to see: Is he not with you?"

---

8. Newport made a total of five voyages to Virginia—the initial one with the first group of colonists in early 1607, then subsequent ones in 1607–08, 1608–09, 1609–10, and 1611. Haile, ed., *Jamestown Narratives*, 50.

9. Smith, "True Relation," 166–67.

Smith explained that he was still aboard ship, but would come the next day. Powhatan asked why Smith had not sent the guns he had requested. Smith explained that he had indeed offered Powhatan's men four huge cannons, since the Indians had requested a "great gun," but the Indians had refused to take them. At this Powhatan laughed heartily. He saw through Smith's ploy. Next time, give his men less burdensome guns! Powhatan realized Smith offered the heavy cannon because he was "sure than none could carry them," Smith noted.[10]

This exchange was part of an ongoing struggle. The Indians wanted English weapons; the English did their best to prevent this. Later the Indians would however get a number of English swords and other weapons, either by barter or theft.

The discourses continued—again a chess game, a high-stakes battle of wits between the shrewd Powhatan and the canny Englishman. Smith was bargaining for more provisions; Powhatan for more control over the English via his alliance with Smith.

In a "loud oration" Powhatan proclaimed that Smith himself was now a Powhatan *weroance*, or chief, "and that the [native] corn, women, and country should be to us [the English settlers] as to his own people." The unstated assumption was that all this was under Powhatan's command and authority. Smith, who was beginning to understand more of the Powhatan speech, used "the best language and signs of thanks" he could in order to show his appreciation. In his 1608 account Smith referred to Powhatan as "this politician," commenting that "Experience had well taught me to believe his friendship till convenient opportunity suffered him to betray us."[11]

Captain John Smith and Chief Powhatan were both highly skilled at the game of diplomacy. Both were very clever chess players. Furthermore, both represented sophisticated and powerful empires (within their respective contexts), and they knew it.

Nevertheless, the Powhatan people—like the Aztecs and Incas confronting the Spanish much further south—were doomed from the start. Given English superiority in numbers, weaponry, and technology, they never really had much of a chance unless the British simply decided to withdraw their American colonies, which was never likely.

The Powhatan people did in fact have "advanced technology," but not the kind the English could recognize, nor the kind that would protect them

10. Ibid., 167.
11. Ibid., 167, 169.

from guns. As Randy Woodley points out, "Indian technology primarily involved housing, planting and harvesting food, medicine plants, fishing, and survival methods such as reading the weather. They considered the English to be as children when they arrived because they could not master what seemed like the most basic survival technologies of that time."[12]

POWHATAN MEETS CAPTAIN NEWPORT

Smith and his men now returned to their ships on the river. An Indian escort accompanied them, carrying food gifts for Smith's "father," Newport. Due to the stormy weather and the fact that one of the ships—actually a barge—had run aground, Powhatan had Smith taken to "a great house . . . hung round with bows and arrows" where Smith was given a feast and overnight lodging.[13]

The next day Captain Newport came ashore. Smith led him to Powhatan's lodge for the important interview. "With a trumpet before him [Newport], we marched to the king, who after his old manner kindly received him, especially [welcoming] a boy of thirteen years old, called Thomas Salvage [or Savage], whom [Newport] gave him as his son."[14] Savage's role was twofold—to secure Powhatan's cooperation, and to learn the Powhatan language and culture so the youth could help the English.[15] Powhatan in turn gave Newport his young aide Namontack in reciprocal exchange (whom Newport later took with him to England). This exchange of "sons" was a sociopolitical transaction, not the exchange of biological

---

12. Randy Woodley, email to author, January 30, 2014. Woodley adds that Native Americans "were far advanced" in several areas, including "dentistry, healing arts, astronomy, oratory, solar and xeriscape energy" (a form of agriculture requiring very little water).

13. Smith, "True Relation," 168.

14. Ibid., 168.

15. Thomas Savage (c. 1595–1633) came from "a fine old English family from Chester." He and another British boy, Henry Spelman (mentioned earlier), lived for a while among the Powhatan and learned their language. Savage later returned to live among the British ("deserted me," Powhatan said). He served for years as an interpreter and probably was the interpreter in the events of Pocahontas's kidnapping. He eventually married, acquired some 9,000 acres of property, had a son, and prospered as a planter and fur trader. Savage Neck on the eastern side of Chesapeake Bay is named for him (Barbour, *Pocahontas*, 30, 88, 139). Cf. McCartney, "Thomas Savage."

sons—a nuance not always understood by the English, other than Smith and others who gained some understanding of Indian culture.[16]

Over the next two or three days the English and the Indians got down to hard bargaining. Both sides had to assess the value of items offered for exchange. The Indians had corn and other food provisions that the English needed, while the Indians desired the settlers' metal objects, including hatchets and large copper cooking pots, and the colored glass beads and other items the strangers had brought from England.

Smith was much more savvy here than Newport. By now Smith had learned a lot about Indian ways. Newport, ignorant of the language and with little understanding the economics involved, was ready to give too much of his store for too little Indian provision—possibly jeopardizing Jamestown's very survival. Newport sought to impress Powhatan by a show of abundant wealth; Smith was canny in not revealing just what the English had, in order to increase his bargaining power. Through some shrewd bargaining Smith managed to get a large amount of corn for a small quantity of blue beads, having convinced the Indians they were especially valuable.[17]

Finally Smith, Newport, and their entourage returned to Jamestown, their ships well laden with supplies. Later they went trading farther up the James River. In early March they were able to bring back another 240 or so bushels of corn, vital for the colonists' survival.[18]

Captain Newport however had a larger commission beyond establishing Jamestown. The investors in England expected him to find gold. During his explorations Newport thought he found some, but the samples he took back proved to be worthless—fool's gold.[19] Newport finally left on his return voyage to England on April 10, 1608.

16. Note the similarities here to the "peace child" in Richardson, *Peace Child*.

17. Barbour, *Pocahontas*, 31; Price, *Love and Hate*, 75; Smith, "True Relation," 169–70.

18. Barbour, *Pocahontas*, 31–32.

19. Price, *Love and Hate*, 75–77. The English investors naturally wanted returns for their venture capital. The most valuable discoveries (they thought at the time, in these pre-tobacco days) would be gold and a water passage from the Atlantic to the Pacific. They pressed the colonists and explorers on both counts, but neither proved successful.

POCAHONTAS IN JAMESTOWN

Spring was now coming to Virginia. With warmer weather and enough to eat, the hundred or so Jamestown settlers felt their prospects improving. The Powhatan seemed friendly and willing to trade. More and more Indians now visited the Jamestown settlement. Relations were cordial, though there were some occasional skirmishes between Indians and Englishmen.

Meanwhile on April 20 the *Phoenix,* commanded by Thomas Nelson, arrived bearing more provisions and another fifty or so colonists. The *Phoenix* had originally set off with Newport's ship for Virginia but during a storm got blown off course and ended up in the West Indies; only now did it make it to Jamestown, four months late.[20] Smith said the ship's "unexpected coming did so ravish us with exceeding joy that now we thought ourselves as well fitted as our hearts could wish, both with a competent number of men as also for all other needful provisions till a further supply should come to us."[21]

About this time, in the spring of 1608, before Newport departed, Pocahontas visited Jamestown several times. She was always accompanied by adult Indians. As a winsome child of eleven or twelve, she made friends with some of the settlers—especially, it seems, with John Smith, whom she had met earlier at Werowocomoco. "Very oft she came to our fort," wrote two of the colonists, "with what she could get for Captain Smith," who "ever much respected" her.[22] Barbour notes that Captain "Newport himself began sending valuable gifts to Powhatan, with Pocahontas often, if not always, flitting back and forth with the Indian porters and messengers."[23]

Price writes that if Pocahontas had at first viewed Smith

> as a captive servant who would spend his days making her bells and jewelry, their relationship had evolved to give her something of greater value: friendship with someone who shared her inquisitive sensitivity. She was curious about the English, and she enjoyed being among them; in Smith, she had found an Englishman who could speak her language and requite her curiosity about these foreigners. Although Smith had practical reasons to encourage the visits—honing his Algonquian, maintaining lines of communication with an ally in Powhatan's court—he also formed an

20. Ibid., 80; Smith, "True Relation," 175–77.

21. Smith, "True Relation," 175.

22. Quoted in Price, *Love and Hate,* 77.

23. Barbour, *Pocahontas,* 28.

admiration for the "nonpareil" and took an avuncular interest in her. [In the Powhatan language] he wrote in his phrase book: "Bid Pocahontas bring hither two little baskets, and I will give her white beads to make her a chaine."[24]

Smith "was conferring special notice on the child, busy man as he was around Jamestown Fort," observes Rountree. "Her father's position had much to do with it, of course, but if she had not had a sparkling personality, it is doubtful that he would have said anything about her at all" in his phrase book.[25]

Townsend notes similarly, "Formally or informally, [Pocahontas] participated in a course of mutual language instruction with John Smith, and it is probably thanks to her that the only full Powhatan sentences that we have are recorded." For example, Smith wrote down the Powhatan for "I am very hungry, what shall I eat?" Smith also recorded a brief dialogue as to where Chief Powhatan was living, perhaps one he actually had with Pocahontas. Pocahontas "clearly participated in conversations very much like this one, revealing something of her interesting and interested self, and demonstrating the strategies each group [the English and the Indians] was attempting to adopt toward the other."[26]

Both Smith and Pocahontas showed a cultural sensibility and curiosity that was lacking in nearly everyone else, Indian and English alike. Both exhibited that rare cross-cultural sensitivity that allows some people to stand above or aside their immediate circumstances and ponder what is really going on culturally.[27]

In these encounters Pocahontas served as a double agent, even as a child. She probably told Powhatan or his lieutenants everything she saw at Jamestown, or was carefully questioned by them. Her later history makes it clear she was a bridge person. Whatever friendship or fondness she developed toward the English, especially John Smith, she never lost her loyalty to or heartfelt concern for her own people and culture.

24. Price, *Love and Hate*, 77.

25. Rountree, *Pocahontas*, 84. Rountree notes that Smith later mentions that Powhatan sent Pocahontas "as one of two emissaries to Jamestown the next spring, knowing that Smith would immediately understand how precious she was to her father" (83–84).

26. Townsend, *Pocahontas*, 74.

27. Though John Rolfe later showed a deep love for Pocahontas, it is not clear that he ever understood her or her people culturally. Thus the Pocahontas-Smith relationship, while not romantic, was unique—unparalleled.

Pocahontas "was not yet on the cusp of womanhood," Price notes, "and her visits found her playing energetically with the few boys of the fort as well as talking with Smith."[28] William Strachey, who was in Jamestown from May 1610 to the fall of 1611, called Pocahontas "well-featured" but mischievous; "sometimes resorting to our fort, of the age of 11 or 12 years, [she would] get the boys forth with her into the marketplace and make them wheel falling on their hands, turning their heels upwards, whom she would follow and wheel so herself naked as she was all the fort over."[29]

Relations were always tense, however, between Jamestown and the Indians. A flare-up of hostilities happened in May of 1608. Chief Powhatan became disgusted with Smith and the settlers for their refusal to trade food for swords. So he launched "a systematic effort to obtain the swords by less direct means. The Indians who came to the fort in a steady stream began by trying to steal them. Failing that, they would ambush the colonists at the gate to the fort and take them by force, or they would catch them off guard when they were working outside the palisade. In this way many swords changed hands, to Powhatan's advantage."[30]

Powhatan no doubt saw this as a justifiable effort to enforce the alliance he had made with his "son," John Smith. He would force compliance on his unruly "son." To Smith's disgust, the Jamestown council refused to take action to stop the thievery, since their London overseers had told them not to "offend" the Indians. Smith put the safety and survival of the colony ahead of any supposed fealty to Powhatan.

One day when a small group of Indians tried to take Smith's own sword, he retaliated. He gathered a few armed men and raided a native town, captured several Indians, and locked them up in the fort. However two of Smith's men were caught by the Indians when they wandered off by themselves foraging. The Indians marched them to the fort and tried to exchange them for their captured comrades, but Smith mustered a large group of armed men before them. Facing a strong force armed with guns, the warriors soon yielded up the two Englishmen and agreed to leave peaceably. The Indian prisoners remained with Smith in Jamestown.[31]

28. Price, *Love and Hate*, 77.

29. Strachey, "History," 630. Strachey probably copied this from an earlier source, since by the time he was in Jamestown Pocahontas would have been a teenager and would no longer have gone about naked but have worn "apronlike deerskin dresses" (Price, *Love and Hate*, 77).

30. Barbour, *Pocahontas*, 33.

31. Ibid., 33–34. The sources give somewhat varying accounts of these conflicts.

Smith was determined to show toughness in order to enforce coexistence with the Powhatan.

Smith questioned and threatened the Indian captives. He discovered Powhatan planned to destroy the English if he could. Price notes, "Smith the realist had long understood that the colony's neighbors [Powhatan and other tribes] hated the English. Not only that, they would hate the English no matter what the English did to make themselves lovable—short of packing up and going back home. Where the colonists saw themselves merely as occupying some fallow, unused ground, the natives plainly had come to regard their presence as an unwanted intrusion."[32]

Three days after Smith had taken the Indian captives, two Indian emissaries showed up at Jamestown. These were personal representatives of Chief Powhatan: Rawhunt, "his most trusty messenger" (as Smith called him), and Pocahontas, Powhatan's daughter. They came with gifts of bread and a deer, apologizing for the "rash, untoward" Indians who had caused trouble, and asked Smith to release the Indian captives. Smith described Pocahontas as a child who "for feature, countenance, and proportion" much surpassed the other Indians and "for wit and spirit" was the "nonpareil of [Powhatan's] country."[33]

Rawhunt, as spokesman, assured Smith that Powhatan still "loved and respected" him, and as proof had sent "his child, which he most esteemed" to entreat Smith for the captive Indians' release. Smith delayed for a day or two in order to underscore who was in charge, but then released the prisoners to Rawhunt and especially Pocahontas, "for whose sake only," he said, he "saved their lives and gave them liberty."[34]

The upshot of these skirmishes and encounters was a brief period of distrustful harmony between the settlers and the Powhatan people.

A few days later—on June 2, 1608—Captain Thomas Nelson departed for England in the *Phoenix*. He carried with him Smith's remarkable 13,000-word firsthand account of his adventures. It was quickly published in London as *A True Relation of Such Occurrences and Accidents of Note as Hath Hap'ned in Virginia Since the First Planting of that Colony*. It was "the

---

32. Price, *Love and Hate*, 83. What was "unused ground" to the colonists was sacred hunting ground to the Indians.

33. Smith, "True Relation," 181; Smith, "General History: The Third Book," 250. Cf. Price, *Love and Hate*, 83.

34. Smith, "True Relation," 181; Smith, "General History: The Third Book," 250.

first published account of the distant colony to reach the public's hands," notes Price.[35]

Meanwhile, Smith used the warm summer weather for further exploration. He took a group of armed men along the coast of Chesapeake Bay and up the lower reaches of the broad Potomac River. They traveled in a two-ton barge with oars and sails that allowed them to navigate shallow rivers. This was partly a survey trip and partly a reconnaissance mission. En route, Smith himself survived a painful and near-fatal stingray attack. Again proving his toughness, he cooked the stingray for supper before the party returned to Jamestown.[36]

After recovering from the stingray attack, Smith set off a second time up the Chesapeake Bay. He explored further north, to the mouth of the Susquehanna River, beyond present-day Baltimore. He was still trying, as commissioned, to find a passage to the Pacific, and the 200-mile long Chesapeake Bay, North America's largest estuary, looked promising.

He of course found no such passage. But for the first time he encountered Iroquoian Indians, a whole different federation from Powhatan's.[37] "Much like the previous exploration, this trip found Smith and his men engaged in diplomacy, hard bargaining, and fending off both illness and occasional enemy attacks."[38] One of Smith's party, Michael Featherstone, died, apparently from illness. Part of the time the party was guided by Mosco, a non-Powhatan Indian or perhaps French-Indian whom Smith had befriended earlier.[39]

Smith arrived back in Jamestown on September 7. The settlers were now much more impressed with his capabilities! The twelve-member Jamestown Council elected him president for a one-year term beginning on September 10.[40] Smith had proved himself both more resourceful and less self-interested than anyone else in Jamestown. One of the colonist-soldiers who served under Smith said "in all his proceedings he made justice his

35. Price, *Love and Hate*, 85.

36. Barbour, *Pocahontas*, 34–35.

37. Ibid., 35.

38. Price, *Love and Hate*, 89.

39. Smith, "General History: The Third Book," 269–71.

40. John Rolfe gives a summary of the political arrangements at this time in a letter from 1617 (Rolfe, "True Relation," 868). The Council consisted of twelve persons, who elected one of their number as president. The system was dysfunctional, Rolfe wrote, largely because of the "envy, dissensions, and jars [that] were daily sown amongst them" (ibid.).

first guide, and experience his second; ever hating baseness, sloth, pride, and indignity, more than any dangers." He would not send his men into any danger "where he would not lead them himself."[41]

Smith set about putting the Jamestown settlement on a better footing and preparing for winter. He reorganized the village, trained men for defense, and saw to it that the colony's few crops were properly harvested. The "church was repaired, the storehouse [reroofed], buildings prepared for the supplies we expected, the fort reduced to a five-square form,[42] the order of the watch renewed," and everyone trained in firearm use, Smith reported. New living quarters were prepared for the expected "Second Supply" from England. The Indians watched with a mixture of concern and bemusement.[43] With Smith in charge, however, "a period of new and closer ties with Pocahontas" began.[44]

Captain Christopher Newport arrived with the Second Supply on September 29, while these preparations were moving ahead. In addition to provisions, Newport delivered seventy more colonists, including twenty-five "gentlemen," fourteen "tradesmen," and twelve "laborers." Among them also were two young boys and Jamestown's first two women. One was the wife of Thomas Forrest, gentleman, and the other was fourteen-year-old Anne Burras, her maid. Tom Forrest may have been related to George Forrest, who came earlier but unfortunately did not last long; he was killed in an Indian attack, "seventeen arrows sticking in him and one shot through him." He lived nearly a week before succumbing.[45]

Anne Burras, "the only unattached woman in a colony of about two hundred" males, by the end of the year was married to John Laydon, one of the original settlers.[46] This was "the first marriage we had in Virginia," Smith noted.[47]

It was now summer, 1608. Pocahontas, about twelve going on thirteen, had visited Jamestown several times. She had built a cross-cultural

41. William Fettiplace, quoted in Price, *Love and Hate,* 122 (spelling modernized).

42. Smith apparently means that two extensions or "points" were added to the original triangular palisade in order to give increased visibility.

43. Smith, "General History: The Third Book," 278.

44. Barbour, *Pocahontas,* 35.

45. Smith, "General History: The Third Book," 330; Woolley, *Savage Kingdom,* 170.

46. Price, *Love and Hate,* 91. One of the tradesmen was John Burras, perhaps Anne's brother.

47. Smith, "General History: The Third Book," 294.

friendship of sorts with John Smith. She sometimes played with the Jamestown boys and had slight acquaintance with several of the adults, who probably viewed her with a mix of curiosity and respect, as Powhatan's daughter. She was a communications link between the English and the Powhatan Indians, a source of intelligence on both sides.

Nothing more, yet. Certainly no romance with John Smith.

Victor Nehlig (1830-1909), *Pocahontas and John Smith*, 1870, oil on canvas, 90 1/2 x 76 1/8 inches. Brigham Young University Museum of Art, 1973. Used with permission.

Chapter Five

The Starving Time

As the days of the summer of 1608 began to shorten, John Smith worried about winter. Smith understood Jamestown's shaky situation. Surviving a second winter was no sure thing.

THE BRITISH "CORONATION" OF POWHATAN

Meanwhile Captain Newport had an odd task to perform. When he had returned to Virginia in late September with supplies and more settlers, he also carried a strange commission, thought up by his sponsors back in London. He was to perform the culturally ludicrous task of crowning Powhatan an English prince, subservient to the British crown. As Barbour puts it, "Someone in the royal council for Virginia conceived the notion that Powhatan could be brought to terms and made subject to King James by the simple expedient of sending him a copper crown, a red woolen robe, and an English bedstead to lie on in place of the pile of mats he used for his throne. Newport was . . . to celebrate a solemn coronation of Powhatan as a subject-king under the overlordship of James I, King of Great Britain, France, and Ireland, and Virginia."[1]

The effort was a measure of English cultural ignorance of the time. It was in fact precisely the opposite of what Powhatan intended in his

1. Barbour, *Pocahontas*, 36.

dealings with the English through John Smith. Powhatan saw *himself* as overlord, not some faraway ruler. Had not Smith himself already become Powhatan's "son"?

Both the British and the Powhatans were maneuvering for dominance. Smith was incredulous. Whose idea was this coronation? he mused.

Nevertheless, the "coronation" went forward, as ordered. First Smith had to visit Werowocomoco and get Powhatan to agree. With only four other Englishmen and accompanied by Namontack, just returned from England with Newport, Smith walked the twenty miles or so through the forest to Powhatan's capital.

Arriving at Werowocomoco, Smith discovered that Powhatan was journeying and had not yet returned. Since Smith was now a celebrity among the Powhatan—a weroance and Chief Powhatan's "son"—the Indians gave him a feast and provided special entertainment that evening.[2]

Smith gives a vivid account. At dusk the Indians led him and his companions to a "fair plain field," a clearing in the forest. A fire was burning, and Smith and the others were seated on mats nearby.

Suddenly from the woods the English heard "such a hideous noise and shrieking" they thought they were being attacked. Grabbing their guns, the English "seized on two or three old men by them" for protection, "supposing Powhatan with all his power" had laid an ambush. But then a young girl rushed to Smith, assuring him all was well; no harm intended. It was Pocahontas. He could kill her, she said, if any harm came. A number of other Indians around gave similar assurances, calming the English. Smith now saw that a group of Indian women and children as well as men were seated in the clearing and a show was about to begin.[3] Smith writes that now "thirty young women came naked out of the woods, only covered behind and before with a few green leaves, their bodies all painted, some of one color, some of another (some white, some red, some black, some parti-color), but all differing. Their leader had a fair pair of buck's horns on her head and an otter's skin at her girdle and another at her arm, a quiver of arrows at her back, a bow and arrows in her hand; the next had in her

2. It is not clear whether this entertainment was already scheduled, or was put on specially for Smith and his companions.

3. Smith, "General History: The Third Book," 280. Cf. Barbour, *Pocahontas*, 38; Price, *Love and Hate*, 92.

hand a sword, another a club, another a pot stick, all horned alike, the rest everyone with their several devices."[4]

The girls "with most hellish shouts and cries" (as they seemed to Smith) rushed to the fire and began circling it, passionately dancing and singing. This continued for an hour, the dancers "oft falling into their infernal passions and then solemnly again [continuing] to sing and dance."

The English were witnessing a mock war dance. Smith called it all a "masquerade," perhaps thinking of the court masques often held in England.[5] Just such a masque figures later in the Pocahontas story, in fact.[6]

The Indian dance over, the performers laid aside their costumes and conducted Smith to an Indian lodge. Here they crowded around him, chanting, "Love you not me? Love you not me?" Then a royal feast was set before them—"fruit in baskets, fish and flesh in wooden platters," plenty of beans and peas. While some of the women served, others sang and danced around the guests. Finally, this "mirth being ended," the English were led with firebrand torches to their lodgings.[7]

Apparently the women were offering themselves to Smith and his companions sexually—as would have been customary in such cases. Smith doesn't say so explicitly, but elsewhere he reports that honored guests on being escorted to their lodgings found a bed prepared and a woman "fresh painted red . . . to be his bedfellow."[8]

When Powhatan returned the next day, Smith explained his mission. The English king had sent him some royal gifts, and Powhatan was invited to Jamestown to receive them properly. The English king was offering to assist Powhatan against enemy tribes, and he also wanted Powhatan's help in finding a passage to "the great salt sea" to the west.

Powhatan's reply suggests his character, his self-image, and his position among the Indians. Powhatan told Smith: "If your King have sent me presents, I also am a king and this is my land. Eight days I will stay [here] to receive them. Your father [Newport] is to come to me, not I to him nor yet to your fort, neither will I bite at such a bait. As for the Monacans, I

---

4. Ibid., 281.

5. Ibid., 281. Rountree calls the drama "a mock war dance" (Rountree, *Pocahontas,* 112).

6. See chapter 10.

7. Smith, "General History: The Third Book," 281.

8. Rountree, *The Powhatan Indians,* 108. Cf. Price, *Love and Hate,* 93; Barbour, *Pocahontas,* 39. For a somewhat parallel situation with Englishmen in Tahiti in the 1770s, see Moorehead, *Fatal Impact,* chapter 2.

can revenge my own injuries. . . . But [as] for any salt water beyond the mountains, the [reports you have heard] are false."[9]

Powhatan certainly was not going to set foot inside Jamestown, where both his dignity and his safety might be in jeopardy. He remained outwardly friendly but still deeply resented the English presence and fully intended to maintain his empire and his dominance.

Smith returned to Jamestown and reported Powhatan's response. If they wanted a coronation, the English would have to go to him. Captain Newport therefore arranged an expedition by ship to bring the English gifts down the James to Chesapeake Bay and up the York River to Powhatan at Werowocomoco.

There the coronation of Powhatan, such as it was, did finally take place. Powhatan graciously accepted the bed, scarlet cloak, and other odd gifts from the English. He refused to kneel to receive the copper crown, but the English managed to get him to stoop a little and placed the crown on his head. The English then set off a celebratory volley of shots. This startled the Indians, but they soon saw they were not being attacked. Chief Powhatan gave a speech thanking the English for their kindness, and he gave Captain Newport his deerskin mantle and his old moccasins.[10]

The coronation in fact accomplished next to nothing. Powhatan still considered himself sovereign in Virginia, not beholden to the English, and the English still had to deal with an indigenous people who resented their presence and could turn hostile in a flash.

By now it was the fall of 1608. Winter was again approaching. Relations between John Smith—now president of the Jamestown Council—and Christopher Newport, who was special commissioner for the Virginia Company back in London, were strained. The two captains had conflicting agendas. Smith was mainly concerned with the safety and survival of Jamestown. Newport's mission was to return to London with some evidence that the colony was prospering (which it wasn't) and some new discoveries—gold, a passage to the Pacific, or something else that could bring profits. London investors were growing impatient for a return on capital, but Jamestown residents were struggling just to survive and to form some kind of viable society.

9. Smith, "General History: The Third Book," 281–82.

10. Ibid., 282; Barbour, *Pocahontas,* 40–42; Price, *Love and Hate,* 93–94; Rountree, *Pocahontas,* 112–14.

Shortly after Smith's and Newport's return from Chief Powhatan's "coronation," Newport commandeered more than half the men in Jamestown to explore further up the James River. They entered hostile Monacan territory and reached the falls of the James (present-day Richmond) but returned just a few days later, finding nothing of value to report back to London, and with many of the men sick.[11]

As soon as Newport returned, Smith put the able-bodied men to work felling trees for more lumber. Since he needed to send something back to London with Newport, he had some of the tradesman try making glass, pitch, tar, soap-ashes, and frankincense as samples of potentially profitable businesses.[12] At some point he set up a "glass house" outside the Jamestown fort to manufacture glass from the abundant sands along the river. Powhatan's spies kept a curious watch. They may have thought the glass house was "a temple or workshop of a whiteman's demon," Barbour suggests.[13]

The Jamestowners hadn't yet discovered the green gold that could be grown right out of the ground. It would be another four years before a newcomer named John Rolfe would prove that *tobacco* was the key to Virginia's prosperity.

Captain Newport sailed on his return trip to England in the ship *Mary and Margaret* in December, carrying off more provisions than Smith felt Jamestown could afford to part with. Nearly half of the remaining two hundred or so colonists were sick or otherwise incapacitated. With winter approaching, Smith was worried.[14]

And Smith found the Powhatans less and less cooperative. Chief Powhatan sensed the colony's vulnerability, and he was unhappy with English incursions further inland, including contact with tribes hostile to him. Powhatan decided that left alone, the colonists would likely starve, and he would be rid of them. Earlier the Spanish had come and gone; maybe the English would, too.

Over the winter however, through a combination of negotiation and intimidation, Smith managed to secure corn from the Powhatan and other Indian tribes. Chief Powhatan made it clear he would trade corn only for

---

11. Barbour, *Pocahontas*, 43. The "falls" are actually a seven-mile stretch where the James River gradually drops over one hundred feet as it runs in a rocky rapids through present-day Richmond.

12. Ibid., 43.

13. Ibid., 58.

14. Ibid., 44; Price, *Love and Hate*, 96.

weapons, which Smith wouldn't do. Smith threatened to dissolve his alliance with Powhatan if the chief wouldn't supply food. Powhatan knew this could mean war, and his men were no match for English guns.

Meanwhile some German craftsmen who were part of the Jamestown colony had at Powhatan's request gone to Werowocomoco to build the chief a new house. The Germans gave Powhatan important intelligence about the precarious conditions at Jamestown, in essence betraying the colony. They also helped the Powhatans acquire some weapons, including guns, from Jamestown during Smith's absence. Barbour suggests that these men—probably "woodsmen and glassblowers from the illimitable forests of central Europe"—had no affection for the English and were actually "more at home" among the Indians, who kept them well supplied.[15]

Early in the new year, 1609, Smith conducted tense negotiations over food with Powhatan at Werowocomoco. Powhatan feigned agreeability, and large quantities of corn were brought to be loaded onto Smith's barge. Smith and his men were treated as honored guests. But Powhatan was planning an ambush. He feared Smith and his men, who refused to lay aside their arms, might try to kill him. Powhatan himself disappeared into the forest, along with "his luggage, women, and children"—presumably including Pocahontas.[16]

Their barge now heavily loaded, Smith and his men had to wait for high tide on the York River in order to depart. They would have to stay the night.

As they were waiting, still being treated as honored guests, Pocahontas appeared at Smith's lodging with a warning of ambush. Now about thirteen, Pocahontas had apparently snuck away from her father's encampment in the woods under cover of the early winter darkness and run back to Werowocomoco. Finding Smith, she told him Powhatan would soon send food for a feast, but that while the English were feasting they would all be killed with their own weapons. Smith should leave at once; she herself was in danger for telling him.[17] Smith gratefully offered her some gifts such as she normally "delighted in." But Pocahontas "with tears running down her

---

15. Barbour, *Pocahontas*, 47, 53.

16. Rountree, *Pocahontas*, 122. Cf. Barbour, *Pocahontas*, 51; Price, *Love and Hate*, 103.

17. Rountree, *Pocahontas*, 123–24. Rountree accepts this story as likely true, "since it appears in two different accounts." Pocahontas's intervention was hardly a rescue, however, since surely Smith and his men had already "guessed Powhatan's intentions."

cheeks . . . said she durst not be seen to have any, for if Powhatan should know it, she were but dead, and so she ran away by herself as she came."[18]

Smith, ever wary, already suspected an ambush. When their food arrived the English ate it—first checking for poison—but kept their weapons at hand and maintained a careful watch through the night. "We spent the night as vigilantly as" the Indians did, Smith noted, yet with a pretense of friendship, acting toward the Indians "as friendly as they to us." Smith and his men departed the next morning as early as possible.[19]

John Smith would not see Pocahontas again for almost eight years, when she was in her twenties. Partly this was because Chief Powhatan as a defensive measure now moved his residence inland to Orapax, a town on the more remote Chickahominy River. Here he was near his childhood home and a good fifty miles from Werowocomoco.[20] For the English, this withdrawal was not a good sign.

THE STARVING TIME

In the ensuing months—spring and summer of 1609—Smith continued trading with various Indian groups, often at gunpoint (actual or implied) in order to keep Jamestown supplied. The settlement was still far from being self-sustaining, and a long drought complicated their agricultural ventures.

As the late spring weather warmed, Chief Powhatan's spies reported that the Jamestown settlers were planting large quantities of corn and beans. Apparently they intended to stay permanently. The Indians also noted the strange birds and animals the English had brought with them—chickens and pigs—which they kept at the settlement for food.

Under Smith's oversight the settlers were working harder—getting more productive and better organized. But there was still much dissension. And more skirmishes erupted between the Indians and the English as Smith tried both to force the Indians (Powhatans and others) to trade for food and to curb the worrisome attacks on settlers when they ventured outside the fort.

18. Smith, "General History: The Third Book," 303. There is no way of verifying the accuracy of Smith's account here.

19. Ibid., 303. Throughout the night "everyone was horribly polite to everyone else," Rountree says (*Pocahontas*, 124). Cf. Barbour, *Pocahontas*, 52.

20. Rountree, *Pocahontas*, 131; Barbour, *Pocahontas*, 51, 57. The Chickahominy River empties into the James several miles upstream from Jamestown.

By early summer 1609, Smith had acquired fairly large quantities of corn from the Indians. But the English hadn't learned to store it properly. To their dismay, much of the supply was ruined by dampness and by the rats and mice that had crossed the Atlantic with them as stowaways. Even though the weather was warm, the colony was already near starvation. Hunting and foraging in the forest was limited by justifiable fear of the Indians, and the settlers were still novices at fishing. They left all fourteen of their fishing nets in the water, where they had rotted.[21] Diminishing supplies of food further fueled tensions and dissensions among the settlers.

Then on July 13, 1609, Captain Samuel Argall arrived—a man much like John Smith in age and resourcefulness. Here was temporary relief. His small ship brought some supplies, and over the next month or so several larger ships arrived.[22] Though the new ships brought supplies, they also brought a flood of more raw settlers, increasing the demand on Jamestown's resources. The English colony now numbered around 500.[23]

Samuel Argall, an excellent navigator who had discovered a faster route across the Atlantic, sailed back to England six weeks later. He would return to Virginia several times and eventually played a key role in the Pocahontas story.

More British Investment

Back in London, Virginia Company leaders were worried. Ships returning from Jamestown brought news of the colonists' struggles and deaths and their conflicts with the Indians.

By 1609 it was clear that the Jamestown experiment was not going well. Realizing more money and settlers were needed, the Virginia Company launched a new fund-raising campaign. A "profusion of propaganda publications" urged people "of all walks of life to emigrate to the New World."[24] One example was *A Good Speed to Virginia,* by the Anglican clergyman Robert Gray. Gray painted a rosy picture of the settlers' lives in North America and on his pamphlet's cover quoted Isaiah 42:4, "He shall

21. Price, *Love and Hate,* 124.

22. Ibid., 112.

23. Barbour, *Pocahontas,* 58–61.

24. Brazil, "More Virginia Propaganda."

not fail nor be discouraged, till he have set judgment in the earth: and the isles shall wait for his law."[25]

Gray recognized the moral and ethical quandaries, however. Though he was sure God was with the colonists, he questioned, "by what right or warrant we can enter in the land of these Savages, take away their rightful inheritance from them, and plant ourselves in their places, being unwronged or unprovoked by them"?[26] His answer: colonization was God's will for the ultimate benefit of the Indians themselves, who should be treated humanely. As Townsend notes, "the central question turned on how the English might colonize the New World and harness the labor of the Indians without cruelly oppressing them" the way the Spanish had in Central and South America. Under the British, the Indians would become Christians and British subjects. They would be more productive, and "ultimately be better off than they were before."[27]

So the fund drive went ahead. This time small shares were offered to the public. The company enlisted clergymen, who saw the New World as a mission field, to promote the stock offering in their churches. Some 659 investors quickly signed up, infusing the project with lots of new cash. The Virginia Company painted a rosy picture of life in Virginia, and soon another 600 people offered to go as settlers in return for a share in company profits.[28]

Promotional material assured doubtful candidates that the native Indians, though primitive and "savage," were "by nature loving and gentle, and desirous to embrace a better condition." The English certainly would not "exercise any bloody cruelty" toward the natives. As one writer put it, "There is no intention to take away from them by force that rightful inheritance which they have in that country, for they are willing to entertain us, and have offered to yield into our hands on reasonable conditions, more land than we shall be able this long time to plant and manure . . . . [Thus] we may have as much of their country yielded unto us, by lawful grant from them, as we can or will desire, so that we go to live peaceably among them, and not to supplant them."[29]

---

25. Gray, *Good Speed to Virginia,* image of title page.

26. Quoted in Townsend, *Pocahontas,* 35.

27. Ibid., 35–36.

28. Price, *Love and Hate,* 110–11.

29. Quotations from ibid. (spelling modernized).

As Price notes, this was "a reasonable description of the company's intentions, but a largely fictitious version of the natives' receptivity."[30]

Expansion of the Virginia Colony

As settlers increased, the English needed more land for additional settlements. Smith sailed upriver and forced the Indians to cede him the site of the village of Powhatan—Chief Powhatan's birth town. The English were again encroaching on the chief's territory, further antagonizing him and the other Powhatans.[31]

On his return Smith was badly burned in a gunpowder accident. While he was traveling in a small boat, the powder bag in his lap exploded, severely burning him. His life hung in the balance for days, but gradually he recovered. Shortly thereafter he disappeared. The Indians were puzzled. Pocahontas heard he had died. Believing this was true, she stopped her Jamestown visits. For four years the English knew nothing of her.

The truth was that Smith returned to England on one of the supply ships that departed around the first of October, 1609. His one-year term as Jamestown Council president had ended on September 10.

Smith's departure was a disaster for Jamestown. In crucial ways, Smith had been an effective leader. Though he didn't yet see tobacco's promise as a cash crop, he had a much more realistic idea of the colony's potential as a profit center than did Newport or the investors and speculators back in London. He knew Jamestown could not supply "*present* profit" to the Virginia Company until the colony was itself self-sustaining.[32]

With Smith gone, the Jamestown Council elected George Percy as his successor. Twenty-nine, Oxford educated, of noble birth, Percy seemed a good choice. But Percy was not as seasoned or culturally astute as Smith. He despised the rough and poorly educated Smith, calling him "ambitious, unworthy and vainglorious." Percy however was less capable of dealing with Jamestown's challenges. Smith was ready to adjust to new realities, but Percy expected to live like a London aristocrat, maintaining a "daily table for gentlemen of fashion." Befitting his new status as council president, he sent back to England for a whole new wardrobe, including five suits,

30. Ibid., 111.

31. Barbour, *Pocahontas*, 60–61.

32. Haile, ed., *Jamestown Narratives*, 291. Cf. Price, *Love and Hate*, 96. Smith's frustration with the Virginia Company personnel is obvious in his caustic language.

multiple pairs of shoes and boots, plus stockings and laces, six nightcaps, and a gold-decorated sword—among other items.[33]

Percy was to serve only until Sir Thomas Gates should arrive from England. According to a new Virginia charter approved in London, Gates would be the colony's first governor, replacing the Jamestown Council president and presumably providing better oversight.[34]

Meanwhile, as always, the Indians were watching. With Smith's disappearance as Jamestown's *weroance*, Powhatan may have felt freer to plot the invaders' annihilation. The chief now had a growing stockpile of weapons—guns, some 200 swords, and other items they had stolen, bartered from disloyal or desperate settlers, or recovered from slain English soldiers.[35]

But Powhatan didn't yet have enough firepower to confront the English in open warfare. Instead his strategy would be gradual eradication through ambush, deception, and assassination, as opportunity allowed. He planned to "contain them, then let them starve."[36] Winter was fast approaching; the weather would be his ally as the settlers battled the cold, dwindling supplies, cultural ineptitude, and dissension.[37]

The full moon on November 1, 1609—All Saints Day—was not a good omen for Jamestown. That day the Indians killed many of the settlers who had been sent to establish other sites—mostly in retaliation for English attacks. Other settlers fled back to Jamestown for safety. The colony's provisions would last only a couple more months—and that only if each person ate a mere half can of meal daily.[38] Council President Percy noted, "So our numbers at James Town [were] increasing and our store decreasing."[39]

Percy concluded that he had to somehow bargain with Powhatan. He sent Captain John Ratcliffe and fifty men by ship to Orapax to negotiate for food.[40]

33. Price, *Love and Hate*, 123.

34. Barbour, *Pocahontas*, 61.

35. William Strachey reported that, "seizing [the settlers'] arms, swords, pieces [guns]," Powhatan had "gathered into his store a great quantity and number, by intelligence above two hundred swords, besides axes and poleaxes, chisels, hoes," and other items ("True Reportory," 435–36).

36. Rountree, *Pocahontas*, 134.

37. Barbour, *Pocahontas*, 61.

38. Ibid., 62; Price, *Love and Hate*, 124.

39. Percy, "Relation," 504.

40. Barbour, *Pocahontas*, 63; Price, *Love and Hate*, 125.

Chief Powhatan was gracious at first and seemed willing to trade. But later when the English (unlike their compatriot Smith) let their guard down, the Indians attacked and killed most of them as they were loading provisions onto their ship. Ratcliffe, as the leader, was taken alive. According to Percy's account, Powhatan "caused [Ratcliffe] to be bound unto a tree naked with a fire before, and by women his flesh was scraped from his bones with mussel shells and, before his face, thrown into the fire; and so for want of circumspection [he] miserably perished."[41]

Jamestown was now truly terrified. Percy sent another colonist, Francis West, and thirty-five men to a town of a different tribe, the Potomacs, to see if they could get food. West was able to acquire a good quantity of corn, probably by force. But then, wanting no more of Jamestown, West and his crew inexplicably set sail for England, leaving the colony in "extreme misery and want."[42]

Over the winter "a world of miseries ensued," Percy reported—so much so that "some, to satisfy their hunger, have robbed the store, for the which I caused them to be executed. Then having fed upon horses and other beasts as long as they lasted, we were glad to make shift with [such creatures] as dogs, cats, rats, and mice, [then devouring] boots, shoes, or any other leather some could come by."[43]

Percy forced settlers to search for snakes, roots, or anything else to eat—but many of the foragers were "cut off and slain by the savages. And now famine [was] beginning to look ghastly and pale in every face," Percy wrote. Some of the English dug up recently buried corpses for food or "licked up the blood" of the injured or dying. Percy added, "To eat, many of our men this starving time did run away unto the savages, whom we never heard of after."[44]

Other eyewitness accounts recorded by Edward Haile in *Jamestown Narratives* underscore the horror. One report says the winter weather was so cold that:

41. Percy, "Relation," 504. Other English captives were similarly treated if the Powhatans viewed them as having wronged the natives.

42. Ibid., 505.

43. Ibid. In recent decades archeologists have found bones of rats, dogs, and poisonous snakes among the Jamestown food remains from this time (Kupperman, *Jamestown Project*, 360).

44. Percy, "Relation," 505–6. Much of Jamestown's misery during the "starving time" was due to the absence of the key leaders and capable settlers who were shipwrecked on Bermuda.

it was not possible for us to endure to wade in the water as formerly to gather oysters to satisfy our hungry stomachs, but [we were] constrained to dig in the ground for unwholesome roots, whereof we were not able to get so many as would suffice us, [due to] the frost at that season and our poverty and weakness; so that famine compelled us wholly to devour those hogs, dogs, and horses that were then in the colony, together with rats, mice, snakes, or what vermin or carrion soever we could light on, as also toadstools, jew's ears [an edible tree fungus], or what else we found growing upon the ground that would fill either mouth or belly; and were driven through unsufferable hunger to eat those things which nature most abhorred: the flesh and excrements of man, as well of our own nation as of an Indian digged by some out of his grave after he had lain buried three days, and wholly devoured him.... One among the rest slew his wife as she slept in his bosom, cut her in pieces, [salted] her, and fed upon her till he had clean devoured all parts saving her head, and was for so barbarous a fact and cruelty justly executed.[45]

His name was Henry Collins, one of Jamestown's "gentlemen." His wife was pregnant; he threw their unborn child into the river. When the deed was discovered, George Percy wrote, "the acknowledgement of the deed [was] enforced from him by torture, having hung by the thumbs with weights at his feet a quarter of an hour, before he would confess," whereupon he was burned to death.[46]

Over the winter a small group of men had been left at a place called Point Comfort, a small lookout fort at the mouth of the James just inside Chesapeake Bay. Toward the end of May, Percy sailed downriver to see if they had survived. To his surprise, he found the men in good health and with so much seafood that they had been able to keep their pigs alive. Their plan was to return to England rather than help the Jamestown community.

Percy put a stop to that and devised a plan to relieve Jamestown. Then the English saw two ships approaching from the Atlantic. Spaniards? No, as it turned out it was two British boats bearing governor-designate Sir Thomas Gates, Sir George Somers, a man named John Rolfe, his wife, and about 140 others.

This group of settlers was supposed to have arrived with Captain Newport months earlier. But their ship, *Sea Venture*, was blown off course

45. Ancient Planters of Virginia, "Brief Declaration," 895–96.

46. Percy, "Relation," 505. Cf. Haile, ed., *Jamestown Narratives*, 473–74; Woolley, *Savage Kingdom*, 257–58.

in a hurricane and wrecked on Bermuda, hundreds of miles across open sea from Jamestown.

The British found enough food on Bermuda to survive. In February of 1610, John Rolfe's wife gave birth to a baby girl, whom the parents named Bermuda. The baby soon died, however, and was buried on the island.

Over several months the survivors under Captain Somers's direction ingeniously managed to build two new ships from the wreckage of the *Sea Venture*, supplemented by local cedar. Named *Patience* and *Deliverance*, the vessels successfully if belatedly carried the survivors the remaining distance northwest to Virginia.[47]

The news of the Bermuda shipwreck eventually reached England. William Shakespeare heard it and got the idea for a new play. The result was *The Tempest*, his final drama, which appeared on stage about a year later, in 1611.

The *Patience* and *Deliverance* arrived at Jamestown on May 24, 1610. There, Percy reported, the newcomers could "read a lecture of misery in our people's faces, and perceive the scarcity of victuals, and understand the malice of the savages who knowing our weakness had divers times assaulted us without the fort, [so that now] of five hundred men we had only left about sixty, the rest being either starved through famine or cut off by the savages and those which were living [were so emaciated] that it was lamentable to behold them."[48]

Barbour notes that as usual, the blame was "always thrust upon the Indians, whose territory [the English] had occupied and whose rights they refused to recognize."[49] One contemporary report put it this way: "It were too vile to say what we endured, . . . but the occasion was only our own, for want of providence, industry, and government, and not the barrenness and defect of the country, as is generally supposed. . . . Had we been in Paradise itself (with those governors) it would not have been much better with us."[50]

Despite the new arrivals from Bermuda, the Jamestown community was still in trouble. The newcomers had only about two weeks' supply of provisions with them, and attempts at gathering food around Jamestown were unsuccessful. Thomas Gates—now in charge, as governor—decided in early June that it was best to abandon the colony entirely and return to

47. Barbour, *Pocahontas*, 66.

48. Percy, "Relation," 507.

49. Barbour, *Pocahontas*, 66.

50. Anonymous report, quoted in Price, *Love and Hate*, 129 (spelling modernized).

England. On June 7, 1610, everyone boarded the four small ships they had available (including *Deliverance* and *Patience*), thankful for the prospect of safety in their native land.[51]

They were in for a surprise. Before they reached Point Comfort and the Chesapeake Bay, the colonists encountered three ships just arriving from England. The newcomers brought lots of food and 150 more settlers. The ships were under the command of Samuel Argall. More importantly, Argall had brought Thomas West, Lord De La Warr (Delaware), with him from London. West, in his early thirties and a cousin of the late Queen Elizabeth, was a tough character who had seen battle with the English in the Netherlands.[52] The colonists learned that West had been appointed governor and captain-general of Virginia for life. West immediately ordered the fleeing colonists back to Jamestown, to their "great grief," and quickly took charge, replacing Gates.[53]

West reorganized the colony, setting up a new Jamestown council. The new council included Thomas Gates, George Somers, George Percy, Captain Christopher Newport, and William Strachey—though Gates and Newport returned to England a month later. West also appointed men in charge of the Jamestown fort and its various operations. He made plain what he thought of the situation: "I delivered some few words unto the [Jamestown survivors], laying some blames upon them for many vanities and their idleness, earnestly wishing that I might no more find it so lest I should be compel'd to draw the sword in justice to cut off such delinquents which I had much rather draw in their defense to protect from enemies, heartening them with the knowledge of what store of provisions I had brought for them."[54]

West had not had time yet fully to assess or understand the situation, but he left no doubt who was in charge. The settlement now had enough rations, but no fresh meat. During the winter they had eaten all their horses and other animals, and the Indians had killed their hogs and driven the

---

51. Price, *Love and Hate,* 137–38.

52. Thomas West was the older brother of Francis West, who had previously sailed back to England with provisions that were supposed to have relieved the Jamestown settlers.

53. Price, *Love and Hate,* 138; Barbour, *Pocahontas,* 75; Haile, ed., *Jamestown Narratives,* 64–65.

54. Governor and Council in Virginia, "Letter to the Virginia Company," 458–59.

deer away. Meat would be scarce until the colony could be restocked with animals and the English learn properly how to fish in Chesapeake Bay.[55]

The Powhatan Indians were of course dismayed to see this resurgence of Jamestown. Chief Powhatan ordered the Indians not to trade with the settlers, but rather to attack them on land or water whenever the foreigners ventured from the fort.[56]

Governor West determined he would force Powhatan to come to terms. He demanded that Powhatan cease all hostilities and return the weapons and tools they had stolen—else he would attack. Powhatan sent back word that the English should either leave Virginia entirely, or at least stay within the confines of Jamestown—or *he* would continue his attacks. Meanwhile the Indians kept up their harassment. Any settlers who went searching for berries or edible nuts might well never return. (John Smith would have gone and negotiated personally with Powhatan—keeping himself well protected—probably with much better results.)

Incensed by Chief Powhatan's belligerence, West sent George Percy on a retaliatory raid to a nearby Indian town. It was plain terrorism, and as often happens, it turned out worse than expected. Percy's men killed about fifteen Indians, burned the village, and shortsightedly destroyed the corn crop. Most of the natives fled, but the English captured several Indians, including one of the *weroance's* wives (Percy called her "the queen") and her children.

Since this attack was revenge, Percy intended to spare no one. Back on shipboard, he consulted with his men, and they decided to take the woman back to Jamestown but kill her children. This "was effected," Percy said, "by throwing them overboard and shooting out their brains in the water." Once the English were back at Jamestown, the "queen" was taken into the woods and put to the sword.[57]

Governor West later ordered other raids, some of which were carried out by Samuel Argall. He burned two more Indian towns, destroying their implements, supplies, and corn crops. In consequence most of the Indians

---

55. Price, *Love and Hate*, 140; Barbour, *Pocahontas*, 76. An attempt to sail to Bermuda and bring back hogs from there failed.

56. Barbour, *Pocahontas*, 77.

57. Percy, "True Relation," 510. Cf. Rountree, *Pocahontas*, 150–51; Barbour, *Pocahontas*, 80; Price, *Love and Hate*, 142–43.

moved further inland where they would be protected by distance and the forests.[58]

The English and the Powhatans were at a virtual stalemate. Jamestown was now large enough and sufficiently provisioned, armed, and organized to withstand Indian attacks. Though the colony was always in danger of running out of food, resupply ships arrived from time to time, and on at least one occasion, around Christmas 1610, Argall managed to buy 400 bushels of corn, peas, and beans, plus "many kinds of furs" from the more distant Potomac Indians.[59]

The colony was thus more secure due to its increasing size and strength. Price writes, "Warfare against Powhatan would continue, with occasional brutality on both sides, for several more years. There would be waves of illness and other setbacks. . . . The formidable challenges still confronting the colony—achieving peace with Powhatan or victory over him, for one, and keeping the investors happy, for another—would not [now be confronted] under the shadow of imminent extinction."[60]

58. Barbour, *Pocahontas,* 84–86.

59. Ibid., 87–88.

60. Price, *Love and Hate,* 143.

Chapter Six

Kidnapped
Pocahontas Betrayed

The Virginia winter of 1610–11—a year after the starving time—was exceptionally cold. "The ground was covered most with snow and the season sharp," wrote Thomas West, the lord governor.[1]

Governor West himself was unwell. As his health declined—a combination of gout, scurvy, and other ills—he thought it best to return to England. He sailed away in March in a ship captained by Samuel Argall. West never fully recovered. He died on an attempted return to Virginia in 1618 at about age 40.[2]

West had left George Percy temporarily in charge of Jamestown, but Sir Thomas Dale arrived on May 12, 1611, in a ship captained by Christopher Newport. Dale immediately took charge. Due to his military commission from England, he in short order became Jamestown's virtual dictator, instituting martial law.[3] "The military discipline which John Smith had labored to inculcate on the colony from within was soon imposed from without."[4] Unlike Smith, however, Dale was unswervingly hostile toward

1. West, "Short Relation," 531.

2. Barbour, *Pocahontas,* 89.

3. Dale apparently instituted a legal code derived mainly from the rules of war of the United Provinces (Netherlands), which had been sent over with Dale by Thomas Smythe, the Virginia Company treasurer, though without the company's endorsement.

4. Barbour, *Pocahontas,* 89. Officially Dale was marshal of the Virginia colony from

the Indians—not interested in trying to understand them or build relationships. Indians were the enemy.

Dale had brought another 300 colonists, plus food and plenty of weapons. Someone thought of the metal armor stored away in the Tower of London—obsolete since the advent of firearms. Such medieval armor offered defense against arrows, so Dale brought some armor along.

The English presence along the James River was about to expand rapidly.

Dale had been knighted by King James in 1606.[5] He was a pious Christian but lacked cultural sensitivity or compassion, and showed little sympathy for the colonists themselves. His harsh legal code, revising and expanding existing laws, made offenses from blasphemy to murder to pilfering corn punishable by death.[6] Duties of Anglican priests were prescribed: "All preachers or ministers . . . shall . . . preach every Sabbath day in the forenoon, and catechize in the afternoon, and weekly say the divine service twice every day, and preach every Wednesday." Ministers were to keep careful records of "all christenings, marriages, and deaths," and to inform the authorities of any settlers who neglected "their duties and service to God."[7]

Dale's harsh enforcement of these laws became legendary. When settlers who ran off to the Indians were captured by the English, Dale had them executed. "Some he appointed to be hanged, some burned, some to be broken upon wheels, others to be staked, and some to be shot to death. All these extreme and cruel tortures he used and inflicted upon them to terrify the rest [from] attempting the like; and some which robbed the store, he caused them to be bound fast unto trees and so starved them to death," Percy reported.[8]

One scholar likens Dale's criminal code to that of the Spanish Inquisition a century earlier. It was "bloodier than the cruelest laws of England in that day" and "sterner than any criminal jurisprudence in all of Western

---

1611 to 1614, and then deputy governor until his return to England in 1616. Lord Delaware (Thomas West) had been named governor, but due to his ailments and early return to England, Dale was the man in charge (Scarboro, *Establisher*, 13).

5. Scarboro, *Establisher*, 20.

6. Scarboro provides some analysis of the laws instituted by Dale, sometimes called the "Dale Code" (ibid., 14–15).

7. "Laws Divine and Moral" section of the 1611 code, quoted in Haile, ed., *Jamestown Narratives*, 29.

8. Percy, "Relation," 518.

Europe in the seventeenth century."[9] Testimony taken for a later British government inquiry declared that Dale's laws for the Virginia Colony were "written in blood," causing "the unjust and undeserved death" of a number of English settlers. Some contemporary accounts picture Jamestown under Dale as being run more as a penal colony than as a town.

From the beginning, Jamestown colonists had been forbidden ever to return to England. Now Dale made leaving the colony—deserting, or attempting to return home—punishable by death. Not until 1617 would colonists be free to go back to England.[10]

Dale's harsh rule was possible because the English Crown in 1609 issued a new charter that in essence made the Virginia Company in England the colony's sole government. The company's laws were supposed to be "as near and as conveniently" as possible "agreeable to the laws, statutes, governments, and policy" of England, but the language and the circumstances opened the door to laws and punishments that had no parallel in contemporary British experience.[11]

Dale seems to have regarded many of the colonists as little more than criminals, clearly considering them his social inferiors. He complained that many were unruly, having been collected in England from unhealthy "riotous" and "infected places."[12] In fact the high mortality rate at Jamestown may have been due in part to the fact that many of the poorer colonists were in weak health already when they arrived in Virginia. Dale saw that the colony needed many more people and sent the suggestion back to England that (in Scarboro's words) "for the next three years all men condemned to die in England [be taken] out of the common jails as the Spanish did to furnish manpower for the West Indies."[13]

FROM SURVIVAL TO EXPANSION

Dale's rule "is condemned for harshness on one hand and praised for order and progress on the other," notes Haile. Dale implemented the Virginia Company's policy of decentralization—establishing new settlements that in

9. Scarboro, *Establisher*, 14.

10. Price, *Love and Hate*, 147.

11. Scarboro, *Establisher*, 17.

12. Ibid., 15–16.

13. Ibid., 17, citing Brown, *Genesis*, 1:506.

time would become plantations.[14] Dale has been described as, next to John Smith, the "ablest soldier and the most sagacious administrator to come to Virginia in the seventeenth century."[15] Yet he was the opposite of Smith in his view of the Indians; a sharp contrast to Smith's willingness to work with the Indians and in his sympathetic interest in the native land and culture.

Dale was essentially a military man. He saw his service in Virginia largely in military—and Old Testament—terms. He was on a great expedition for God and country. In a letter to Sir Thomas Smyth, Dale likened his mission to Joshua's conquest of the promised land.[16] Remaining in Virginia until May 1616, he would play a key role in the Pocahontas story.[17]

Dale mounted fresh attacks on the Indians, sometimes leading them himself. The Indians were mystified that the English soldiers no longer fell when struck by arrows. George Percy reported that seeing this, the Indians "did fall into their exorcisms, conjurations, and charms, throwing fire up into the skies, running up and down with rattles, and making many diabolical gestures with many necromantic spells and incantations, imagining thereby to cause rain to fall from the clouds to extinguish . . . our men's matches [for firing muskets] and spoil their powder."[18]

All to no avail. "For our men cut down their corn, burned their houses and, besides those which they had slain, brought some of them prisoners to our fort."[19]

The English colony was now spreading out. More settlements and forts were established along the James and adjacent rivers. Dale's goal was to gain full control of the land between the James and the York—that is, from what is now Richmond down to Chesapeake Bay.[20]

Meanwhile Governor Thomas Gates returned to Virginia with a fleet of nine ships. Dale turned the governorship of the colony back over to Gates but remained as military commander and in fact continued as dominant leader. The colony was again reorganized with plans laid for further

---

14. Haile, ed., *Jamestown Narratives,* 46. Haile notes that Dale's "program of decentralization of settlements, in fact a policy assignment of the Council of Virginia, was only temporarily interrupted after the massacre of 1622."

15. Scarboro, *Establisher,* 13, quoting W. Gordon McCabe.

16. Ibid., 21.

17. Barbour, *Pocahontas,* 90.

18. Percy, "Relation," 515.

19. Ibid.

20. Barbour, *Pocahontas,* 94.

expansion. First came the founding of the colony's second town, Henrico, named for the English Prince Henry.[21] Dale marked out more sites for plantations up the James River as far as the falls where Richmond now sits. Fearing Indians and possibly Spaniards, he fortified the colony from the mouth of Chesapeake Bay to the falls, eighty miles upstream.[22]

Henrico, about sixty miles upriver from Jamestown, was much better suited for settlement than was swampy James Island. The Virginia Company had instructed Dale to move the colony's seat of government to a healthier site, and one less vulnerable to potential Spanish attack by sea. Dale chose a high piece of land at a horseshoe bend in the James River. Across the neck of the horseshoe he built a stockade and cut a deep ditch, the ditch forming a kind of moat. Dale used a technique he had learned in Holland, and the ditch soon became known as Dale's Dutch Gap. On this well-protected site the town of Henrico was built.[23]

Dale intended that the English would take complete possession not only of all the land between the York and the James rivers, but additional Indian lands as well. He built forts and mapped out numerous large tracts, called "hundreds," for future settlement. He also instituted new policies that offered incentives for people to raise their own food and thus become self-sufficient, rather than depending upon the common store to which all contributed. New settlers were promised a four-room house with twelve acres of land, tools, livestock, and enough food to see them through the first year.[24] The experiment in freer enterprise worked.

21. Ibid., 94–95.

22. Scarboro, *Establisher*, 22.

23. Ibid. Henricus Historical Park now stands at the approximate site of Henrico. This area saw action during the Civil War and then in 1870 the US government built the Dutch Gap Canal—expanded later during the twentieth century to farther shorten the river and accommodate larger ships. Today therefore the original site is much altered; a huge Dominion Virginia Power plant fed by a constant string of coal cars covers much of the area. See "Henricus Historical Park," lines 16–23.

24. Scarboro, *Establisher*, 26–29. "Whereas the colonists had formerly been fed from the common store and had labored jointly in the production of food, Dale had now 'taken a new course' in the whole colony by allowing each man three acres of ground upon which to bestow his own labor for eleven months of the year with one month a year to be given to the common labor. Hamor promised to any new settler a house of four rooms, rent free, with twelve acres of ground attached to it and a year's provision of food from the common store. In addition he promised tools in order that after the first year the settler might become self-sufficient, and he also promised poultry and swine, and to the deserving settler, a goat or two and a cow" (ibid., 28–29).

The Virginia colony, now extending well beyond Jamestown, survived the 1611–12 winter much better than the previous winter's "starving time." Settlers began experimenting with various crops, including tobacco. Still, the colony was far from being self-sustaining.

GOOD NEWS FROM VIRGINIA

The Virginia colony of 1612 was remarkably different from the struggling Jamestown settlement of just a few years earlier. To counter the bad press still circulating in London, the young Anglican priest and missionary Alexander Whitaker wrote "Good News from Virginia" and sent it off to England. Whitaker, whom a later Anglican churchman described as "faithful and true-hearted," had helped Dale lay the foundation of Henrico.[25]

Whitaker's pamphlet was actually a long sermon on Ecclesiastes 11:1—"Cast thy bread upon the waters: for after many days thou shalt find it." He addressed it to the Virginia Company in London but sent it to his friend William Crashaw. In 1613 Crashaw quickly got it into print, together with his own lengthy introduction, as *Good News from Virginia*.[26]

Whitaker reported that since the starving time, "this English colony hath taken better root; and as a spreading herb whose top hath been often cropped off renews her growth, and spreads herself more gloriously than before, so this plantation, which the devil hath so often trodden down, is by the miraculous blessing of God revived, and daily groweth to more happy and hopeful success."[27] Whitaker celebrated the colony's emerging prosperity as a vine of God's planting. He challenged the Virginia Company and its investors to do more, and offered a stirring missionary challenge that predated William Carey's *Enquiry into the Obligations of Christians to use Means for the Conversion of the Heathens* (1792) by well over a century and a half.[28]

---

25. Anderson, *History*, 1:225 (quotation), 234.

26. Crashaw says *Good News from Virginia* was actually preached as a sermon in Virginia and was intended "rather for the private use and encouragement" of the colony's supporters (actual or potential) "than with any intent to make it public" (William Crashaw's Epistle Dedicatory in Whitaker, *Good News*, 698).

27. Whitaker, *Good News*, 730.

28. For this and other reasons, it is highly misleading to call William Carey "the father of modern missions." Carey himself pointed to the prior missionary work of the Moravians, David Brainerd, John Wesley, and others.

Alexander Whitaker is an intriguing figure who deserves to be much better known. He probably would be, had he not died just six years after arriving in Virginia. He drowned while crossing the James River, probably in a small boat while attending to his parish duties. But for several crucial months he played a key role in Pocahontas's life.

Whitaker (1585–1617) was an Anglican missionary with a vision for converting America's Indians to Christianity—very much like John Wesley 112 years later.[29] His father, the Rev. Dr. William Whitaker, was Master of St. Johns College, Cambridge, and Regius professor of divinity. A respected Puritan author,[30] the elder Whitaker was "the champion and spokesman of the Calvinistic interpretation of the Church's teachings," notes William Littleton.[31] Alexander's mother, Susan Culverwell, had family connections with some of London's wealthiest families. She died, however, when Alexander was only four, and the elder Whitaker himself died in 1595, when Alexander was ten.[32]

Alexander entered Cambridge University in about 1604. It was "an exciting moment to be a student of religion: the professors were in the midst of the agitating and inspiring work of debating the nature of Protestantism and writing the King James Bible."[33] Alexander's uncle was a member of the translation and revision committee.

Whitaker was ordained in 1609. He began serving as parish priest in northern England near York[34] but soon left his "comfortable life" there to accompany Thomas Dale to Virginia in 1611.

---

29. "Wesley went to Georgia explicitly to convert the Indians to Christianity" (Hammond, *John Wesley in America,* 148). Wesley traveled to the Georgia Colony in 1735 as a missionary of the Anglican Society for the Propagation of the Gospel (SPG); Whitaker went to Virginia about eighty years before the SPG was founded. Hammond discusses Wesley's contacts with and views of the Indians in *John Wesley in America,* 148–53 ("The Indian Mission").

30. William Whitaker (1548–1595) has been described as "one of the first great gifted Cambridge Puritan theologians" who wrote "the best rebuttal and debate on the authority of Scripture against the Roman Catholics" (Whitaker, W., "Mediator," lines 1–3).

31. Littleton, "Alexander Whitaker," 328. Cf. Bailyn, *Barbarous Years,* 45.

32. The best source is Porter, "Alexander Whitaker." Cf. Townsend, *Pocahontas,* 111; Haile, ed., *Jamestown Narratives,* 65–66. Due to his parents' deaths, Alexander had some personal financial resources by inheritance.

33. Townsend, *Pocahontas,* 111.

34. Possibly in or near the town of Burton Agnes, Yorkshire; in his will Whitaker mentions a debt of seven pounds owed him by "Sir Henry Griffith of Burton Agnes . . . for a chest of viols which I sold him" (Whitaker, Will).

Knowing his future was uncertain and "sea voyages most dangerous," Whitaker executed his will on February 16, 1610, as he prepared to leave England, so that "I might have my soul more free for heavenly contemplation," as he phrased it. He appointed his brother Samuel as executor, giving him twenty-four pounds, all his moveable goods, and "my Bill of Adventure to Virginia and all profits therefrom."[35]

Whitaker intended to return to England after three years. But he continued on, remaining until his untimely death in 1617. By then he was serving as priest at the Bermuda Nether Hundred settlement, downriver a ways from Henrico.[36] He would later be called the "Apostle to Virginia."[37]

Much like John Wesley a century later, Alexander Whitaker went to America to convert the Indians. That was his primary aim, and in that regard he was more successful than Wesley in Georgia.

Whitaker landed with Dale at Jamestown but was soon posted further inland, up the James River at the new Henrico settlement. In an early letter to his friend William Crashaw in England, dated August 9, 1611, Whitaker described his early encounters with the Indians and his fascination with their customs and beliefs. He wrote, "I think that the Lord has spared this people and enriched the bowels of the country with the riches and beauty of nature that we wanting them might in the search of them communicate the most excellent merchandise and treasure of the gospel with them." Whitaker hoped that now God would "fulfill his purpose and set up the kingdom of his son" in Virginia.[38]

Whitaker served as preacher at Henrico from 1612 to about 1616. At the time of writing *Good News from Virginia* he was performing "daily and diligent service" as Anglican pastor. He "diligently preacheth and catechizeth," wrote Crashaw.[39]

Whitaker's duties would have included "holding services twice daily, preaching on Wednesday and Sunday, catechising on Sunday afternoon," meeting regularly with his four parish wardens, and keeping the official record book. He delighted in gardening—a duty as well as a pleasure, since

35. Ibid. Whitaker left small amounts to his sisters and another brother and listed money owed him and some small debts to be paid from his estate.

36. Littleton, W., "Alexander Whitaker," 336; Haile, ed., *Jamestown Narratives*, 65–66.

37. Porter, "Alexander Whitaker."

38. Whitaker, letter to William Crashaw (English modernized).

39. Crashaw, Epistle Dedicatory, in Whitaker, *Good News*, 707.

he was expected to provide most of his own food. He also became a skilled fisherman as he discovered many varieties of fish in the James River.[40]

Whitaker's *Good News from Virginia* is a remarkable missionary manifesto. He makes the case for converting the Indians, but not before raking over the coals those who invested in the colony with wrong motives and priorities. Virginia had not prospered earlier, Whitaker charged, because many of the investors "have not been reconciled to God nor approved [by] Him." In fact, said Whitaker, sounding like a true Puritan, "Some of our adventurers [investors and backers] in London have been most miserable covetous men, sold over to usury, extortion, and oppression. Many of the men sent hither [as settlers] have been murderers, thieves, adulterers, idle persons, and whatnot besides, all which persons God hateth even from His very soul. How then could their alms or anything else which they do be pleasing unto God?"[41]

But now the time has come for redoubled efforts to support the colony, Whitaker says, and above all to convert the Indians. "Surely if there were ever an opportunity given of setting forward this plantation, the season is now most fit. Strike then whilest the iron is hot; do this good work whilest you may, before it is too late."[42]

Whitaker urges his readers to "remember the poor estate of the ignorant inhabitants of Virginia. Cast forth your alms, my brethren of England." Those too poor to help financially "may venture their persons hither, and here not only serve God but help also these poor Indians, and build a sure foundation for themselves."[43]

Whitaker stressed the common humanity of the British and the Indians, noting that the British were much like the Indians before England was evangelized. "One God created us: They have reasonable souls and intellectual faculties as well as we. We all have Adam for our common parent."[44]

Yet the present condition of "these naked slaves of the devil" is "miserable," Whitaker laments, and should "move you to compassion toward them. They acknowledge that there is a great good god, but know him not, having the eyes of their understanding as yet blinded. Wherefore they serve

---

40. Littleton, "Alexander Whitaker," 341–42 (quotation on 341).

41. Whitaker, *Good News*, 722.

42. Ibid., 723.

43. Ibid., 727.

44. Ibid., 731.

the devil for fear, after a most base manner, sacrificing themselves (as I have here heard) their own children to him."[45]

Whitaker would soften his view of the Powhatan Indians with time as he got to know some of them, especially Pocahontas. The rumor of child sacrifice turned out to be false, or at least contested. John Rolfe said a few years later (in 1616), after his marriage to Pocahontas, that he doubted Whitaker still believed this was true.[46]

Whitaker in fact balanced his negative portrayal of the Indians' spiritual condition with many positive comments about their life and culture. They are not nearly "so simple as some have supposed." Physically they are strong and nimble, "quick of apprehension, . . . subtle in their dealings, exquisite in their inventions, and industrious in their labor." The Indians have a form of "civil government amongst them which they strictly observe." They "encroach not upon their neighbors' dwellings." Murder is "a capital crime scarce heard of among them," and adultery and other offenses are "most severely punished." The Indians are perhaps the world's best marksmen. With their powerful bows and arrows they can "kill birds flying, fishes swimming, and beasts running." Whitaker had himself seen an Indian "of 12 or 13 years" fell a bird with an arrow. On one occasion an Indian shot a colonist "quite through the body and nailed both his arms to his body with one arrow."[47]

Whitaker was optimistic that the Indians could be converted and the colony would thrive. "He that was powerful to save us by His word, when we were nothing, will be merciful also to these sons of Adam in His appointed time, in whom there be remaining so many footsteps of God's image."[48]

Good News from Virginia ends with further description of the Indians and of the fertile land from the Atlantic coast to the Appalachian Mountains. The land was rich in all kinds of birds, fish, and animals, including such strange creatures as the flying squirrel and "the female *possown*, which will let forth her young out of her belly and take them up into her belly again at her pleasure without hurt to herself." Though the various Indian tribes are "a people to be feared," they are "easy to be subdued" since the British have superior weapons.[49]

45. Ibid., 730–31.
46. See Haile, *Jamestown Narratives*, 731, 882.
47. Whitaker, *Good News*, 732–33.
48. Ibid., 733.
49. Ibid., 742–43.

So the British challenge is clear:

> Wherefore you, right wise and noble adventurers of Virginia, whose hearts God hath stirred up to build Him a temple, to make Him an house, to conquer a kingdom for Him here—be not discouraged with those many lamentable assaults that the devil hath made against us. . . . Go forth boldly, and remember that you fight under the banner of Jesus Christ, that you plant His kingdom who hath already broken the serpent's head. God may defer His temporal reward for a season, but be assured that in the end you shall find riches and honor in this world and blessed immortality in the world to come.[50]

What better statement of the British Christian world view of the time?

In all this extended discourse Whitaker makes no mention of Pocahontas. Probably he had not yet met her, though he likely had heard stories. Soon he would meet the young woman.

BETRAYED!

In September of 1612, just six weeks after Whitaker penned *Good News from Virginia*, Captain Samuel Argall returned in a large and well-armed ship, the *Treasurer*. This was his third voyage to Virginia.[51]

Argall quickly put his navigational and logistical skills to good use by helping the colony acquire more food from the Indians—by force, if necessary. Commander Dale wanted to be sure the colonists were well supplied for the approaching winter. Sailing further north up Chesapeake Bay beyond the range of the Powhatans, Argall entered the Potomac River, where he found Indians willing to trade. He returned to Jamestown in February, 1613, with more than a thousand bushels of corn.[52]

Again in March Argall and his men boarded the *Treasurer* and sailed up Chesapeake Bay. This was a voyage of exploration. He found he could ascend the wide Potomac nearly two hundred miles northwest from the Bay. He thus reached the vicinity of present-day Washington, DC. Argall went exploring onshore with a group of men and was surprised to find that

---

50. Ibid., 744–45.

51. Barbour, *Pocahontas*, 97–98.

52. Ibid., 101–2; Argall, "Letter," 753.

the local Indians had a "great store of cattle as big as kine"—one of the first mentions of bison in Virginia.[53]

Even more surprising, however, was the intelligence Argall received. Powhatan's daughter Pocahontas was in the vicinity! She was visiting a town of the Patawomeck (as in "Potomac") Indians.

This was big news. The English had heard nothing of Pocahontas for over three years. As the Virginia colony grew, Pocahontas disappeared. In fact, she had gone to live at Orapax, Chief Powhatan's more remote capital. In 1610, around the age of fourteen, she married a man named Kocoum—not a chief, but a capable warrior whom she seems to have wed by choice. He may have been part of Powhatan's personal guard. There is no record of any children from this marriage.[54]

Pocahontas had now traveled more than seventy miles north, Argall learned, to the Patawomeck town of Passapatanzy. Perhaps her husband Kocoum was originally of the Patawomeck tribe, which could account for Pocahontas's travel so far north from Orapax, probably mostly by foot. Or there could have been other reasons, such as security concerns. One account says she had been with the Patawomecks for three months, trading "some of her father's commodities for theirs"—in other words, part of a trade mission, in which case she would have been accompanied by a number of others. Rountree suggests, "People for miles around" would have known "that the great Powhatan's daughter was visiting" in the area.[55]

Whatever her reasons for being in Patawomeck rather than Powhatan territory, Pocahontas had now been discovered by the English—specifically, by Samuel Argall and his men. Though still only about seventeen, Pocahontas was now a married woman, no longer a frolicsome child.

Argall himself later wrote that while he and his men were exploring in the area, "I was told by certain Indians my friends that the Great Powhatan's daughter Pokahuntis [sic] was with the Great King Patowomeck [that is, the high chief of the Patawomecks], whither I presently repaired, resolving to possess myself of her by any stratagem that I could use for the ransoming of so many Englishmen as were prisoners with Powhatan, as also to get such arms and tools as he and other Indians had got by murther

53. Argall, "Letter," 754; Barbour, *Pocahontas,* 102.

54. Strachey, "History," 620; Rountree, *Pocahontas,* 141–43; Townsend, *Pocahontas,* 85–87; Barbour, *Pocahontas,* 98–99. All later authors cite Strachey's 1612 "History" as their source.

55. Rountree, *Pocahontas,* 156.

and stealing from others of our nation, with some quantity of corn for the colony's relief."[56]

Argall laid an elaborate trap. Shrewd as John Smith, Argall knew that if he held the paramount Powhatan chief's daughter hostage, she would be a powerful bargaining chip in securing peaceful coexistence with the Powhatan nation. Certainly this was wiser than constant warfare.

Argall and his men traveled to the Patawomeck town of Passapatanzy, about two miles south of the Potomac River.[57] There he negotiated with the Patawomecks for the capture of Pocahontas. Taking hostages was a familiar practice among the Indians, often used as a negotiating tool. In fact, both Smith and Argall, wiser in the ways of the Indians than were most Englishmen, sometimes used the exchange of hostages as a means of guaranteeing that no harm would come to either side when the English visited Indian villages. A young Englishman might be exchanged for a young Indian, for example, and later returned.

But taking the paramount Powhatan chief's daughter captive was much different. It was a high-stakes move, and not to the liking of the Patawomeck Indians. The remarkable thing is that the Patawomeck, after talking it over in council, went along with it. They certainly felt coerced; as Rountree writes, "of the two powers," the Powhatans and the English, "the Patawomecks preferred to cooperate with" the English, "especially if they could convince Powhatan that they had been coerced, which indeed they had been."[58]

The local Patawomeck *weroance*, Iopassus, and one of his wives became coconspirators with Argall. Captain Argall already knew Iopassus—the two were "friends" in a mutually self-serving way. So that prior relationship also factored in the dynamics of Pocahontas's kidnapping.

Someone told Pocahontas that an English ship from Jamestown was moored nearby. She was immediately curious. She wanted to see for herself and perhaps get firsthand news of the settlement.

Iopassus and his wife obligingly walked with Pocahontas to the riverside. Here Iopassus's wife, by prearrangement, begged to go aboard the ship and see what it was like. Iopassus said no; she couldn't board alone. But

---

56. Argall, "Letter," 754. Cf. Barbour, *Pocahontas,* 103.

57. Today Passapatanzy is an unincorporated village in King George Country, Virginia, just east of Fredericksburg, with a population of about 1,200, roughly fifty miles south of Washington, DC.

58. Rountree, *Pocahontas,* 156.

perhaps Pocahontas would accompany her. Sensing a possible trap, Pocahontas was reluctant. She finally agreed, however, persuaded in part by Iopassus's wife's tears after her husband refused to let her board without Pocahontas. So Iopassus and his wife clambered onto the ship, Pocahontas following.

Once aboard, the three guests were shown around the ship, then given supper and invited to stay the night. Pocahontas was given the gunner's room as her guest quarters.

She probably didn't sleep much. She was up early the next morning, anxious to get back on land. Captain Argall sent Iopassus and his wife ashore, but refused to let Pocahontas go. Feigning surprise, Iopassus asked why. Argall said Pocahontas must remain a hostage until the Powhatans released eight Englishmen and their store of stolen weapons.

Like a trapped squirrel, Pocahontas was terribly upset—"exceeding pensive and discontented," in Ralph Hamor's words. Unaware she had been betrayed by the Patawomeck, Pocahontas fell into Argall's trap. Argall somewhat resembled Smith physically, and that may have made Pocahontas more vulnerable to his deception. He assured Pocahontas she would be treated as an honored guest, perhaps suggesting she could be a peacemaker between the Powhatan and the English.[59]

Argall sailed back to Jamestown with his young prize. The date was April 13, 1613. Argall also sent a runner to Chief Powhatan with news of Pocahontas's capture.[60]

Pocahontas was now a hostage at Jamestown. As Powhatan's daughter, and because of her strategic value, she was treated well. The whole power balance between the English and the Powhatan had suddenly shifted. As Edward Haile comments, "Argall's brilliant stroke—the capture of Pocahontas—proved to be the key to solving the whole Indian problem." So it appeared.[61]

Over two hundred years later the Anglican historian James Anderson observed, "It was a cruel and shameful act to ensnare and take captive one who had rendered such signal services as these; and although in the end overruled for good, the contrivers of the scheme must bear the burden of its reproach."[62]

---

59. Pocahontas's abduction is related in several sources. See especially Argall, "Letter," 754–55; Hamor, "True Discourse," 802–04; Rountree, *Pocahontas,* 156–57; Barbour, *Pocahontas,* 106–9; Price, *Love and Hate,* 149–51.

60. Barbour, *Pocahontas,* 108–9.

61. Haile, ed., *Jamestown Narratives,* editorial comment, 792.

62. Anderson, *History,* 1:239.

Chapter Seven

True Love

Pocahontas and John Rolfe

Things moved quickly now. Within a year Pocahontas converted to Christianity and married John Rolfe.

But matters of the heart are complex. Is it possible to disentangle Pocahontas's conversion and her romance—her relationships to John Rolfe and to Jesus Christ?

Not really. Yet they are different tales. In order to understand the conversion, we certainly must understand the romance. Pocahontas's relationship with Rolfe is in fact key to comprehending her conversion.

POCAHONTAS, JAMESTOWN HOSTAGE

By the time of her capture, Pocahontas was already famous in England. Popular reports about the Virginia colony and the charismatic "Indian princess" had been circulating in London for several years. Pocahontas was described as "the Nonpareil of Virginia"—the unparalleled, the incomparable one. She was the great Chief Powhatan's "delight and darling."[1]

Thus the romantic Pocahontas myth was born. British ignorance of Native American culture, and for that matter of the real Jamestown situation, made romanticizing easy.

---

1. Smith, "True Relation," 181; Hamor, "True Discourse," 802.

It was not her physical beauty so much as her charisma and personality that attracted people to Pocahontas. All the accounts agree. For these traits we have to thank primarily her father and her unknown mother. To the English Pocahontas was an exotic, and she seemed perfectly suited to the role.

So when Pocahontas turned up in Jamestown it was big news in England.[2]

Though held against her will, Pocahontas "was treated with respect and kindness." This was due mainly to Powhatan's status as "emperor" or paramount chief, but also to her previous contacts with the English—and maybe a little English embarrassment at her kidnapping by Argall, which hadn't been anticipated. A few of the early Jamestown survivors must have remembered Pocahontas's playful visits to Jamestown several years earlier, when she was still a child. Officially, from the British standpoint, "Pocahontas was the daughter of the ruler of the land. She was therefore a princess."[3]

Very quickly, Pocahontas had to cope with big changes. First would have been her clothes. Certainly the English would quickly have "put more clothes on her," says Rountree. By now a sizable number of women lived at Jamestown, and some probably tried to befriend Pocahontas. Karen Robertson points out that "women must . . . have been involved" in Pocahontas's transition, "particularly in supervising her change of clothing from the fringed doeskin apron of the Powhatans to the full skirts and bodice of English dress." Robertson notes how important clothing was to the English as a marker of social status. "With her change of clothes, the daughter of Powhatan moves toward her place in English social structures." She is now both "visually and verbally defined as a princess."[4]

Pocahontas would have been dressed according to current English styles. "The foreigners' clothes were distinctly uncomfortable until one got used to them; we would not like them today," notes Rountree. They "constricted a woman's movements," especially the tight and multilayered dress-up clothing that the English colonial women would by this time have been wearing. Pocahontas saw immediately that such clothing was not designed for outdoor work and activities or the warm summer weather she was used to.[5]

2. Hamor, "True Discourse", 802.

3. Barbour, *Pocahontas,* 109.

4. Robertson, "Pocahontas at the Masque," 568.

5. Rountree, *Pocahontas,* 160.

Other wrenching adjustments came in quick succession: English food and eating customs; almost total separation from the forests and rivers and wildlife Pocahontas had grown up with. "This kind of confinement would have been very hard to bear," notes Rountree, "judging by the reactions of other traditional Native Americans over the centuries when they were captured and jailed."[6]

And yet the various accounts agree that, as Barbour puts it, "from resignation to her fate, [Pocahontas] gradually came to welcome her new role in the relations between the colony and her people." She was, and could be, a bridge person. She understood the English and their language better than did the other Indians, and she certainly understood and cared deeply about her own people—their welfare and their future. Her new life was a kind of sacrifice. We have only English firsthand accounts, however; Pocahontas never shared publicly what was on her heart at the time.

The next nine months were a dramatic turning point for Pocahontas—and consequently for English-Powhatan relations and for Virginia itself. For Pocahontas, her young age (now approaching eighteen) and her previous contacts with the English, especially John Smith, probably made change easier. Pocahontas was still a teenager, Rountree points out, at an age when "new languages can still be learned fast and new cultural practices can be fairly readily adapted to, for they may be seen more as an adventure than as a trial. Pocahontas had had friendly, interesting experiences among the denizens of Jamestown in 1608, so the groundwork had been laid for her to have a positive attitude in 1613–14. She seems, as a personality, to have been lively and adventurous anyhow, and her ability to make friends and entertain people would have served her well in captivity."[7]

CHRISTIANIZING POCAHONTAS

Pious but iron-willed Thomas Dale was still very much in charge at Jamestown. He took immediate steps to have Pocahontas instructed in the Christian faith, placing her under the tutelage of the Rev. Alexander Whitaker. Whitaker had arrived in Jamestown with Dale, as noted previously, and was about twenty-eight (the same age as John Rolfe) and single. He became the person most directly responsible for Pocahontas's conversion.[8]

6. Ibid., 160.

7. Ibid., 162.

8. "Alexander Whitaker, a [twenty]-eight-year-old minister from Cambridge, was

In fact, both Dale and Whitaker—temperamentally opposites—played key roles. Whitaker described Sir Thomas Dale as "our religious and valiant governor" who "labored a long time to ground" Pocahontas in the Christian faith.[9] That at least was his public view.

Alexander Whitaker was the ideal person to tutor Pocahontas, Dale felt. Off he sent the young woman to Henrico so Whitaker could begin her instruction—that is, her catechesis.[10]

Henrico was Governor Dale's pet project. He was determined to turn it into the Virginia Colony's model settlement. Now with plenty of men and equipment, Dale could build a substantial town. Once the place was secure, Ralph Hamor reported, Dale "began to think upon convenient houses and lodgings for himself and men, which, with as much speed as was possible, were more strongly [built] and more handsome than any formerly . . . contrived and finished" in Virginia. As construction went on Hamor reported that there were already three streets of "well-framed houses, a handsome church" and the foundation of "a more stately" brick one, and also "storehouses, watchhouses, and suchlike."[11]

In four months Dale "made Henrico much better and of more worth" than the other settlements, including Jamestown. Unlike the original settlement, Henrico was soon a growing town of women and children, not just men.[12]

By the summer of 1613 the Virginia colony had grown remarkably. The English population was now several hundred, and additional settlements were being established up and down the James and other rivers. More and more land was cleared for crops. Rather than a few hundred male adventurers, the colony was now inhabited by growing families of permanent settlers.

---

assigned the task of polishing Pocahontas's English and teaching her the ways of a Christian lady" (Price, *Love and Hate*, 152). Price mistakenly gives Whitaker's age as thirty-eight.

9. Alexander Whitaker, quoted in Haile, ed., *Jamestown Narratives*, 848.

10. Barbour, *Pocahontas*, 118. Some accounts imply that Pocahontas remained in Jamestown during this whole period, but this does not seem to have been the case.

11. Hamor, "True Discourse," 824–25.

12. Ibid., 824. Cf. Townsend, *Pocahontas*, 108. Hamor describes the other settlements and plantations also that were being established at this time. Henrico was abandoned after the devastating Indian attack of 1622. It is now a historical park with a partial restoration of the original town, as noted earlier.

Further north, the French were establishing colonies at the same time, moving inland along the St. Lawrence River, laying the foundation of what we know today as the Canadian province of Quebec.[13]

Virginia's brightened fortunes were due in large measure to a series of reforms that Thomas Dale instituted on his own authority, beginning in 1613. Essentially Dale introduced a free-enterprise, entrepreneurial model, though under his tight control, apparently without consulting either the colonists or the stockholders back in England. Growing crops communally had not worked. So Dale allocated three-acre plots to the colony's "ancient planters" (the earlier settlers) and smaller plots to more recent arrivals. With greater security and increased numbers, this system succeeded. More crops were raised and food production increased. More and more land was put under cultivation—land which the Indians of course regarded as theirs. In this context John Rolfe began his experiments with growing tobacco and improving its taste.

At the Henrico site, one hundred acres of land were set aside as church land. Here "a handsome church" building and "a fair framed parsonage" were built. Whitaker called the site Rock Hall. The land was intended for the support of Whitaker and future Anglican preachers.[14]

Whitaker quickly established a Sunday pattern of preaching in the morning and catechizing in the afternoon. He served communion once a month. He and Thomas Dale apparently developed a close relationship; he wrote in 1614, "Every Saturday night I exercise in Sir Thomas Dale's house."[15]

With stockade walls and watchtowers all around, plus armed guards, Henrico was quite secure from the Indians. Here Pocahontas could be safely held.[16]

Social and moral considerations, too, may have played a role in moving Pocahontas to Henrico. As Townsend notes, the Jamestown settlers were nearly all male, and archeological evidence suggests that at least some

---

13. Cf. Barbour, *Pocahontas,* 119–21.

14. Haile, ed., *Jamestown Narratives,* 825; Anderson, *History,* 1:235.

15. Alexander Whitaker, quoted in Haile, ed., *Jamestown Narratives,* 849. Whitaker doesn't explain whether he is referring to physical or spiritual exercises, or both.

16. Hamor, "True Discourse," 824–25. As the Virginia Colony was expanding and increasing in number, there were numerous other contacts and interactions with the Indians (primarily the Powhatans) that are not detailed here.

of them "cohabited with Indian women." In Henrico "there were white women and children present to socialize her" the way Dale intended.[17]

For several months, beginning shortly after Pocahontas's kidnapping in April 1613, Whitaker met regularly with the prize hostage. He carefully instructed her in the Christian faith as well as English language and ways. Now Pocahontas makes a new friend: the widowed John Rolfe.

Meanwhile, Chief Powhatan tried to regain his daughter's freedom. He freed the seven Englishmen he'd been holding and sent them back to Jamestown, their muskets broken. He promised that if Pocahontas was released he would return the stolen weapons and send 500 bushels of corn. The Powhatan people and the English would be friends forever.[18]

Thomas Gates replied for the English. Pocahontas was being treated kindly, he said, but would not be released until the weapons were returned. No reply came from Powhatan. A stalemate ensued for several months. In the spring of 1614 Gates returned to England, leaving Deputy Governor Thomas Dale as the sole governing authority in the Virginia Colony.[19]

Pocahontas had now been held hostage for nearly a year. Frustrated that Powhatan had not come to terms, Dale decided to confront the Indians directly. He intended to gain a clear upper hand and insure the permanent security of the English colonists. Scarcely had Gates's ships sailed off toward England than Dale took several ships and about 300 armed men down the James to Chesapeake Bay and then up the York River to Werowocomoco, Powhatan's former capital. He brought along Pocahontas ("who had been long prisoner with us," he noted) as his main bargaining chip.[20] John Rolfe was also on board.

A day or two later the Indians sent to ask what the English were up to. Dale replied that he had Pocahontas on board, and he was ready to release her if Chief Powhatan would comply with his terms: The return of weapons, tools, and any Englishmen they still held.[21] As Dale himself put it tersely several weeks later, "I [told the Indians] that I came to bring [Powhatan] his daughter, conditionally [i.e., on condition that] he would—as had been agreed upon for her ransom—render all the arms, tools, swords, and men

---

17. Townsend, *Pocahontas*, 108.

18. Barbour, *Pocahontas*, 118–19.

19. Ibid., 119, 124.

20. Ibid., 124–25, 267; Thomas Dale to "Mr. D. M.," June 18, 1614, in Hamor, "True Discourse," 843.

21. Barbour, *Pocahontas*, 124–25.

(that had run away), and give me a ship full of corn for the wrong he had done unto us. If they would do this, we would be friends; if not, burn all."[22]

Perhaps Dale didn't know that Powhatan had left Werowocomoco many months earlier. Powhatan's half-brother Opechancanough was nearby, however. He served as a key Powhatan weroance under the paramount chief's authority; John Smith had encountered him some years earlier. Opechancanough could negotiate with the English in Powhatan's place.[23]

But Dale refused to meet with Opechancanough. He was determined to deal directly with Chief Powhatan. He landed at Werowocomoco with a detachment of armed men. The Indians attacked but Dale's men launched a counter assault, killed several Indians, burned some of their houses, and carried off a supply of corn.[24]

The next day Dale sailed further up the York River. Encountering more Indians, Dale threatened to destroy all the native towns he found if the Indians did not come to terms.[25] One can only wonder what Pocahontas, aboard Dale's ship, thought of all this, or indeed to what extent she realized what was happening. It seems likely she understood very well, and wanted to find a way to make peace before things got even worse.

The Indians eventually sent word that they would indeed comply with Dale's demands. Dale went ashore to await Powhatan's next steps.[26]

Pocahontas herself then went ashore with the English. According to Dale, Pocahontas conversed with the Indians but would talk only "to them of the best sort" (probably, that is, those who officially represented Powhatan). She told them, Dale said, that "if her father had loved her, he would not value her less than old swords, [artillery] pieces, or axes; wherefore she would still dwell with the Englishmen, who loved her."[27]

Pocahontas was probably sincere in this, for by this time she had a secret: she was in love with John Rolfe.

Pocahontas's message, carried back to Chief Powhatan, who was still fifty miles or so further inland, must have come as a shock. Powhatan

---

22. Thomas Dale to "Mr. D. M." in Hamor, "True Discourse," 843.

23. Barbour, *Pocahontas,* 125.

24. Ibid., 125.

25. Ibid., 125.

26. Ibid., 125.

27. Thomas Dale to "Mr. D. M." in Hamor, "True Discourse," 844. Cf. Rountree, *Pocahontas,* 164. This is one of very few cases in which we have Pocahontas's own words. Although they are reported secondhand from a one-sided source, subsequent events suggest that they are in substance accurate.

decided it was time to establish peace with the English, whom he now had no chance of defeating. He sent a message to Dale promising to deliver the tools and weapons to Jamestown within fifteen days, along with corn. He also specified that the Indian people and chiefs under his authority or in league with him should "be included and have the benefit of the peace." As for Pocahontas, he would consider her now to be Dale's "child" to "ever dwell with" him and the English. Thus Powhatan and Dale (in other words, the Powhatans and the English) would be "ever friends."[28] Pocahontas became, in effect, a peace child.

Chief Powhatan was now a relatively old man of about seventy, twice the average Indian life span. He kept his part of the bargain. Chief Opechancanough also reluctantly complied, proclaiming his "love" for Dale. Under the circumstances he had little choice. "So the bargain was made," Thomas Dale wrote home triumphantly, "and every eight or ten days I have messages and presents from [Chief Powhatan], with many appearances that he much desireth to continue friendship."[29]

Dale didn't realize that in fact Opechancanough was biding his time, still hoping for revenge.

A significant period of peace with the Indians did begin in the spring of 1614. Pocahontas played a key role—not just passively as a bargaining chip, but actively, taking the initiative to secure peace with her father and thus with the Powhatans generally. She knew what she was doing. Her message to her father was, it appears, a calculated move to work around Dale's belligerence and make the best of a dangerous situation. David Price comments, "However unexpected her decision, it was true to form: Pocahontas had found a way, against the odds, to remain master of her fate. In electing to stay with the English, she had several evident motives. One was her longtime affinity for the English, going back to December 1607 when she first laid eyes on John Smith, and her subsequent girlhood visits to converse with Smith and to play with the boys at the fort. Another was her attraction to Christianity, which had struck a resonant chord in her; she proved an eager student of the English faith."[30]

28. Thomas Dale to "Mr. D. M." in Hamor, "True Discourse," 844. Cf. Barbour, *Pocahontas*, 126.

29. Thomas Dale to "Mr. D. M." in Hamor, "True Discourse," 844–45. Cf. Barbour, *Pocahontas*, 126.

30. Price, *Love and Hate*, 154.

Pocahontas was really the only person in a position and with the wits to see both sides of the equation. She discerned both the good and the vile among the English but also among her own people. She of course cared about the fate of the Indians. And she had her own personal reasons, as was daily becoming more clear.

What happened to Pocahontas's husband Kocoum remains a mystery. He disappears from the accounts. He may well have been killed in conflicts with the English, or there could have been a divorce.[31] Or it could have been a forced separation due to Pocahontas's kidnapping or other events.

The dates as the story unfolds now are key. Dale sailed up the York River to confront Powhatan in March 1614. Pocahontas married John Rolfe just a few weeks later, on April 5. This means that in short order Pocahontas had already made three key, interlaced decisions: to profess the Christian faith, to marry John Rolfe, and to remain permanently with the English. Of course these decisions were long incubating. But each is significant in its own right.

Between her kidnapping in early 1613 and these events almost a year later, Pocahontas changed in several ways. This was the period of her introduction to the Christian faith, but it is impossible to separate the strand of her conversion from the other events in her life at this time—especially her relationship with John Rolfe.

In order to understand Pocahontas's conversion to Christianity (the focus of the next chapter) we'll try to grasp what happened between her and John Rolfe.

We don't know all the details, but the romance with Rolfe—the mutual attraction—seems to have begun shortly after Pocahontas's kidnapping and confinement in Jamestown and then Henrico. John Rolfe actually visited Pocahontas many times during the months Alexander Whitaker was catechizing her.

MATTERS OF THE HEART: "ENTHRALLED IN SO INTRICATE A LABYRINTH"

John Rolfe, now twenty-eight, had fallen deeply in love with seventeen-year-old Pocahontas. This is crystal clear from the astonishing letter he wrote to Thomas Dale. Rolfe's letter is one of the most remarkable documents in all English literature—combining at once personal introspection, romantic

31. Rountree, *Pocahontas*, 166.

passion, cultural issues, as well as questions of intent and motivation and of faith and salvation. Everything intersects here—faith, politics, love, sexuality and gender issues, ethics, moral responsibility, power, empire.

Rolfe was attracted to Pocahontas virtually from the moment he saw her, which was probably shortly after her kidnapping. He quickly found himself in turmoil as he wrestled with his growing fascination with and affection toward the young Powhatan woman. What were his real motivations? What were the implications of any possible relationship with her for himself, for his own soul, for the Jamestown colony and its reputation in England, for relations with the Indians, even for his own economic well-being? These matters greatly troubled Rolfe for some time, as his letter shows. Could he marry Pocahontas? Rolfe talked with Pocahontas numerous times, and a relationship began to blossom.

Toward the end of 1613, apparently, Rolfe wrote a long open letter to Sir Thomas Dale, who as deputy governor would have to authorize a marriage. Rolfe filled four large foolscap sheets (each about thirteen by sixteen inches) with his plea. The letter is partly soul searching, partly biblical and theological debate—and certainly fascinating from the perspective of Christ and culture.[32]

Ralph Hamor—who knew Rolfe and watched the romance blossom— said that "long before" Rolfe wrote his letter to Dale, he "had been in love with Pocahuntas [sic] and she with him." In fact Hamor himself carried Rolfe's letter to Dale, he claims. For her part, Pocahontas sent word to her family of the romance and intended marriage.[33]

The word "romance" fits. A deep love surpassing all the complicating factors and difficulties really seems to have blossomed between Pocahontas and Rolfe. "All the accounts agree that she and Rolfe fell in love with each other," notes Rountree,[34] and there seems no reason to doubt this. As noted earlier, both had been previously married; Rolfe had lost his wife and baby daughter about three years earlier.

The romance developed over several months—a "long time," said Rolfe—during Pocahontas's captivity. John Rolfe won the young woman by

32. Rolfe letter (undated) to Thomas Dale in Hamor, "True Discourse," 850–56. Barbour discusses and quotes from the letter and also includes it as an appendix. Barbour, *Pocahontas*, 128–30, 247–52.

33. Hamor, "True Discourse," 809.

34. Rountree, *Pocahontas*, 163. Though Barbour says there seems to be "no record anywhere" that in fact Pocahontas "*was* willing" to marry Rolfe (Barbour, *Pocahontas*, 131; emphasis in the original), most accounts suggest the attraction was mutual.

his love—by his gentleness and by showing more sympathy than most English men. Perhaps his own recent loss of a wife and daughter played a role.

Pocahontas saw Jesus in Rolfe. Unknowingly at first, she met Jesus through his love and consideration. She had befriended and admired John Smith, but clearly Smith was not Jesus; nor was Rolfe. But in their sensitivity to her, so unlike most of the English and even many of her own people, she must have seen some intimations of Jesus. Call it God's prevenient, drawing grace.

The most convincing proof of John Rolfe's true love for Pocahontas is his agonized but carefully diplomatic letter to hard-fisted Thomas Dale, seeking permission to marry Pocahontas. Dale at this point was effectively Pocahontas's guardian, since she was his hostage. In his letter to Dale, Rolfe "is virtually writing to the father of his bride-to-be," notes Haile.[35] In fact Rolfe addresses Dale as "the patron and father of us in this country."[36]

Rolfe frankly confesses he has fallen deeply in love. He believes the affection is mutual; he speaks of Pocahontas's "great appearance of love to me."[37]

But how can a Christian marry a pagan? He recalls biblical injunctions against taking "strange wives." He examines his own motives. What is it that has provoked him "to be in love with one whose education hath been rude, her manners barbarous, her generation accursed, and so discrepant in all nurtriture from myself"? He thought, "Surely these are *wicked* instigations, hatched by him who seeketh and delighteth in man's destruction!"[38]

But then it occurred to Rolfe, "Why dost thou not endeavour to make her a Christian?" Was this not his Christian duty? He concluded that this was God's word to him. His calling was Pocahontas's conversion. And so she might also become his wife. He asked himself, "Shall I be of so untoward a disposition as to refuse to lead the blind into the right way?" By his "faithful pains and Christian-like labor" he could be the catalyst in Pocahontas's salvation.[39]

So Rolfe wrote to Dale, in essence asking Dale's approval of Rolfe's project to convert and then marry Pocahontas. He was motivated, he said, not by "the unbridled desire of carnal affection." Rather, he was pursuing

35. Haile, ed., *Jamestown Narratives*, 793.

36. Rolfe letter in Hamor, "True Discourse," 851.

37. Ibid., 854.

38. Ibid., 853.

39. Ibid., 853–54.

this project "for the good of this plantation, for the honor of our country, for the glory of God, for my own salvation, and for the converting to the true knowledge of God and Jesus Christ an unbelieving creature, namely Pocahontas, to whom my heart and best thoughts are and have a long time been so entangled and enthralled in so intricate a labyrinth, that I was even a-wearied to unwind myself thereout." Now, he felt, God had "opened the gate and led me by the hand." He would work for Pocahontas's conversion and marry her.[40]

Rolfe told Dale that he humbly submitted himself to God and the governor "for His glory, your honor, our country's good, the benefit of this plantation, and for the converting of one unregenerate to regeneration— which I beseech God to grant for His dear son Christ Jesus His sake."[41]

Rolfe frankly admitted, or at least implied, his sexual attraction toward Pocahontas. This is what led him to question his own motives, and in fact lends credibility to his letter. Rolfe says that "from the very instant that this [his attraction toward Pocahontas] began to root itself within the secret bosom of my breast" he was concerned that it might be inconsistent with his Christian commitment. He was well aware of the dangers of "hypocrisy and dissimulation," he said, but so far as he could tell, "these passions of my troubled soul" proceeded "from an unspotted conscience." He carefully reflected on these things in his "holiest meditations and prayers."[42]

Rolfe said that his "settled and long continued affection" for Pocahontas had "made a mighty war in my meditations!" So "I have never failed to offer my daily and faithful prayers to God for His sacred and holy assistance," recognizing "the frailty of mankind, his proneness to evil, his indulgency of wicked thoughts."[43]

Rolfe was very troubled for some months. Thoughts of Pocahontas intruded upon his "holiest and strongest meditations." He pondered these matters "daily, *hourly*." They troubled his sleep, at times "even awaking me to astonishment." When he didn't see Pocahontas for some period of time he found he thought of her all the more rather than forgetting her.[44]

If he were "sensually inclined," Rolfe said, rather than acting with pure intentions, he could "satisfy such desire" easily enough in the Virginia

40. Ibid, 851.
41. Ibid., 855.
42. Ibid., 850.
43. Ibid., 851, 853.
44. Ibid., 853–54.

Colony—indirect reference to some colonists' cohabitation or affairs with Indian women. But he could not so indulge himself "without a seared conscience." Another option he had considered would be returning to England and finding a suitable wife there. He knew that "the vulgar sort" of men in Virginia would certainly put the worst possible construction on his attraction to Pocahontas.[45]

Was John Rolfe's interest in young Pocahontas lust, cultural fascination, genuine love, or something else? Or a mix of all these? Who knows the human heart?

To me Rolfe's affection appears pure-intentioned, but not single-intentioned. His own testimony suggests he fell deeply in love with Pocahontas. But he also wanted to see her saved—converted to Christianity—and he was well aware also of the larger implications for Indian-English relations.

It is easy to dismiss Rolfe's letter as mere self-justification or as purely self-serving. Yet all evidence suggests that Rolfe was a man of integrity, character, and genuine Christian commitment (by the lights of English Protestants at the time). Her letter shows that he strongly hoped to get what he wanted, but for honorable reasons.

What do others say? Helen Rountree acknowledges "Pocahontas and John Rolfe's feelings for each other," suggesting a genuine mutual love, despite all the cultural issues.[46] Camilla Townsend says that by the time he wrote his letter to Dale "John was in love, and had been for months" and that his letter was "written in the heat of passion, when, according to the writer himself, Pocahontas was still staunchly unconverted." She adds,

> Rolfe says much that is honest and self-revealing, even airing his doubts about Pocahontas and her background. Some have quoted from the letter to prove his love was lacking, a stunted, grudging thing, with the implication that Pocahontas should have steered clear. All lovers have doubts about their partners, though. For Rolfe to have incorporated none of the fears and prejudices of his era would have been impossible. What seems more remarkable is that, given those fears and prejudices, he rose to the task of announcing to his social peers that he loved her. [In his negative comments on Indian culture he] was not saying, though, that the woman herself was inherently rude or evil, only that her education and acculturation, the customs taught her, were not what his had been—and certainly he thought his had been superior. Despite all

45. Ibid., 855.
46. Rountree, *Pocahontas*, 166.

that, apparently, he admired her for herself. He published to the world that he was in love with her anyway.[47]

Linwood "Little Bear" Custalow, trying to unravel the story from the native point of view and citing oral history, tells quite a different story. He claims Pocahontas was raped shortly after being kidnapped, was already pregnant when she was moved to Henrico, and "was forced to wear English clothing to conceal her pregnancy." Custalow says Indian "oral history is adamant that [Pocahontas's son] was born out of wedlock, prior to the marriage ceremony between Pocahontas and Rolfe." The true father is unknown, "but one likely candidate appears to be Sir Thomas Dale."[48]

There is nothing inherently implausible about this alternative version of events, given what we know about contacts between native peoples and invading foreigners, including the English. On the other hand there is very little evidence to back up Custalow's account, and it is hard to know how much weight to give to oral history, as he reports it, in this case.

Other authors have differing opinions. Ann Uhry Abrams says in *The Pilgrims and Pocahontas*, "Although the marriage of Pocahontas and John Rolfe . . . is often given a romantic gloss, there is ample reason to believe it was arranged for economic and political reasons. . . . Rolfe himself acknowledged that he needed to placate the Indians in order to save his nascent tobacco enterprise."[49]

Yet however complex the dynamics and motivations involved, the preponderance of evidence suggests a bond of true love between Pocahontas and John Rolfe.

THE MARRIAGE: POCAHONTAS BECOMES MRS. JOHN ROLFE

Thomas Dale read John Rolfe's letter with keen interest. He quickly approved the marriage. Its advantages for the Virginia Colony were obvious.[50]

Old Chief Powhatan also agreed. As with his daughter, both personal and political considerations intertwined. He was concerned about

47. Townsend, *Pocahontas*, 114–15.

48. Custalow and Daniel, *True Story*, 62–64. Custalow claims that at Jamestown Pocahontas was visited by her eldest sister Mattachanna and that "Pocahontas confided in Mattachanna that she had been raped" (62).

49. Abrams, *Pilgrims and Pocahontas*, 20.

50. Hamor, "True Discourse," 809.

Pocahontas's personal welfare as well as the security of his people. Having Pocahontas among the English would perhaps mean less hostility from the foreigners. When the time came for the marriage, Powhatan sent Pocahontas's "old uncle" Opachisco as his representative and two of his sons as witnesses.[51] He did not attend himself, still very wary of the English.

Details of Pocahontas's actual marriage to John Rolfe are scanty. Apparently the wedding took place on Tuesday, April 5, 1614, in Jamestown. Pocahontas's baptism, in which she was given the Christian name Rebecca, may possibly have occurred the same day.

The wedding ceremony, conducted according to the prescribed liturgy in the *Book of Common Prayer,* was performed by the Rev. Richard Bucke. As Townsend pictures it,

> [Pocahontas] stood before the pastor in fine clothes made of fabric brought from England and responded to the words in English. John promised only to love, honor, and keep her; she also promised to obey and serve. "Wilt thou have this man to thy wedded husband, to live together after God's ordinance in the holy estate of matrimony?" the pastor asked. "Wilt thou obey him and serve him, love, honor and keep him, in sickness and in health? And forsaking all other, keep thee only unto him, so long as you both shall live?" She answered, as had been rehearsed, "I will."[52]

Richard Bucke, the officiating clergyman, was the Anglican priest at Jamestown and a friend of Rolfe's. Rolfe considered him "a very good preacher."[53] Bucke had been on Bermuda with the Rolfes (John and his first wife) and the others shipwrecked there; in effect he was Rolfe's pastor on Bermuda. He had christened baby Bermuda Rolfe on February 11, 1610. He probably conducted the baby's funeral on Bermuda and possibly also that of Mrs.

51. Ibid., 809.

52. Townsend, *Pocahontas,* 128. Price gives a fairly detailed account of Pocahontas and John Rolfe's wedding and wedding night, based on marriage customs in England at the time. Though plausible, it is speculative, since we don't have direct sources. Price, *Love and Hate,* 157–68.

53. Haile, ed., *Jamestown Narratives,* 44. Haile notes that there is "no evidence" that the service was performed by Alexander Whitaker, Pocahontas's catechist (ibid., 65).

Rolfe later in Jamestown.[54] Barbour calls Bucke "a staunch Puritan,"[55] though in England he was also said to be a close friend of William Shakespeare.[56]

Alexander Whitaker probably participated in the wedding service as well, considering his key role in Pocahontas's conversion.[57] By this time John Rolfe owned property across the river in the Jamestown vicinity, as well as further downriver, and probably viewed Jamestown as his parish church.

Just weeks after this important cross-cultural union, Ralph Hamor wrote that "ever since we have had friendly commerce and trade not only with Powhatan himself but also with his subjects round about us; so as now I see no reason why the colony should not thrive apace."[58]

Anthropologist Helen Rountree says that after the marriage, Rolfe and Pocahontas would almost certainly have gone to visit her father, Chief Powhatan. Peace had come, and "keeping up with relatives was highly valued in both cultures. Rolfe also met and became friends with Opechancanough during this period, for in a later letter he indicated that although relations between the two peoples were strained, Opechancanough still 'loved' him. The in-law relationship was a good one—but then, John Rolfe was as good at drawing people to him as Pocahontas was."[59]

The peace was partly due to Thomas Dale's efforts. The governor did what he could to capitalize on the Rolfe-Pocahontas union. The marriage proved to be the catalyst for a peace treaty that Dale negotiated with the semi-independent and more democratic Chickahominy Indians of the area. Seeing the power shift between the Powhatans and the English, the Chickahominy initiated the negotiations. They offered to become the

54. See ibid., 55, 412. Captain Christopher Newport, William Strachey, and Mrs. Horton were baby Bermuda's sponsors at her christening (ibid., 55; Woodward, *Brave Vessel*, 82).

55. Barbour, *Pocahontas*, 133. Fischer also calls Bucke "a staunch Puritan," adding however that "Virginia did not attract many of that persuasion" (Fischer, *Albion's Seed*, 233).

56. "REV Richard Buck," line 18.

57. Rountree says Whitaker "most likely performed the ceremony," which presumably would have been true had it occurred at Henrico. Whitaker almost certainly would have gone to Jamestown for the wedding, and probably would have had some role in the service (Rountree, *Pocahontas*, 166).

58. Hamor, "True Discourse," 809. The union thus became a part of the age-long history of reconciliation or peaceful coexistence and trade enabled by a cross-cultural marriage alliance.

59. Rountree, *Pocahontas*, 167.

English King James's subjects in exchange for relative autonomy, protection from the Powhatans, and trade with the English. So peace was established with the Chickahominy as well as the Powhatans—for a time, at least. So John Rolfe could write in 1617 that "a peace was concluded and still continueth so firm that our people yearly plant and reap quietly, and travel in the woods a-fowling and a-hunting as freely and securely from fear of danger or treachery as in England. The great blessings of God have followed this peace, and it next under Him hath bred our plenty: every man sitting under his fig tree in safety [cf. Zech 3:10], gathering and reaping the fruits of their labors with much joy and comfort."[60]

This was indeed a monumental change from just five years earlier. Perhaps the English colonists and the native people really could live harmoniously and to mutual benefit, everyone thriving, as a new nation was born.

60. Rolfe, "True Relation," 869.

Chapter Eight

Pocahontas Meets Jesus

The first week of April 1614, Pocahontas was baptized as a Christian and married John Rolfe. Her new name, given at baptism, was Rebecca. The conversion and marriage occurred in the middle of Lent; Easter was on April 24.[1]

We know a few other key facts about Pocahontas's conversion. The earliest account comes from Sir Thomas Dale—effectively Virginia's governor at the time, as we have seen. In a letter of June 18, 1614, just months after the event, Dale wrote to a friend in London: "Powhatan's daughter I caused to be carefully instructed in Christian religion, who after she had made some good progress therein renounced publicly her country['s] idolatry, openly confessed her Christian faith, was as she desired baptized, and is since married to an English gentleman of good understanding. . . . She lives civilly and lovingly with him, and I trust will increase in goodness as the knowledge of God increaseth in her. She will go into England with me, and were it but the gaining of this one soul, I will think my time, toil, and present stay well spent."[2]

As do other accounts, Dale's summary closely links Pocahontas's conversion and marriage. But in what sense was Pocahontas actually converted to the Christian faith? Did she personally come to know Jesus Christ, in an evangelical sense?

1. Townsend, *Pocahontas*, 124. Cf. 201.
2. Rolfe letter in Hamor, "True Discourse," 845.

Other accounts of the conversion and marriage provide few clues. Alexander Whitaker, who probably spent more time with Pocahontas during these months than anyone else, reports little. In a letter written the same day as Dale's he merely repeats the same thing: "Pocahuntas, or Matoa[ka], the daughter of Powhatan, . . . openly renounced her country['s] idolatry, confessed the faith of Jesus Christ, and was baptized." In reporting the now-prospering state of the colony Whitaker describes Pocahontas's conversion as the "best" news he has to report.[3]

Whitaker gave considerable credit to Thomas Dale for Pocahontas's conversion. He described Dale as "a man of great knowledge in divinity and of a good conscience in all his doings."[4]

John Rolfe, in his 1613 Pocahontas letter (quoted in the previous chapter), spoke of his concern "for the converting to the true knowledge of God and Jesus Christ an unbelieving creature, namely Pocahontas." Compared with the English, Rolfe said, Pocahontas's "education hath been rude, her manners barbarous." As Rolfe struggled with his own feelings for Pocahontas, the thought occurred to him, "Why dost thou not endeavour to make her a Christian?"[5] Rolfe wrestled with his own motivations here. Yet he recognized Pocahontas's "desire to be taught and instructed in the knowledge of God, her capableness of understanding, her aptness and willingness to receive any good impression." How could he in good conscience "refuse to lead the blind into the right way?" He was ready to do his "duty" for the sake of "the converting of one unregenerate to regeneration—which I beseech God to grant for His dear son Christ Jesus His sake."[6]

Rolfe cited a passage from John Calvin's relatively recent *Institutes of the Christian Religion* (1536; first English edition, 1561). He felt the passage

---

3. Alexander Whitaker, quoted in Haile, ed., *Jamestown Narratives*, 848. The main point of Whitaker's letter was to defend Dale, "our religious and valiant governor," who through "war upon our [Indian] enemies and kind usage of our [Indian] friends" had brought the Indians "to seek for peace of us, which is made, and they dare not break." It is curious that Whitaker does not provide more details of Pocahontas's conversion and his conversations with her, at least in the sources that have survived. Rountree says that Dale's and Whitaker's brief reports comprise "all the information we are given by eyewitnesses" regarding Pocahontas's conversion. She implies that the conversion took place while Pocahontas was still in Jamestown (Rountree, *Pocahontas,* 159).

4. Alexander Whitaker, quoted in Haile, ed., *Jamestown Narratives*, 849.

5. This suggests that Rolfe's attraction for Pocahontas probably predated Whitaker's sessions with her.

6. Rolfe letter in Hamor, "True Discourse," 851–55.

was relevant, especially if he ended up marrying Pocahontas and they had children.

Calvin wrote, based on the Abrahamic covenant and the Apostle Paul's writings, that "the children of Christians, or those who have only one believing parent, are called holy" and thus "differ from the impure seed of idolatry." This was comforting assurance, though of course Rolfe fervently hoped Pocahontas would herself become a believing Christian. Rolfe promised he would "never cease" his efforts until he had "accomplished and brought to perfection so holy a work," which he hoped God would bless to both his and Pocahontas's "eternal happiness."[7]

John Smith, in his 1624 *General History of Virginia, New England, and the Summer Isles*—written while Pocahontas was in England but published after her death—gave considerable credit to Rolfe "and his friends" (presumably including Whitaker) for Pocahontas's conversion. By their "diligent care," Smith says, Pocahontas "was taught to speak such English as might well be understood, well instructed in Christianity, and was become very formal and civil after our English manner." He described Pocahontas (in his introductory letter to Queen Anne) as "the first Christian ever of [the Powhatan] nation, the first Virginian [that] ever spake English, or had a child in marriage by an Englishman"[8] (thus a kind of trophy of colonial success).

This is not fully accurate. Some of the Powhatan men had learned at least a smattering of English, and one or two Powhatan in earlier years reportedly had professed Christianity (Roman Catholicism) under the Spanish. Smith's careful wording that Pocahontas "had a child *in marriage* by an Englishman" is significant, since a number of Englishmen apparently fathered children by Indian women outside marriage. Pocahontas was not the first Indian woman to bear an English child.

There was good reason to rename Pocahontas Rebecca, the name of the patriarch Isaac's wife in the Old Testament. Most likely the name was Alexander Whitaker's choice, or suggestion. He would have worked through the Old Testament stories with Pocahontas as part of her Christian instruction. In the Genesis account Rebecca, or Rebekah (though related to Isaac) left her own place and people to be united with Isaac in what was to

7. Ibid., 854–56. Rolfe cites the exact reference in Calvin's *Institutes*, bk. 4, ch. 16, section 6. See Calvin, *Institutes*, 2:523. The definitive edition of the *Institutes* had been published in 1559, fifty-four years before Rolfe's letter.

8. Smith, "General History, Fourth Book," 861, 863. Years earlier, as a child, Pocahontas got a start with English through her contacts with Smith.

her a strange land. Rebecca voluntarily consented to go marry Isaac. Her family blessed her as she went: "May you, our sister, become thousands of myriads; may your offspring gain possession of the gates of their foes" (Gen 24:60). She would become the mother of a chosen race.

If Whitaker chose the name, he may have been thinking also of the Genesis account of Rebecca's sons, Jacob and Esau. Genesis 25:22–23 relates:

> The children struggled together within her; and she said, "If it is to be this way, why do I live?" So she went to inquire of the LORD.
>
> And the LORD said to her,
>
> "Two nations are in your womb,
> and two peoples born of you shall be divided;
> the one shall be stronger than the other,
> the elder shall serve the younger."

When the twins were born, the first, Esau, "came out red" and was nick-named Red (Edom). "Afterward his brother came out, with his hand gripping Esau's heel; so he was named Jacob" (Gen 25:25–26).

Townsend suggests, quite plausibly: "It is more than likely that Whitaker thought the parallel perfect. Pocahontas's children would be by nature both Indian and Christian, both red and pale. But if she was like the Rebekah of the Bible, she would devote herself to a next generation whom she envisioned as the heirs of Jacob, who were younger in the land than their red brethren."[9]

Pocahontas might have read the Genesis account quite differently! Townsend points out, "She could easily have focused her attention on the passages narrated from the perspective of Rebekah's people, in which the great decision is left to the young woman herself, and her siblings bless her for being willing to go and bear children" among a far-off people. "The parallels with her own people's worldview were striking."[10]

Receiving a new name would not have seemed strange to Pocahontas. Multiple names were common among the Powhatan and often a sort of status symbol. She told Whitaker that in fact her secret Indian name was not Pocahontas but Matoaka; Pocahontas was a nickname. She was named Amonute at birth but Matoaka was her hidden name, which may have meant "One Who Kindles." One account suggests she would have

9. Townsend, *Pocahontas*, 126–27.
10. Ibid., 127.

previously kept this name secret from the English for fear of it being used magically against her.[11]

Revealing her secret name to Whitaker, and no doubt to John Rolfe, may well signal the seriousness of her decision to become a Christian and Rolfe's wife. Certainly this would be consistent with the love she and John now shared.

Pocahontas was now Rebecca. She was now Mrs. Rolfe, the wife of an Englishman.

THE KEY ROLE OF ALEXANDER WHITAKER, MISSIONARY AND CATECHIST

Spring was sprouting in Virginia when Pocahontas professed her faith and was baptized as a Christian that first week of April, 1614, and married John Rolfe. Her baptism and marriage were performed according to the rubrics of the Church of England's *Book of Common Prayer*, the official and pre-scribed manual of doctrine and liturgy.

As Pocahontas's teacher, Alexander Whitaker took his task very seriously. The Cambridge-educated Whitaker was by his own desire an Anglican missionary to Virginia. It is not likely he would have departed from the church's prescribed ceremonies.

Like John Rolfe, Whitaker was a kind and sympathetic man with genuine concern for the conversion of the Indians, which in fact he regarded as a solemn duty. In terms of doctrine and official instruction it was Whitaker who led Pocahontas to Jesus, however Pocahontas herself understood his role.

According to Benjamin Woolley in *Savage Kingdom: The True Story of Jamestown*, Whitaker's task was not only to teach Pocahontas Christian doctrine but also "to read and write, so she could study the newly published King James Bible, and take notes for her studies." The education process, Woolley notes, "was not all one way. Regular contact with the Indian princess [sic] produced something of a conversion in Whitaker, his attitude to the 'savages,' initially superstitious and histrionic, approaching respect."[12]

Camilla Townsend speaks of Pocahontas's "confusing relationship" with Whitaker. In this earnest young clergyman "she found a jailer who was determined to treat her with such kindness that her gratitude would be

11. Ibid., 127–28; Rountree, *Pocahontas*, 37–38.

12. Woolley, *Savage Kingdom*, 316.

infinite, and who wanted at the same time to control her hopes, her thoughts, her very life. He gave her regular lessons in English and Christianity."[13]

Control is too strong a word. Nor was Whitaker really Pocahontas's "jailer." But certainly Whitaker aimed to influence and shape this young Indian woman, whom he regarded as a sincere seeker and the harbinger of a much greater harvest.

As Whitaker took up the task of instructing and catechizing Pocahontas, the English Bible and the *Book of Common Prayer* would have been primary curriculum. It's highly likely that Whitaker, perhaps with Rolfe's help, taught Pocahontas not only to speak but also to read and write English—to become a proper literate English Christian.[14]

All contemporary witnesses who write of Pocahontas's conversion stress that it was voluntary—whatever that would have meant, given her circumstances. Pocahontas renounced idolatry, professed faith in Jesus Christ, and said she desired baptism. Townsend points out that the language used in these accounts

> suggests that Whitaker stuck closely to the ceremony in the Book of Common Prayer, as might be expected: "Dost thou forsake the devil and all his works, the vain pomp, and glory of the world, with all covetous desires of the same, the carnal desires of the flesh, so that thou will not follow, nor be let by them?" And Pocahontas would have given the prescribed answer: "I forsake them all." "Dost thou believe in God the Father Almighty, maker of heaven and earth? And in Jesus Christ his only begotten Son our Lord, and that he was conceived by the Holy Ghost, born of the Virgin Mary . . . ?" And she would have responded, "All this I steadfastly believe." "Wilt thou be baptized in this faith?" pressed the minister. "That is my desire."[15]

Unlike most Anglicans, Pocahontas was baptized as an adult. Back in England nearly all Anglicans, men and women alike, were baptized as babies, then given some doctrinal or catechetical training when they came to their "years of discretion"—generally about age eleven or twelve.

---

13. Townsend, *Pocahontas*, 110–11.

14. Helen Rountree notes however that "the historical record is silent about whether she ever became literate" (Rountree, *Pocahontas*, 161). Whitaker and Rolfe surely would have wanted Pocahontas to be able to read the Bible and other Christian literature.

15. Townsend, *Pocahontas*, 125. This may not have been the exact wording, but it is close and essentially correct.

Very few Anglicans ever received any further doctrinal instruction as adults. Their understanding of Christian doctrine and of Scripture was often shaky. If they attended Sunday worship regularly—which a great many British folk did not—they would have learned something from sermons if the preaching was any good, and if they paid attention. But for a great many, probably the majority, neither was true. The Church of England was the state church, inseparable from the government, and most people attended services no more than required.

In Pocahontas's conversion, then, we face a most remarkable irony. Through her personal daily catechesis under Whitaker, her participation in Christian worship, and her eventual profession of faith and life with the earnest John Rolfe, Pocahontas probably knew and understood more Christian doctrine than the great majority of British Christians! If her Christian theology was mixed some with pagan myths and superstitions, so was that of most Anglicans. "Sixteenth-century ecclesiastical visitation records show" that the common people, though nominally Christians, "had no sense of any meaningful division between religion and magic" in their everyday lives and followed many superstitious practices.[16]

Plus, unlike most Anglicans, Pocahontas was instructed one-on-one. So Pocahontas as Mrs. Rebecca Rolfe may well have been a more informed and more genuine Christian in an evangelical sense than were the huge majority of professed Christians she would later meet in England.[17]

In addition, Pocahontas had gained deeper spiritual and theological insights through her cross-cultural experiences. These came first when she was an alert and curious child interacting with John Smith and the Jamestown settlers. These experiences then provided the grounds for further cross-cultural insights during her three years in the Virginia colony and later her short but intense time in England.

CATECHIZING POCAHONTAS

Pocahontas's conversion came during a high tide of interest in catechesis in the Church of England. Catechesis meant teaching basic Christian doctrine to children or adults in preparation for baptism or confirmation. Usually

16. Rowlands, "Conditions of Life," 41–42.

17. Pocahontas is therefore a type of the critical bridge person who frequently appears in the history of Christian mission.

this was done using a Catechism, a summary of doctrine in question-and-answer form.

Alexander Whitaker knew of and promoted this reform. His father William Whitaker and other Puritan divines played a role in this new concern for doctrinal training. Future bishop Lancelot Andrewes gave a popular series of catechetical lectures in Cambridge in 1578, claiming, "By our catechizing the papists have lost ground of us, and can never recover it again unless by a more exact course of catechizing than ours."[18]

A brief Catechism was included in the very first *Book of Common Prayer* in 1549—the historic prayer book of Edward VI. The Catechism was intended for use in confirmation classes and covered mainly the Apostles' Creed, the Ten Commandments, and the Lord's Prayer.

But Puritans wanted something better. Largely through their influence, the Catechism was revised and expanded in 1604. Teachings on the sacraments were added. Doctrines were presented in question-and-answer form.[19] Puritans had often complained that "candidates were insufficiently prepared for Confirmation," notes T. W. Drury.[20]

When Alexander Whitaker began meeting with Pocahontas in late 1613[21] to instruct her in the Christian faith, he was thus using the recently updated *Book of Common Prayer* Catechism. For Scripture, Whitaker would have proffered to Pocahontas either the new King James Bible (1611)

---

18. Green, *The Christian's ABC*, 1. The Council of Trent, in issuing its own catechism, complained that Protestants had done great "mischief . . . especially by those writings called catechisms" (ibid.).

19. Hefling and Shattuck, *Oxford Guide*, 176. Two chapters in this book are especially useful as background: "The Colonies and the States of America" (176–85) and "Catechisms" (500–508). "Catechism" is here capitalized when referring specifically to ones included in the *Book of Common Prayer*, but not when referring in a general way to catechisms.

20. Drury, *How We Got Our Prayer Book*, 90. The Hampton Court Conference of 1604, convened by King Henry I, brought together "Episcopal and Puritan divines" and resulted in few changes to the *Book of Common Prayer*, but those made generally reflected Puritan concerns. The conference's main historic importance is that it recommended a revision of the English Bible, which resulted in the "Authorized" or "King James" Version of 1611. Hampton Court thus became "the birthplace of our present English Bible" (Drury, *How We Got Our Prayer Book*, 36, 86).

21. Custalow says that "within three months" of her abduction to Jamestown, Pocahontas was moved to Henrico where later in the year "Rolfe started helping Reverend Alexander Whitaker teach Christianity to Pocahontas"(Custalow and Daniel, *True Story*, 110). This is consistent with the chronology presented by Barbour, *Pocahontas*, xix–xx.

or more likely the Geneva Bible (1560), in common use among British colonists in America.[22]

Actually the *Book of Common Prayer* Catechism was just one of hundreds of catechisms published in the later 1500s and early 1600s—evidence of an upsurge in concern with Christian instruction in the wake of the Reformation.[23] "The Catechism in the Book of Common Prayer was the basic text in the period, and additional catechisms served to expand on the Prayer Book's content and (it was hoped) to present the content in more effective language."[24]

This explosion of doctrinal manuals in the Reformation era owed much to the spreading new technology of moveable-type printing. This happened first on the Continent, then in England. Both Luther and Calvin wrote catechisms. "More than one hundred thousand copies of Luther's *Small Catechism* were printed over the forty years following its first publication," note J. I. Packer and Gary Parrett. In fact the Reformation itself can be understood as "a response to centuries of catechetical decline." By the time of Jamestown, however, catechesis within Anglicanism, after the upsurge in the 1500s, "was waning again."[25]

With Pocahontas, Whitaker would have used the Prayer Book Catechism, but likely had other catechisms at hand. Alexander Nowell's *A Catechism, or First Instruction of Christian Religion* (1570) was a best-seller, often reprinted. *The ABC with the Catechism* (1551) and *The Primer and Catechism* (1570) were also popular. The first was intended for children; the second was a devotional book. It would be unsurprising if Whitaker had one or more of these, and others besides.[26]

---

22. Whitaker's biblical quotations in "Good News from Virginia" are from the Geneva Bible.

23. Green's careful study documents the publication of between 600 and 1,000 different catechisms in England during this period, depending on precisely how "catechism" is defined. Most of these were considerably longer than the *BCP* Catechism and were intended to supplement it; and some emphasized particular theological points. Decade by decade, between 20,000 and 100,000 copies of various catechisms were printed, Green estimates (Green, I., *Christian's ABC*, 4, 50–53).

24. Hefling and Shattuck, *Oxford Guide*, 500.

25. Packer and Parrett, *Grounded in the Gospel*, 61, 59, 65. "The use of printed catechisms was a staple among the growing communities of the Reformation, including the Anglicans in England and Presbyterians in Scotland" (65). Packer and Parrett give a very useful overview in chapter 3, "The Waxing and Waning of Catechesis" (51–73).

26. Hefling and Shattuck, *Oxford Guide*, 500–501.

Within the Church of England, knowledge of the *BCP* Catechism was officially required as a condition of being confirmed and receiving the Lord's Supper. In practice this was widely ignored, and "for the most part, the church hierarchy showed scant interest in enforcing confirmation as a prerequisite for communion," note Hefling and Shattuck.[27]

But this was not so in Pocahontas's case. Her experience was the first in what became common practice: In the colonies, "missionaries and other clergy catechized the youth and through that prepared them for adulthood in the church," so that catechizing in effect "served as the rite of passage into adulthood."[28]

King James I himself promoted catechesis. In 1622 he ordered that Sunday evening sermons focus on the main sections of the Catechism, and this served further to raise its public profile.[29] Toward the end of the century, Bishop John Tillotson said that catechizing and the popular Foxe's *Book of Martyrs* had become "the two great pillars of the Protestant religion."[30]

Whatever the degree of catechetical practice or neglect across the scattered parishes of England, it is clear that in Virginia, Whitaker took it most seriously. How much more so in the case of Pocahontas, the firstfruits of a hoped-for great harvest of native peoples?

Whitaker knew that the Anglican 59th canon of 1604 instructed priests "not only to examine the children in the catechism . . . but 'to instruct them therein,' that is, to teach them the meaning, and make them understand the weight of every word." He was to provide "the plainest and clearest explications and illustrations of every point" as concisely as possible so that the teaching "might easily be carried away and remembered."[31]

What did Whitaker actually teach Pocahontas? How did she respond? The main focus was the Bible and the Catechism itself. The Ten Commandments and the Lord's Prayer were part of the Catechism and would of course have been stressed.[32] Presumably Pocahontas memorized them, as required. The Catechism also included the Apostles' Creed and teaching

---

27. Ibid., 503.

28. Ibid., 503–4.

29. Ibid., 504.

30. Green, *Christian's ABC*, 1.

31. Ibid., 148–49.

32. Unfortunately we have little direct evidence as to how much Bible content figured in catechetical teaching. Some catechisms included biblical references, though not the one included in the *Book of Common Prayer* (1604).

on the sacraments, as already noted. With this instruction, Pocahontas was now ready to answer all Whitaker's catechetical questions.

FIGURE 3
The Baptism of Pocahontas, by John Gadsby Chapman (1836–40), U.S. Capitol Rotunda

"WHAT IS YOUR NAME?"

Following the prescribed instructions, Whitaker asked: "What is your name?"

The simple question immediately got Pocahontas's attention! Names were a big deal among the Powhatan. Whitaker and Pocahontas likely had some interesting discussion at this point. Here (if not earlier) she would have to explain that Pocahontas was actually a nickname, and that her birth name was Amonute.

The next question was also tricky: "Who gave you this name?" The prescribed answer was, "My Godfathers and Godmothers in my Baptism, wherein I was made a member of Christ, the child of God, and an inheritor of the kingdom of heaven."[33] Since this didn't apply, Pocahontas needed to explain Powhatan naming customs.

---

33. "A Catechisme" from the *Book of Common Prayer*, 1604. Spellings modernized here and in what follows from the Catechism. The English of the time tended to put the letter *e* at the end of words like *child, kingdom,* and *Christ.*

In Anglican infant baptism, godparents vowed on behalf of the child to "forsake the devil, and all his works and pomps, the vanities of the wicked world, and all the sinful lusts of the flesh," to "believe all the articles of the Christian faith," and to "keep God's holy will and Commandments, and walk in the same all the days of my life." Since this also didn't apply, Whitaker would have asked the question directly of Pocahontas. Then he asked, "Dost thou not think that thou art bound to believe and to do, as they have promised for thee?"

She would have responded as taught: "Yes verily, and by God's help I will. And I heartily thank our heavenly Father, that he hath called me to this state of salvation, through Jesus Christ our Saviour. And I pray God to give me his grace, that I may continue in the same unto my life's end."

Pocahontas was to next recite the Apostles' Creed and the Ten Commandments. These, Pocahontas was to say, taught her "my duty towards God, and my duty towards my neighbour." Her duty toward God, the Catechism taught, was "to believe in him, to fear [reverence] him, and to love him with all my heart, with all my mind, with all my soul, and with all my strength. To put my whole trust in him. To call upon him. To honor his holy name and his word, and to serve him truly all the days of my life." And toward neighbor:

> To love him as myself; And to do to all men as I would they should do unto me. To love, honor, and succor my father and mother. To honor and obey the King, and his ministers. To submit myself to all my governors, teachers, spiritual Pastors and Masters. To order myself lowly and reverently to all my betters. To hurt nobody by word, nor deed. To be true and just in all my dealings. To bear no malice nor hatred in my heart. To keep my hands from picking and stealing, and my tongue from evil speaking, lying and slandering. To keep my body in temperance, soberness, and chastity. Not to covet nor desire other men's goods. But learn and labor truly to get my own living, and to do my duty in that state of life, unto which it shall please God to call me.

The words of Pocahontas, as she was taught to recite. Did she at some point in this process ponder the contradiction between the command "to do to all men as I would they should do unto me" and English treatment of her own people? Did she discuss this with Whitaker or her fiancé John Rolfe?

Since it is impossible to keep these commandments without God's help, the Catechism taught, prayer was essential. So here Pocahontas would recite the Lord's Prayer.

The Catechism finally proceeded to teaching on the sacraments. Just two are "generally necessary to salvation," baptism and the Lord's Supper. Pocahontas was asked: "What do you mean by the word Sacrament?"

Her reply, in the words of the Catechism, was the classic Anglican formula: "I mean an outward and visible sign of an inward and spiritual grace given unto us; ordained by Christ himself, as a means whereby we receive the same, and a pledge to assure us thereof." Thus every sacrament consists of two parts, "the outward visible sign, and the inward spiritual grace." In the case of baptism, Pocahontas had learned, the outward visible sign is water, and the inward spiritual grace is "A death unto sin, and a new birth unto righteousness: for being by nature born in sin, and the children of wrath, we are hereby made the children of grace."

In her Powhatan culture Pocahontas was familiar with signs of various sorts, such as the tobacco pipe (a symbol of peace), so we may well wonder what she made of these Christian "signs."[34]

The Catechism concludes with further teaching about the sacraments.

Whitaker knew well the instructions at the end of the Catechism that "The Curate of every parish, or some other at his appointment, shall diligently upon Sundays and holy days, half an hour before Evening prayer, openly in the Church instruct and examine so many children of his parish sent unto him, as the time will serve and as he shall think convenient, in some part of this Catechism." Further, "there shall none be admitted to the holy communion; until such time as he can say the Catechism and be confirmed." Like John Wesley in Georgia a century later, Whitaker presumably observed these instructions much more conscientiously than did most clergy in England.

Pocahontas was now ready for baptism. Then marriage to John Rolfe. She had had months of instruction in the Christian faith and in British ways.

---

34. The Powhatan used various rattles to signify power or priestly office, and particular birds, animals, or roots, as well as beads and shells, might carry symbolic meaning (Rountree, *Powhatan Indians,* 51, 90–91, 97). When a man and woman married, "The groom's father or 'chief friend' . . . brought a long string of shell beads and broke it over the couple's heads, after which the beads belonged to the bride's father" (ibid., 90).

CONVERSION OR ACCOMMODATION?

Despite all we *do* know, we are left wondering how fully Pocahontas understood the Christian faith or really comprehended the Scriptures. We can wonder how deep her conversion went, and especially whether she could distinguish between biblical faith in Jesus Christ and British cultural Christianity.

The King James Bible subtly if unintentionally revealed Christendom assumptions in the way it translated the original Hebrew and Greek. Terms which in the New Testament were largely functional, such as *deacon* and *bishop*, now meant official positions of authority in the church hierarchy. Pocahontas was reading the Bible through layer upon layer of the centuries of Christendom.

Nor do we know what was really going on in Pocahontas's mind and heart. Camilla Townsend draws upon accounts of other Indian conversions, however, to offer some plausible insights. She writes,

> [N]umerous other converted Indians throughout the hemisphere wrote or spoke of their experiences, and many pastors who came to know them better than Whitaker ever [knew Pocahontas] analyzed the situation thoroughly. These other texts tell us that Indians who converted in the first months of contact were virtually always incorporating the Christian God into their previously existing pantheon. Even the story of a god's spirit impregnating an unsuspecting woman was an old one in many of their cultures. Pocahontas almost certainly was agreeing to set aside her town's *okee* [local deity] in favor of Jesus Christ; she would have had to do something similar if she had been carried off by Iroquoian Indians or any other enemy. But nothing she said that day [of her baptism] is proof that she was in fact renouncing all that she had previously known and loved, or that her own personality had been obliterated. In her conversion and in her married life she continued to assert herself.[35]

And yet, given her prior contacts with the English over several years, Pocahontas's conversion was probably more thorough than that of other Indians. She seems to have been sincere, both in her Christian profession and in her love for John Rolfe, whatever her level of understanding. Certainly her understanding, and likely her personal faith, would have deepened during her brief years as Mrs. Rebecca Rolfe.

35. Townsend, *Pocahontas*, 125–26.

From this distance, it is easy to suppose that Pocahontas's Christian instruction was superficial. Yet the evidence points to much more thorough instruction than most committed Western Christians today receive! How many Christians today get up to a year of regular, almost daily, personal instruction in the Christian faith? Pocahontas received careful catechetical instruction under devoutly Christian, moderately Puritan auspices.

Certainly cultural elements were mixed in. Pocahontas must have seen the stark contradiction between the Christian ethics taught by Whitaker and the English lives Pocahontas saw lived around her—with the notable exceptions of her husband and her catechist.[36] Whitaker himself would have been at pains, it seems from what we know of him, to point out the discrepancy between the way of Jesus and the ways of the British colonists.[37]

In sum, Pocahontas's conversion seems to have been sincere and in its own way genuine. She likely had a real encounter with Jesus.

Indian oral tradition tells a very different tale here, however. According to some Indian accounts, Pocahontas was depressed among the English. Her becoming more "formal and civil" among her captors was a symptom of fear and depression. It wouldn't be the first time that a depressed woman found solace in Jesus. Yet there is no real evidence of depression, and psychological analysis based on somewhat similar experiences of others is always suspect.[38]

The story of Pocahontas is a story of love—for John Rolfe, and through him and missionary Whitaker, for Jesus.

36. Pocahontas's later outburst at John Smith (chapter 11) shows she was very good at spotting ethical contradictions.

37. As the Jesuit missionary Francis Xavier did with his Roman Catholic converts in India earlier.

38. See Custalow and Daniel, *True Story*, 55–62.

Chapter Nine

John Rolfe, Tobacco Man

John Rolfe and Pocahontas, husband and wife, now began their lives together—an integral part of the Virginia Colony, since Rolfe was already
well established there. Pocahontas continued learning English ways.

And now John Rolfe was discovering the key to Virginia's big success.
Not gold or a passage to the Pacific, but tobacco.

Meanwhile a brief, covert story played out—a drama John Rolfe and
Pocahontas knew nothing about.

POCAHONTAS'S LITTLE SISTER

The curious incident involved Pocahontas's younger half-sister. In May
1614, Sir Thomas Dale quietly sent Ralph Hamor to visit Chief Powhatan
with a fresh request. Hamor was to see if "by any means [he] might procure
a daughter" of Powhatan, in addition to Pocahontas, "for surer pledge of
peace." Dale had heard that Powhatan had a younger daughter—a sort of
second Pocahontas, still unmarried—and he was curious.

Hamor and a few companions traveled overland to Powhatan's current residence to deliver Dale's inquiry. Powhatan gave Hamor an audience,
passed the peace pipe, and asked about "his brother Sir Thomas Dale" and
about Pocahontas. Powhatan wanted details of "his daughter's welfare, her
marriage, his unknown son [Rolfe], and how they liked, lived, and loved
together."

Hamor assured Powhatan that Pocahontas was "so well content that she would not change her life to return to live with him." At this Powhatan "laughed heartily," Hamor said, "and said he was very glad of it."[1] But why had Hamor come?, the old chief asked.

Hamor revealed his mission—to deliver Powhatan's younger daughter to the English. Dale's real motives became clear when Hamor met privately with Powhatan (or as privately as Powhatan would permit). He told Powhatan, "The bruit [i.e., report] of the exquisite perfection of your youngest daughter, being famous through all your territories, hath come to the hearing of your brother Sir Thomas Dale, who for this purpose [sent me] to entreat you by that brotherly friendship you make profession of, to permit her with me to return unto him, partly for the desire which [he] himself hath, and partly for the desire her sister [Pocahontas] hath to see her. . . . [Dale] would gladly make [her] his nearest companion, wife, and bedfellow."[2]

Hamor said Dale had decided to remain in Virginia "so long as he liveth" (a lie). So now this proposed additional "natural union" between the English and the Powhatan—two proud peoples now peacefully "made one" through Pocahontas's marriage—would further cement the peace. It would be a clear sign from Powhatan of his "perpetual friendship" with the English. The marriage would personally bind together two great men, Dale and Powhatan, to the good of everyone. To Dale, now in his fifties, it looked like a win-win situation: peace with the Indians, and a comely teenage Indian girl (whom he had never met) in his bed.[3]

Governor Dale saw the happy companionship of John and Pocahontas, and perhaps he was envious. There were a couple of complications, however, which he failed to mention. He already had a wife back in England. Further, he was committed to return to England as soon as he could.[4] Already having a wife would have been no problem to Powhatan, of course, so Dale need not mention it. But it would be an issue among the English.

1. Hamor, "True Discourse," 832.

2. Ibid., 833.

3. Ibid. Dale's birth date is unknown. However he was already a mercenary in Holland by 1588.

4. "Dale was already married. His wife Elizabeth, Lady Dale, was at home in England; they had wed on the eve of his departure for Virginia" (Price, *Love and Hate*, 160; cf. Barbour, *Pocahontas*, 153, 269; Brown, *Genesis*, 2:870–71, 873; Scarboro, *Establisher*, 42). His wife was the well-connected Elizabeth Throckmorton, a cousin of the wife of Sir Walter Raleigh (cf. Barbour, *Pocahontas*, 269; Scarboro, *Establisher*, 42–43, 76).

Perhaps Dale thought he could keep his relationship with Powhatan's younger daughter a secret. It is difficult to see how he could have formally married her, as Rolfe did Pocahontas, since he was already married. Even if his wife in England had died—which does not seem to have been the case—the marriage or liaison would raise eyebrows, for the daughter in question seems to have been only about thirteen. To his patron in England Dale described himself as a "good and honest" husband much concerned about his wife's poor health.[5]

Powhatan was disgusted at Dale's audacity. Yet he remained polite. He told Hamor that only days earlier he had sold his daughter to be the wife of "a great weroance," and she was already three days' journey away. Hamor responded that certainly Powhatan had the authority to call her back, and Dale was willing to pay three times as much for her.

At this Powhatan responded that "he loved his daughter as dear as his own life," delighting in "none so much as in her, whom if he should not often behold, he could not possibly live."[6] If this second daughter went among the English he would never see her again, for he had determined "upon no terms whatsoever" ever to visit the English. Surely Pocahontas was enough of a pledge of peace. Should Pocahontas die, only then would he consider Dale's request. It was very unbrotherly of Dale "to desire to bereave me of two of my children at once," Powhatan said.[7]

The chief insisted that for now, no further pledge of peace was needed. "Too many" men had been killed on both sides, "and by my occasion there shall never be more. . . . I am now old and would gladly end my days in peace." If the English felt they needed still more land, "I will remove myself farther from you."[8]

With that, Powhatan closed the issue, and food was brought. Hamor returned to the English colony two days later, leaving behind a fuming Chief Powhatan and bearing a list of items Powhatan wanted sent to him, including a shaving knife, a cat, and a dog. Never again would Powhatan give an Englishman an audience.[9]

---

5. Brown, *Genesis*, 2:871.

6. One thinks here of Jacob and his sons Joseph and Benjamin in the book of Genesis.

7. Hamor, "True Discourse," 834. Cf. Barbour, *Pocahontas*, 141–42.

8. Powhatan's personal narrative would be played out again and again by weary, battle-worn chiefs of many other tribes as the white settlers and pioneers expanded steadily westward toward the Pacific over the next three centuries.

9. Hamor, "True Discourse," 835–37. Cf. Barbour, *Pocahontas*, 142–45.

Nothing came of Thomas Dale's proposed union with Pocahontas's younger sister. In fact, Ralph Hamor, Dale's envoy to Powhatan, seems to be the only one to have reported the incident. It was probably unknown to Alexander Whitaker or John Rolfe. Perhaps Pocahontas learned of it later from her Powhatan contacts.

JOHN ROLFE, COLONIAL ENTREPRENEUR

Pocahontas's marriage to John Rolfe proved to be tragically brief—less than three years. But they were very busy and productive years. Rolfe cultivated a tract of land he had acquired along the James River, not far from Jamestown. Where he and Pocahontas lived following their marriage is uncertain; most likely it was in or near Jamestown.

Rolfe was clear in his mission: "to labor in the Lord's vineyard, there to sow and plant, to nourish and increase the fruits thereof, . . . that in the end the fruits may be reaped to the comfort of the laborer in this life and his salvation in the world to come." This is "the service Jesus Christ requireth of his best servant," and Rolfe intended to be faithful to this calling in all the ways he could, both spiritually and materially.[10]

This was consistent with the original charge given the Virginia colonists. In England five years earlier, Rolfe had heard a sermon reinforcing the mission. On April 25, 1609, Rolfe, his pregnant first wife possibly at his side, assembled with other Virginia colonists at Whitechapel, London, to hear a two-hour farewell sermon by the Reverend William Symonds. Symonds exhorted the colonists to be good English Christians and go to America with high purpose and resolve. The band of about 200 or so colonists were soon to embark on the adventure of their lives.[11]

Symonds laid out a robust biblical and theological rationale for the colonial venture, defending it in the face of various criticisms. Were the colonists robbing the Indians of their land? No, said Symonds, for the English would plant "a peaceable colony in a waste country, where the people do live but like the deer," without settled property. Might not the natives nevertheless be hostile? If so, the English need not fear, for the Indians had nothing stronger than reed mats to protect themselves, and their "most fearful weapon of offence" was "an arrow of reed" (or so he thought). [12]

10. Rolfe letter in Hamor, "True Discourse," 854.

11. Townsend, *Pocahontas*, 90.

12. Quoted in ibid., 90 (spellings modernized).

True, Symonds noted, the colonists would face "diverse difficulties" when living "among barbarous people," especially in maintaining their piety and religious zeal. Like God's people in the Old Testament, they must keep themselves pure from the allurements of native women. "They may not marry nor give in marriage to the heathen, that are uncircumcised." Break this rule, Symonds said, and you "may break the good success of this voyage."

To live safely among the natives, the colonists might have to use force. But Symonds said, in effect, the end justifies the means. God was on their side. "The sum is, what blessing any nation had by Christ, must be communicated to all nations." One effective means would be to capture some Indian children and raise them as Christians so they in turn could win their elders. This had precedent in Scripture and in church history: "A captive girl brought Naaman to the prophet. A captive woman, was the means of converting Iberia, now called Georgia. Edesius & Frumentius, two captive youths, were the means of bringing the gospel to India. God makes the weak things of the world confound the mighty, and gets himself praise by the mouth of babes and sucklings. Be cheerful then, and the Lord of all glory, glorify his name by your happy spreading of the gospel, to your commendation, and his glory, that is Lord of all things."[13]

Capturing native children as an evangelistic tool was in fact explicitly recommended in Virginia Company instructions: "If you perceive that [the Indians] upon your landing, fly up into the country and forsake their habitation, you must seize into your custody half their corn and harvest and their werowances and all their known successors at once whom if you entreat well and educate those which are young and to succeed in the government in your manners and religion, their people will easily obey you and become in time civil and Christian."[14]

John Rolfe went to Virginia with these instructions and expectations in mind. Educated and with his own signet ring for letters, he could reasonably expect to become a successful merchant trader.[15]

Rolfe was the first to foresee the commercial success of tobacco. Crucially, he was also the first to figure out how to make it actually happen.

13. Quotations from ibid., 91 (spellings modernized).

14. "Instructions, orders and constitutions by way of advice" for the Virginia colonists (1609), quoted in ibid., 92 (spellings modernized).

15. Townsend, *Pocahontas,* 93.

He began raising tobacco experimentally. His experiments with different strains eventually opened the floodgate to Virginia's economic prosperity.

The Powhatan grew and smoked tobacco ceremonially. The English, however, found the native variety much too bitter or "biting." Within a year of arriving in Jamestown and meeting Pocahontas, Rolfe started growing tobacco as a crop, seeking ways to improve it.

The key turned out to be seeds from the West Indies. Rolfe discovered that Trinidad and Orinoco tobacco thrived in Virginia's temperate climate. Soon he "developed cultivation as well as curing methods, and successfully marketed the result in England such that at Jamestown was born the world's first commercial tobacco culture." As a result, "Virginia after Rolfe had a reason for being. Even the Indians smoked Orinoco" for pleasure, though retaining the native strain for religious rituals.[16]

By the end of the summer of 1612, notes Linwood "Little Bear" Custalow, "John Rolfe's first crop of West Indies tobacco was curing. It was taller than the Powhatan type."[17] By the time Rolfe later met Pocahontas, he was beginning to prosper in this pioneering venture.

It took a few years for Rolfe's tobacco to become fully competitive on the British market. He continued experimenting and refining. During his and Pocahontas's visit to England in 1616 he reported that in Virginia tobacco "thriveth so well that no doubt but after a little more trial and experience in the curing thereof it will compare with the best in the West Indies." By this time tobacco was already the colony's "principal commodity."[18]

Rolfe started exporting tobacco to England about the same time he married Pocahontas. He sent samples in 1612 and began exporting in 1614. Price notes, "From the first four barrels of tobacco leaf that Rolfe sent to England in March 1614, the Virginia tobacco trade had grown (according to customs records) to 2,300 pounds in 1616, 18,839 pounds in 1617, and 49,528 pounds in 1618."[19] Rolfe's tobacco was just as good (but cheaper than) the high-priced leaf imported by Spain from Central America. A successful business was born and Rolfe was thriving.

In England, King James I was heartily opposed to tobacco. Nevertheless, its use spread rapidly. Rolfe could not have seen any ethical problems with producing and selling the crop. Its harmful effects were not yet known,

16. Haile, "Introduction," in Haile, ed., *Jamestown Narratives*, 55.

17. Custalow and Daniel, *True Story,* 110.

18. Rolfe, "True Relation," 869, 872.

19. Price, *Love and Hate,* 186. Cf. Morison, *Oxford History,* 52.

though King James had his opinions.[20] The king even published a pamphlet, *A Counterblaste to Tobacco.* He was sure tobacco polluted men's "inward parts." Using tobacco was "a custom loathsome to the eye, hateful to the nose, harmful to the brain, dangerous to the lungs."[21] But by now market dynamics and tobacco's addictive power had won out.

In Virginia, nearly every colonist now wanted in. "Virginia went tobacco mad," for a time neglecting other essential crops. In 1626, 500,000 pounds were exported. Three years later the total reached an amazing 1.5 million pounds, then remained at about that level for the rest of the century. A global trade developed; major investors entered the market; tobacco prices fluctuated wildly.[22] This was seventeenth-century globalization.

Tobacco had been introduced to England about fifty years earlier, when a man named John Hawkins brought some good tobacco from Florida. The taste for tobacco "caught hold rapidly" and the tobacco habit spread throughout the British Isles. Since tobacco could not successfully be grown in England, the British were dependent upon Spanish American imports. For both political and economic reasons they wanted their own source. This was Rolfe's golden opportunity.[23]

During this period of perfecting his tobacco, Rolfe served as secretary and recorder of the colony for almost two years. This put him at the center of Virginia affairs.[24] And he became a father for the second time. Pocahontas gave birth to a son in 1615. John and Pocahontas named him Thomas, perhaps in honor of Sir Thomas Dale.

ROLFE'S VISION FOR VIRGINIA

By now some 350 colonists were scattered up and down the James River in various settlements. Rolfe penned "A True Relation of the State of Virginia," addressed to the king. He wanted to set the record straight, especially now that the colony was finally thriving. "How happily and plenteously the good blessings of God have fallen upon the people and colony" in recent years, in contrast to earlier much publicized difficulties.

20. Price, *Love and Hate*, 186.
21. Quoted in ibid., 177 (spelling modernized).
22. Vaughan, *American Genesis*, 99.
23. Ibid., 98.
24. Barbour, *Pocahontas*, 152.

Rolfe responded to those who asked skeptically, "How is it possible Virginia can now be so good, so fertile a country, so plentifully stored with food and other commodities" when just a few years earlier "men pined with famine? Can the earth now bring forth such a plentiful increase?"

It is true, Rolfe said, that "Virginia is the *same* it was, I mean for goodness of the [location] and fertileness of the land, and will no doubt so continue to the world's end, . . . a country spacious and wide, capable of many hundreds of thousands of inhabitants: for the soil, most fertile to plant in; for air, fresh and temperate, somewhat hotter in summer and not altogether so cold in winter as in England—yet so agreeable it is to our constitutions that now 'tis more rare to hear of a man's death than in England." The water is good and plentiful, and there are "fair navigable rivers and good harbors," with fine places and resources "for buildings and fortifications and for building of shipping." In fact, "scarce any or no country known to man" is "more abundantly furnished."

There is still some shortage of livestock, Rolfe reports. Yet already the colony has "cattle, horses, mares, and goats, which are carefully preserved for increase," and also "great store of hogs, both wild and tame, and poultry great plenty."

Rolfe goes on,

> But the greatest want of all is least thought on, and this is good and sufficient men as well of birth and quality to command soldiers to march, discover, and defend the country from invasions, as also artificers, laborers, and husbandmen with whom, were the colony well provided, then might trial be made what lieth hidden in the womb of the ground. The land might yearly abound with corn and other provisions for man's sustenance; buildings, fortifications, and shipping might be reared, wrought, and framed; commodities of divers kinds might be reaped yearly and sought after; and many things (God's blessing continuing) might come with ease to establish a firm and perfect commonweal.[25]

Much of this vision would, with time, come to pass.

Commenting on this report, Edward Wright Haile writes, "Rolfe believes in orderly development under wise absolutism, each man at his appointed task. He wants Virginia to be a place where honest people with modest means can get a start." Haile adds, "Up to now, America has been

25. Rolfe, "True Relation," 866–68.

described by Englishmen. Rolfe married an American [Pocahontas] and is the first Englishman to sound to me like an American."[26]

Rolfe could not foresee that the very struggles of the Virginia Colony would shortly lead to the birth of American democracy. In 1618 the Virginia Company in London passed a series of reforms and sent as governor Sir George Yeardley to implement them. Yeardley was instructed "to abolish arbitrary rule, introduce English common law and due process, encourage private property, and summon a representative assembly."[27]

As a result, the Virginia House of Burgesses was created in 1619, with twenty-two members. Until 1632 this first legislative assembly in America met in the choir of the Anglican church building in Jamestown. Though operating under the authority of the governor and ultimately the Crown, the House of Burgesses set the precedent for other legislative bodies that would with time develop in America.[28]

These were changes Pocahontas would not live to see. Now however, in the spring of 1616, prospects for John Rolfe, Pocahontas, and baby Thomas—and in fact for the colony itself—looked bright. These were in fact the best years for John and Pocahontas (now called Rebecca).

For the Rolfe family personally, things started changing dramatically about a year after baby Thomas's birth. Thomas Dale decided to return to England and to take all three Rolfes with him as prime specimens of Virginia's emerging prosperity and bright prospects.

Dale, the Rolfes, and a number of others departed from Jamestown on the ship *Treasurer*, still captained by Samuel Argall, around the end of April, 1616.[29] Dale's entourage included about a dozen Indians—in particular Uttamatomakkin, essentially a Powhatan ambassador and one of Pocahontas's many brothers-in-law.[30] The ship arrived safely in England in early June.

By now Pocahontas was accustomed to life in the Virginia Colony. In London she would find a totally new and strange world.

---

26. Haile, introduction to Rolfe's "True Relation," 865.

27. As summarized by Morison, *Oxford History*, 52.

28. Ibid., 52–53; Anderson, *History*, 1:253.

29. On the date, see Rolfe, "True Relation," 866. Barbour, *Pocahontas*, gives the date as "April 21 (?)" (*Pocahontas*, xx).

30. Rountree, *Pocahontas*, 176; Scarboro, *Establisher*, 38.

Chapter Ten

London Celebrity

Virginia was in full spring bloom as Pocahontas sailed off to London with her husband John and year-old son Thomas. Weeks on the Atlantic Ocean lay ahead.

If plans went as expected, she would be back in her homeland within a year.

Again Pocahontas was being conveyed on a ship captained by Samuel Argall, her captor just three short years earlier. Pocahontas knew the ship—the very one used in her kidnapping. Argall was its partial owner.

The voyage to England lasted seven weeks, about average for eastbound journeys. The party was large and Argall's ship, *Treasurer*, was crowded. In addition to the Rolfes, Thomas Dale, and the ship's crew, nearly 100 people were aboard. A dozen of these were Powhatan Indians, both men and women. Chief among them was Uttamatomakkin, Chief Powhatan's personal representative. Powhatan sent Uttamatomakkin (whom the English generally called Tomocomo) to England specifically to gather intelligence on the numbers and strength of the English.

The other Powhatans included Uttamatomakkin's wife Matachanna, also Pocahontas's half-sister, who served as nurse for young Thomas Rolfe. Others in the native party included a second half-sister and half a dozen or so other men and women who served as attendants to Pocahontas and Uttamatomakkin.[1]

1. Woodward, *Pocahontas*, 174–75.

Pocahontas faced this new adventure with a mix of curiosity, excitement, and apprehension. John had probably explained to her what such a voyage would involve.

There was plenty of unpleasantness. On the way over Thomas Dale had a man hanged from the yardarm. His name was Francis Lymbry, but he called himself Francisco Lembrai, pretending to be Spanish. He was discovered to be a renegade Irishman serving as a Spanish spy.[2]

Approaching England, *Treasurer* sailed along the Cornwall coast and up the English Channel. It docked at Plymouth on June 12, 1616.[3]

Pocahontas now caught her first glimpse of a large, bustling English port. "As it turned out, England was gray," notes Townsend. "Everything about it was gray—the stonework, the weathered wood, the filthy water slapping the docks."[4] So different from Virginia. Pocahontas "was met with pomp and ceremony by Sir Lewis Stukley, the Vice-Admiral of Devon, and other gold-braided officials."[5]

Soon the Rolfes were jostling along on a coach to London. It would have taken about a week to cover the 180 or so miles. Though a dusty, jolting ride, this gave Pocahontas a chance to see the lovely open English countryside—meadows, croplands, cattle, and wooded fencerows rather than the dense forest of Virginia.[6]

The scene changed as the party neared London. "Pocahontas's disconcerting first view would have been of a slum, the borough of Southwark, across the Thames from the city proper." Not far away was Shakespeare's Globe Theater. Then on across London Bridge, still crowded with shops and dwellings, and into the old city.[7]

Soon the carriage pulled up to the well-known Belle Savage Inn, where the Rolfes were to lodge. Someone perhaps explained to Pocahontas that "savage" was not a demeaning reference to the Indians but rather the name of the original proprietor.

News preceded them! Pocahontas found herself already famous. Within days she was being "fêted at public and private gatherings, appearing at masques, and parties where she was very much admired," wrote John

---

2. Townsend, *Pocahontas,* 135–36; Percy, "True Relation," 516.

3. Townsend, *Pocahontas,* 137–38; Woodward, *Pocahontas,* 174.

4. Townsend, *Pocahontas,* ix.

5. Woodward, *Pocahontas,* 174.

6. Price, *Love and Hate,* 164–65.

7. Ibid., 165.

Yardley in *Before the Mayflower*. Lady Delaware, the wife of Thomas West, presented her to King James and Queen Anne.[8]

On arriving in England Governor Dale had quickly dispatched a letter to Sir Ralph Winwood, the British secretary of state. Dale announced, "I am by the mighty power of the Almighty God safely returned from the hardest task that ever I undertook, and by the blessing of God have with poor means left the colony in great prosperity and peace, contrary to many men's expectations." He had brought with him on the *Treasurer*, he said, "exceeding good tobacco," sassafras, potash, sturgeon, "and suchlike commodities" that the colony was already providing. Virginia was a great place, Dale said, and would serve well "both for the emptying of our full body [that is, crowded England, through emigration] and the maintenance of our shipping." Dale urged His Majesty's government to accelerate "to inhabit there" and "to possess one of the goodliest and richest kingdoms of the world and indeed so fit for no state as ours." Surprisingly, he made no mention of Pocahontas or John Rolfe.[9]

POCAHONTAS SEES LONDON

Pocahontas had arrived at one of the world's biggest and most cosmopolitan cities, home to some 225,000 souls. It was well on the way to becoming a global trading center and "a great emporium of data."[10] Crowded and unsanitary, it was not a healthy place. The Indians were soon coughing with respiratory ailments. They knew wood smoke in their native homes, but not the acrid, sulfurous coal smoke that hung heavily in London's air.

The Belle Savage Inn, just off Fleet Street outside the old city wall, was a popular stopping place for travelers—partly for its location but also because its inner court served as a playhouse where strolling players performed. Here "you shall never find a word without wit, never a line without pith," said one observer. Entertainment in the courtyard ranged from bearbaiting to Christopher Marlowe's *Faustus*.[11]

Pocahontas's visit only upped the Belle Savage's fame. A few years later Ben Jonson in his play *The Staple of News* referred to the Indian celebrity. A tavern is "too unfit for a princess," says one character. No, a second replies;

8. Yardley, *Before the Mayflower*, 160.

9. Dale, "Letter to Winwood," 878–79.

10. Darwin, *Unfinished Empire*, 270.

11. Barbour, *Pocahontas*, 159–60. Cf. Townsend, *Pocahontas*, 139.

"the blessed Pokahontas, as the historian calls her, and great king's daughter of Virginia, hath been in womb of a tavern."[12]

The Rolfes' lodging thus was popular and well-known, though not high class.

Word spread quickly through London's streets and parlors that the "Indian princess" had arrived. Soon she was famous for being famous. Londoners wrote about her in their letters and diaries. John Chamberlain, a compulsive letter writer with many well-placed friends, wrote on June 22, 1616, "Sir Thomas Dale is arrived from Virginia and brought with him some ten or twelve old and young of that Country, among whom the most remarkable person is Pocahuntas (daughter to Powhatan a King or cacique of that Country) married to one Rolfe an Englishman."[13] Many of the English were eager to learn more about these exotic primitives, as they viewed them. "Londoners regularly came to gape whenever captive Indians, or even Indian artifacts, were displayed."[14]

For his part, John Smith was concerned—both for Pocahontas's sake and for England's—that she should be well treated. In a letter to Queen Anne he advised, "If she should not be well received, seeing this kingdom may rightly have a kingdom by her means, her present love to us and Christianity might turn to such scorn and fury as to divert all this good to the worst of evil."[15] Smith knew that Pocahontas was no passive simple "primitive."

In England, Pocahontas was Lady Rebecca Rolfe—"Lady" in recognition of her father's status and importance in colonial politics. The Virginia Company provided her with four pounds a week to help cover expenses. As Townsend puts it, "If the [Rolfes'] tour was to be a success, she would have to dress like a Jacobean grand dame and feed her attendants decently." To appear in status-conscious fashionable society "she would have to go beyond anything she had worn in Virginia, with canvases to hold out her skirts, sleeves so large they nearly immobilized her, and a wooden board placed along her stomach and the lower part of her breast to ensure a

12. Quoted in Townsend, *Pocahontas*, 135. The Belle Savage served both as an inn and a tavern; many taverns were also inns.

13. Brown, *Genesis*, 2:789 (English modernized).

14. Townsend, *Pocahontas*, 144.

15. Smith, "General History, Fourth Book," 863 (Smith's summary of the letter he claimed to have sent to Queen Anne). It is interesting in light of a later encounter that Smith, who knew Pocahontas well, refers to her (potential) "fury."

certain shape once she was dressed."[16] Socially she outranked her husband, who boasted no royal blood.

Sir Edwin Sandys, Member of Parliament, a founder of the Virginia Company and now its treasurer, acted more or less as the Rolfes' sponsor and host in London. Many in London wanted to meet Pocahontas. Invitations to dinners and parties arrived at the Belle Savage. Samuel Purchas, a clergyman and publisher of travel accounts, certainly wanted to meet her to satisfy his curiosity and gain more information about Virginia and its Indians.[17] He was present on several social occasions involving the Rolfes and also Uttamatomakkin, with whom he conversed several times.

Purchas was especially taken with Pocahontas. Not only did she "accustom herself to civility, but still carried herself as the Daughter of a King, and was accordingly respected, not only by the Company . . . but of diverse particular persons of Honor, in their hopeful zeal by her to advance Christianity. I was present, when my Honorable and Reverend Patron, the Lord Bishop of London, Doctor [John] King, entertained her with festival state and pomp, beyond what I have seen in his great hospitalities afforded to other Ladies."[18]

What did Pocahontas make of all this? There are hints she enjoyed the attention and status even as she was troubled by the superficiality of British high society and the looming question of her own people's fate.

The Bishop of London's palace, Samuel Purchas's church at Ludgate, and the Belle Savage Inn were all within walking distance of each other. But it was an unhealthy place to live, especially for people accustomed to the Virginia forests. Pocahontas needed a more wholesome setting, so in late summer the Rolfes moved to the country estate of the Percy family in Brentford, nine miles further up the Thames. This was the ancestral home of George Percy, an early Jamestown colonist who likely remembered Pocahontas as a child. Percy was now back in London and may have offered the Rolfes this much more pleasant place.[19]

16. Townsend, *Pocahontas*, 139, 140.

17. Purchas had earlier described Virginia itself as a "virgin" of whom the English colonists would make "an honest and Christian wife," as we note in chapter 13 (Townsend, *Pocahontas*, 141).

18. Purchas, *Purchas, His Pilgrimes*, 19:118, quoted in Townsend, *Pocahontas*, 142 (English modernized).

19. Townsend, *Pocahontas*, 142–43. On George Percy, see chapters 5 and 6, above. Townsend says Pocahontas "was tired and sick. She had no way of knowing that she was being attacked by thousands of foreign microbes, against which she had no built-up

Townsend imagines this more hospitable suburban setting: "Strolling the country lanes, Pocahontas improved in spirits. By that time little Thomas must have been walking and talking, mixing the Algonkian words of his caretakers with the English he heard everywhere."[20]

POCAHONTAS AT THE COURT MASQUE

When Pocahontas was twelve she hosted John Smith at an Indian dance spectacle in Virginia.[21] Now, nine years later in a 180-degree cultural turnaround, the King and Queen of England hosted Pocahontas at an elaborate British court entertainment called a masque.

Christmas 1616, with its endless round of social events, had come and gone. For the nobility the capstone was the annual Twelfth Night Masque, held on January 6, 1617 at the royal banqueting house, Whitehall Palace. Pocahontas and Uttamatomakkin were honored guests by invitation of Queen Anne herself; John Rolfe was also included. Pocahontas sat near the king on the royal dais.[22]

The annual Twelfth Night Masque at the Court of King James was the current fad in royal entertainment. It was a prestigious social event to which only the most favored and well connected were invited. *Masque* meant not a masquerade but rather a courtly spectacle that grew fashionable in the late 1500s and early 1600s. Such masques developed first in Italy; and in their elaborate costumes and sets reflected the opulence of Italian opera, though court masques were usually performed just once.[23]

"A masque was neither a play nor a dance but rather a spectacular show lasting as long as three hours. Dancers and musicians paraded and performed, some with lines to say or sing, all relying on extraordinary settings and costumes to create a magical effect."[24] Masques typically took the form of fanciful allegory climaxing in flattering homage to the king. The main characters were usually based on classical mythology. Characters

---

immunities" (Townsend, *Pocahontas*, 142).

20. Ibid., 143.

21. See chapter 5.

22. Townsend, *Pocahontas*, 144–45.

23. The masque Pocahontas attended, *The Vision of Delight*, was however performed a second time, on January 19.

24. Townsend, *Pocahontas*, 146.

might be named Fortune, Folly, Delight, and so forth, or given names of Greek or Roman gods or goddesses.[25]

Masques were musical fantasies combining singing, dancing, acting, and elaborate stage sets and machinery. Guests often participated in the dances, though key roles were played by professional actors backed by skilled musicians.[26] Masques embodied "self-congratulation within conspicuous consumption on a massive scale. It was not uncommon for the king to spend £3000 (the equivalent of several hundred thousand dollars today) on a production that would be performed once or twice, and witnessed by a thousand people."[27]

Pocahontas earlier had an audience with King James and Queen Anne, so she knew the courtly protocols. But she had never witnessed anything like *The Vision of Delight*, the masque written for this occasion by playwright Ben Jonson. The elaborate fantasy would have been nearly unintelligible without some knowledge of Greek mythology. Yet Pocahontas was probably able to follow the drift of the drama, picking up on some of the mythic symbolism.

Playwright and poet Ben Jonson was a favorite of James I. He wrote and produced several masques for the royal court. *The Vision of Delight* was especially elaborate, though not untypical. The text was by Jonson with music by Nicholas Lanier and elaborate costumes and staging by the celebrated Inigo Jones.[28]

Jonson took masques seriously as literature, insisting upon their "uplifting ethical character."[29] His courtly audiences, however, saw them main-

25. David Lindley describes the masque more fully: "Its heart is the appearance of a group of noble personages dressed in elaborate disguise to celebrate a particular occasion and to honour their monarch. They perform some specially designed (and well-rehearsed) masque dances, and then take out the members of the court audience in the communal dance of the revels. The fundamental job of the masque writer was to provide a fiction to explain the disguised arrival, and the basic symbolic assertion of all court masques derived from the moment of the dissolution of the masque's fiction into the social reality of the court. The antimasque (also called the ante-masque, or antic masque) became a fixed part of the masque's pattern after 1609, when Ben Jonson, in answer to Queen Anne's request for 'some Daunce, or shew, that might praecede hers, and have the place of a foyle, or false-Masque' responded with the presentation of twelve witches [etc.]. . . . Most frequently, of course, the formal pattern of the masque became an image of harmony and order, and an idealisation of the court by whom and for whom it was performed" ("Introduction," in Lindley, *Court Masque*, 1–2).

26. Lindley, *Court Masque*; Limon, *Masque*.

27. Orgel, *Ben Jonson*, 3.

28. Meagher, *Method and Meaning*, 78.

29. Ibid., 79.

ly as fashionable entertainment. Pocahontas must have been fascinated, if somewhat mystified.

Like Jonson's other masques, *The Vision of Delight* was on one level a morality tale, an idealized drama of harmony overcoming chaos. Its central dance portrayed a "complex idea of the harmony of nature, being reminiscent of Zephyr and Flora, of Venus, of the spring itself," writes John Meagher. Jonson the "humanistic poet" himself referred to the "sweet *union*, . . . the harmonious laws of Nature and Reason" and sought to reflect this in his productions.[30] In this sense masques breathed the spirit of the dawning Enlightenment.

There was nothing Christian about *The Vision of Delight*, either explicitly or implicitly. Rather, as Jerzy Limon writes, masques of this type represented

> the fullest single manifestation of early Stuart culture. In actual productions [the masque] fused together all the arts—poetry, painting, music, architecture, sculpture, dancing, and acting— each created by the leading talents of the period. Its appearance was made possible only by the royal patronage . . . ; with the disappearance of this patronage the masque [in this sense] ceased to exist. From James's accession in 1603 [the dramatic masque] served an important ideological function at the Stuart court. Basically it presented in an allegorical and emblematic form the doctrine of Divine Right, the fundamental component of Stuart ideology.[31]

What exactly did Pocahontas see on this Twelfth Night evening? David Price writes, "Once the crowd settled down for the performance, Pocahontas would have observed a street scene and elegant buildings onstage, constructed and painted in perspective so the street appeared to recede into the distance. From 'afar off' entered a bare-breasted woman representing Delight, joined by Grace, Love, Harmony, Revel, Sport, and Laughter. Delight gave a rhythmic exhortation to the players to 'play and dance and sing.'"[32]

Delight introduces the action, singing Jonson's lines. Soon a large monster appears, pulled onstage by unseen stagehands. From its belly six comic dancers burst forth and perform a long dance routine.

Next the dark, star-covered chariot of Night rises, lifted by overhead wires, followed by the moon. Night sings out, "Break, Fantasy, from the

30. Ibid., 88, 89, 186 ("humanistic poet").

31. Limon, *Masque*, 200.

32. Price, *Love and Hate*, 177.

cave of cloud, and spread thy purple wings; now all thy figures are allowed, and various shapes of things."

The backdrop changes to clouds. Fantasy appears, launching into a strange, bawdy monologue including double entendres. Various "phantasms" enter and dance onstage. The scene changes again to the bower of Zephyrus, god of gentle winds. Peace sings a song, and Wonder recites a poem full of allusions from mythology and nature which ends:

> Behold! How the blue bind-weed doth itself enfold
> With honeysuckle, and both these entwine
> Themselves with bryony [a broad-leave vine] and jasmine,
> To cast a kind of odoriferous shade.

So the action continues, the whole entertainment ending in dancing in which the court guests participate. Pocahontas, Uttamatomakkin, and John Rolfe watched in wonder. What they thought at the end of the long night we'll never know.[33] An acute cultural observer, Pocahontas may have thought back to the evening dance entertainment she helped stage for John Smith and his companions at Powhatan's town years before. The contrast was huge. Yet there were parallels.

FIGURE 4
Simon Van de Passe's engraving of Pocahontas from life (1616)

33. Description based mainly on Townsend, *Pocahontas*, 146–49; Price, *Love and Hate*, 176–78; Robertson, "Pocahontas at the Masque," 551–83.

POCAHONTAS'S PORTRAIT

What did Pocahontas really look like? In London, of course, she was dressed like a noblewoman. The letter writer John Chamberlain described her, somewhat disdainfully, as "no fair Lady, and yet with her tricking up and high style and titles you might think her and her worshipful husband to be somebody, if you do not know that the poor [Virginia] company out of their poverty are fain to allow her four pound a week for her maintenance."[34]

The most authentic image of Pocahontas is the one drawn from life while she was in London. The respected Dutch-German engraver Simon Van de Passe was working in London at the time, doing portraits and engravings of well-known figures, including John Smith and King James I. He was engaged to draw a portrait of Pocahontas that could be engraved and printed in multiple copies, as memorabilia or souvenirs of Pocahontas's London visit.

Van de Passe was young, about the same age as Pocahontas. On his portrait he lists her age as twenty-one, though she may have been a year or so younger. His engraving is widely viewed as the only authentic likeness we have of Pocahontas and is the basis of Mary Ellen Howe's 1994 color portrait[35] and also of the full-size standing portrait of Pocahontas by Richard Norris Brooke in the Virginia Museum of Fine Arts in Richmond.[36]

In the engraving Pocahontas appears in costly attire, dressed for court. The unusual hat, called a high capotain, then in vogue, was a woman's version of the popular men's beaver hat. Stylistically the high capotain was still somewhat edgy, though Queen Anne had worn one decorated with an ostrich feather, giving it legitimacy.[37]

Townsend notes that Van de Passe portrays Pocahontas "as indigenous," not European, clearly showing "her high cheekbones, almond eyes, and black hair." Yet clearly she is someone of regal status: "Long, delicate fingers hold a fan of ostrich feathers, a symbol of royalty."[38]

Interestingly, the name *Pocahontas* does not appears on the work. Rather, the engraving's legend reads, "Matoaka alias Rebecca daughter of the mighty Prince Powhatan Emperor of Attanoughskomouck alias Virginia

34. Quoted in Townsend, *Pocahontas*, 148–49 (spelling modernized).

35. Lewis, "Pocahontas Revealed," lines 233–60.

36. Richard Norris Brooke, *Pocahontas* (1889 and 1907), Virginia Museum of Fine Arts. The portrait forms the cover of Allen, *Pocahontas*.

37. Townsend, *Pocahontas*, 152; Robertson, "Pocahontas at the Masque," 573.

38. Townsend, *Pocahontas*, 152, 153.

converted and baptized in the Christian faith, and wife to the worthy Mr. John Rolfe."[39] An oval inscription around the portrait in Latin likewise identifies Pocahontas as "Matoaka alias Rebecca," daughter of Powhatan.

Probably Pocahontas herself had a hand in the inscription. She may have explained to Van de Passe that "Pocahontas" was a childhood nickname; her real name was Matoaka, even though the English knew her as Lady Rebecca (and popularly still as Pocahontas). The inscription may have been her way of asserting her own identity. She probably also sounded out for Van de Passe the correct Indian name for Virginia, which the English rendered in various ways.[40]

Pocahontas, alias Matoaka, alias Lady Rebecca Rolfe, was now indeed a London celebrity, with a recognizable image.

FIGURE 5
Pocahontas, by Mary Ellen Howe (1994)

39. Spelling modernized.

40. Townsend writes, "This rendition was obviously the result of Matoaka's sounding it out for a Dutchman, just as it was undoubtedly the woman herself who insisted on using Matoaka rather than her more famous and attention-grabbing nickname, which everyone else was using" (Townsend, *Pocahontas,* 154).

Chapter Eleven

—————

Last Days of Pocahontas

The Rolfes had now been in England almost six months. Spring 1617 was approaching. Pocahontas and her family would soon return to America. Preparations were underway.

SHAKESPEAREAN DAYS

William Shakespeare (1564–1616) was Pocahontas's contemporary. He died at Stratford-upon-Avon just as Pocahontas and her family were setting out from Virginia on their voyage to England. The two never met.

Even so, these parallel lives—the "princess" and the playwright—were multiply linked. Both were born before 1600 and passed away before 1620.

Shakespeare died on April 23, 1616, at the age of fifty-two. Ben Jonson (1572–1637), author of satirical plays and lyric poetry as well as high-style court masques like the *Vision of Delight,* was still at the height of his career. Shakespeare had acted in one of Jonson's early hits, *Every Man His Humour,* in 1598.

The main link between Shakespeare and Pocahontas is the playwright's great last masterpiece, *The Tempest*—which gave us the phrase "brave new world," a comment on colonialism. Though Shakespeare set the play on a Mediterranean island, the inspiration came from the 1609 Atlantic hurricane that sent *Sea Venture,* part of the Jamestown fleet, off course and stranded John Rolfe and his first wife on Bermuda.[1] Mrs. Rolfe gave birth to a daughter shortly after the shipwreck. The Rolfes named her Bermuda. Sadly, the baby died on the island, and not long after the Rolfes arrived in Jamestown the mother died also.

The Tempest was first performed before King James I at Whitehall on November 1, 1611. Pocahontas was then a mere teenager of about fourteen. Only five years later, she herself would watch a spectacular drama in King James's presence.

Jonathan Bate, in his introduction to a modern edition of *The Tempest*, notes how the play "conjures up the spirit of European colonialism" in multiple ways. Shakespeare knew members of the Virginia Company. He learned of the Bermuda disaster by late 1610, and set to work writing. The resulting play "intuits the dynamic of colonial possession and dispossession with such uncanny power," Bate suggests, that the key characters Prospero and the native Caliban are sometimes taken as prototypes of the cultural dynamics and contradictions of colonialism.[2]

The Tempest actually reflects the adventures of the Virginia colony in several ways:

> Arrival on an island uninhabited by Europeans, talk of "plantation," an encounter with a "savage" in which alcohol is exchanged for survival skills, a process of language learning in which it is made clear who is master and who is slave, fear that the slave will impregnate the master's daughter, the desire to make the savage seek for Christian "grace" (though also a proposal that he should be shipped to England and exhibited for profit), references to the dangerous weather of the Bermudas and to a "brave new world": in all these respects, *The Tempest* conjures up the spirit of European colonialism [and the new Jamestown colony in particular].[3]

Historian Karen Kupperman notes similarly that Shakespeare's language in *The Tempest* "paralleled the descriptions in the vivid report published by those who had experienced the momentous 1609 hurricane" off Bermuda. Shakespeare in fact uses his key character Caliban—perhaps *The Tempest*'s most intriguing figure—to offer veiled criticism of colonialism. Caliban "castigated Prospero for having taken the island from him and made him his slave. Like the Chesapeake Algonquians [and Powhatans], Caliban

1. See Woodward, H., *Brave Vessel*.
2. Bate, "Introduction," in Shakespeare, *The Tempest*, xiv–xv.
3. Ibid., xiv.

eventually vowed no longer to provide food for Prospero, and referred to the intricate and irreplaceable native-built weirs on which the colonists depended: 'No more dams I'll make for fish.'"[4]

The Tempest, even with its veiled critique of British colonialism, is fiction and fantasy. Yet it prefigured the real-life drama that played out a few years later when Pocahontas and her family arrived in London.

JOHN SMITH'S SURPRISE

Spring in the south English countryside is beautiful, but the time for the Rolfes' return voyage was drawing near. Where was John Smith, Pocahontas wondered. She had not seen him for nine years. Back in Jamestown she'd been told he was dead. People in London said he was alive and living in England. Surely he would want to see her. Why had he not come?

The likely reason was social protocol. Pocahontas was now a lady and a celebrity. She was considered royalty. Smith had heard about the court masque. Roles were now reversed. John Smith was Lady Rebecca's social inferior, and he felt it. He seems to have been in turmoil over seeing Pocahontas due to the astonishing events in her life since they'd last met.[5]

Smith no doubt heard that Pocahontas would soon be returning to America. He himself was about to set sail for New England.[6] So one day Smith showed up with several friends at Brentford, hoping to see her. Smith felt Pocahontas deserved more "service" from him than a brief unannounced visit (he said later), but time was short.

Smith's surprise visit triggered the longest, most dramatic and emotional outpouring of words from Pocahontas that we have on record. Smith himself describes the encounter.

When she saw John Smith, Pocahontas was overcome with emotion. "After a modest salutation, without any word," Smith says, "she turned about, obscured her face, as not seeming well contented." Pocahontas was upset and Smith was probably embarrassed. John Rolfe was present, and he

---

4. Kupperman, *Jamestown Project,* 249.

5. Possibly also his health and appearance had been impaired by the gunpowder explosion that sent him back to England.

6. Barbour, *Pocahontas,* 165–66; Price, *Love and Hate,* 180; Townsend, *Pocahontas,* 154.

led Smith and the others back outside or to a different room while Pocahontas recovered herself. They "all left her for two or three hours," Smith reports.[7]

When they returned Smith found Pocahontas with "a well set countenance" and a speech ready for him. The outburst of words and emotion is worth quoting just as Smith reported it.[8]

Pocahontas first reminded John of all the ways she had helped him in the early Jamestown days. "You promised Powhatan what was yours should be his, and he did the like to you," she said. "You called him father, being in his land a stranger, and by the same reason so must I do you."

Smith recoiled. He interrupted Pocahontas. Given her status as royalty—a king's daughter—he could not now allow her to call him father. Think of who she was in England! This was not Jamestown. Smith was conscious also of the others present. Though he could excuse this title "father" personally, in this context he could not.

His objection only upset Pocahontas more. She retorted, "Were you not afraid to come into my father's country, and to cause fear in him and all his people, except for me? And you're afraid now to have me call you father? I tell you I will, and you shall call me child, and so I will be forever and ever your countryman. They always told me you were dead, and I knew nothing else till I came to Plymouth. Powhatan had commanded Uttamatomakkin to seek you, and know the truth, because your countrymen lie much."[9]

"Except for me"! Here again, Pocahontas's exceptional self-possession—she insists. Despite all that had happened, John Smith was still her "father." She meant two things. First, her remarkable bond of love and affection for Smith dating back to her preteen years was still in her heart—in some sense lying deeper even than her love for her husband. But also she meant that the bond between John Smith and her father, Chief Powhatan—the adoption—still held. Smith had not honored or lived up to it. Yes, the English "lie much," but she had expected better of Smith—the man who owed her his life, and to whom she owed her insider understanding of the English. As Karen Robertson puts it, Pocahontas "tellingly reprimands

7. Smith, "General History, Fourth Book," 864. Cf. Townsend, *Pocahontas,* 154; Price, *Love and Hate,* 180.

8. Smith, "General History, Fourth Book," 864.

9. Ibid., 864 (English slightly modernized and paraphrased for clarity).

Smith for his failure to uphold a set of reciprocal obligations that derive from kinship—his adoption as Powhatan's brother."[10]

Smith probably had brought his friends along to show Pocahontas off and to bask in the glow of her celebrity. He did not find what he expected. When he and his friends left Pocahontas alone for some time he found himself "repenting" for having told them "she could speak English"—apparently misunderstanding her silence.

Seeing Smith was probably the jolt that released in Pocahontas a flood of mixed emotions built up over past weeks through the whirl of events and new experiences and her exalted social status.

Townsend summarizes,

> [Pocahontas] was clearly expressing profound sadness and anger, not unrequited love. She spoke rather of political matters. Her father had established a kin relationship with this man, implying reciprocity and honesty. Smith had defaulted on both counts. He had not prevented the depredations of the English or kept his promises. He had simply slipped away, leaving a lie to explain his absence and his failure to live up to his word. At the same time Pocahontas reminded him that she herself had honored the claims of reciprocity and honesty and intended to continue doing so. It is hard not to hear the note of judgment and superiority: she embodies her people's virtues, while she deprecates not just Smith but all the English [who] "lie much."[11]

Smith left Pocahontas's presence disconcerted and dismayed.

But Pocahontas herself was unwell. Young Thomas was also ill. Still, they had to pack for the long voyage back to America. Departure from London was planned for mid-March.

A GRAVE AT GRAVESEND

The day came. The Rolfes and their fellow passengers would sail down the Thames to Gravesend, then around the south coast of England through the English Channel and head west into the Atlantic. Once again Samuel Argall was the captain, though this time his ship was the *George*. Argall now had added status and responsibilities; he had recently been appointed deputy governor of Virginia.

10. Robertson, "Pocahontas at the Masque," 578.

11. Townsend, *Pocahontas*, 155–56.

Before leaving, John Rolfe met again with Sir Edwin Sandys, Virginia Company treasurer. The company had collected funds for Indian evangelism, and Sandys delivered 100 pounds personally to Rolfe. The money was given, Sandys reported, to "Mr. Rolfe and his Lady, partly in doing honor to that good example of her conversion, and to encourage other of her kindred and nation to do the like, and partly upon promise made by the said Mr. Rolfe on behalf of himself and the said Lady, that both by their godly and virtuous example . . . as also by all other good means of persuasions and inducements, they would employ their best endeavors to the winning of the people to the knowledge of God."[12]

As the *George* sailed down the Thames, Pocahontas felt increasingly ill. Most of the Virginia Indians were suffering colds or worse. Some may have had pneumonia.

Near the mouth of the Thames sits the small town of Gravesend where, 121 years later, John Wesley would arrive on his return voyage from Georgia. The town had a three-story inn, and John Rolfe insisted that Pocahontas go ashore to rest and see a doctor.

Too weak to walk, Pocahontas was carried to the inn and put to bed. Presumably a doctor was called—though medical diagnosis and treatment were still quite primitive in England. Native Indian herbal medicine was in some ways more advanced and might have done Pocahontas more good. She was probably suffering from pneumonia, virulent flu, or some other respiratory disease. One account says it was smallpox.[13]

Pocahontas died at the inn on Friday, March 21, 1617. Samuel Purchas wrote, "At her return towards Virginia [Pocahontas] came at Gravesend to her end and grave, having given great demonstration of her Christian sincerity, as the first fruits of Virginian conversion, leaving here a goodly memory, and the hopes of her resurrection, her soul aspiring to see and enjoy presently in heaven, what she had joyed to hear and believe of her beloved Savior."[14] Far away in Virginia, Alexander Whitaker died at almost the same time, drowning in the James River.[15]

Both Pocahontas and Whitaker died far from their native shores.

12. Quoted in Townsend, *Pocahontas*, 156 (English modernized).

13. Pennington, *Church of England*, 20.

14. Purchas, *Pilgrimes*, 19:188, quoted in Barbour, *Pocahontas*, 181–82.

15. Whitaker drowned sometime during March, 1617 (Price, *Love and Hate*, 186; Littleton, "Alexander Whitaker," 347). His will was proved in London by his brother Samuel on August 4, 1617 (Whitaker, Will).

John Rolfe and two-year-old Thomas remained at Pocahontas's bed-side until she died. Toward the end Pocahontas told John, "All must die. It is enough that our child lives."[16] Earlier Uttamatomakkin had told Samuel Purchas that the Powhatans "held it a disgrace to fear death, and therefore when they must die, did it resolutely."[17]

For John, Thomas's survival helped cushion "the sorrow of her loss," he said, though the boy was still ailing. Writing to Edwin Sandys on his arrival back in Jamestown, Rolfe said he was sure Pocahontas's soul "rests in eternal happiness." In Thomas John could see "the living ashes of his deceased Mother." For his part, he had learned "such temperance . . . in prosperity, and patience in adversity, that I will as joyfully receive evil, as good at the hand of God: and assuredly trust that He, who has preserved my child, even as a brand snatched out of the fire, has further blessings in store for me, and will give me strength and courage to undertake any religious and charitable employment" that the Virginia Company might require. He requested that the "liberal stipend" Pocahontas had been receiving from the Virginia Company might be continued "for her child's advancement, which will the better enable myself and him hereafter to undertake and execute" whatever the Virginia Company might desire.[18]

Pocahontas was given last rites from the *Book of Common Prayer* at St. George's Church, Gravesend. Rolfe, Uttamatomakkin, and several others, Indians and English, were present. The parish register recorded (mistaking John's name): "[March] 21 Rebecca Wrothe wyffe of Thomas Wroth gent. A Virginia Lady borne, was buried in the chauncell."[19] Unfortunately the grave was left unmarked.

What should he do now about Thomas, John wondered. He was torn. With most of the remaining Indians quite ill and no one properly able to care for Thomas, Rolfe found himself in "such fear and hazard of his health" that he wondered if it would be better to leave the toddler in England. Captain Argall, Rolfe said, persuaded him this really was best, so when the ship reached Plymouth on the English Channel Rolfe left Thomas in the care of

---

16. John Rolfe to Sir Edwin Sandys, June 8, 1617, from Jamestown, in Kingsbury, *Records of The Virginia Company*, 3:71. Rolfe wrote that Pocahontas died "saying all must die, but tis enough that her childe liveth."

17. Purchas, *Pilgrimage*, 3rd ed., 955, quoted in Townsend, *Pocahontas*, 157.

18. Rolfe to Sandys, June 8, 1617 (English modernized), in Kingsbury, *Records of The Virginia Company*, 3:71–72.

19. Quoted in Anderson, *History*, 1:244n24.

Sir Lewis Stukely, who offered to keep him until John's brother Henry could come for him.[20]

That settled, Rolfe finally left from Plymouth aboard the *George* on April 10.

Thomas Rolfe would return to Virginia only as an adult, a dozen years after his father's death.[21]

Pocahontas's remains stayed in England. Like Jesus, she had a three-year public ministry among folks who saw themselves as God's chosen people.

20. Rolfe to Sandys, June 8, 1617 (English modernized), in Kingsbury, *Records of The Virginia Company*, 3:71.

21. Barbour, *Pocahontas*, 184.

Chapter Twelve

Twisting the Gospel

Pocahontas and Jesus—what a tangled web!

And Alexander Whitaker. A key player in Pocahontas's conversion, Whitaker was a sincere Christian and a theologically trained Anglican missionary. A conscientious seeker for truth, Whitaker earnestly wanted to ground Pocahontas in the Christian faith. He did his best to genuinely introduce the young woman to Jesus, as we have seen.

But like most missionaries, Whitaker faced prickly obstacles. How could he help Pocahontas understand the gospel and truly meet Jesus under such culturally odd circumstances? Could he make Pocahontas understand that what went under the name of *church* and *Christianity* in Jamestown was oceans apart from the Christian faith of the earliest Christians? How much was Whitaker himself aware of the disparity?

It was a twisted gospel Pocahontas received. This chapter shows how, in three critical ways, the gospel Pocahontas came to embrace was a distortion of the biblical good news.

Actually, some of Pocahontas's native understandings and values were closer to Jesus' good news than was the gospel she saw played out before her in Jamestown and then in London.

KINGDOM OF GOD OR BRITISH IMPERIALISM?

The most obvious problem was that in Anglicanism, the kingdom of God, and the British Empire were conjoined. Church and state were firmly wedded, all bound up together.

This church-state alliance is often called Constantinianism, referring to the Roman Emperor Constantine of 1,300 years earlier.

Constantine, ruler of the Roman Empire, converted to the Christian faith in 312 AD. This was a big tipping point. By 300 AD the early Christians had so multiplied throughout the empire that they could not be ignored. The conversion of the Emperor Constantine (c. 272–337) brought sudden and historically critical shifts. Christianity moved from a despised minority to the favored religion. The Christian Church had conquered the Roman Empire, people said.

Constantine's conversion and official endorsement of the Christian faith soon afterwards eased the lives of most Christians. But over time, church and state became so intertwined that in practical terms they were indistinguishable. The result was Medieval Christianity—Christendom—with all its pluses and minuses; its pageantry and superstition; all its myths and mystics and relics, its great monastic orders and massive, soaring cathedrals.[1]

The toxic problem was the mixing together of faith dynamics and raw state power. Faith could be, and was, backed up by force—armies, police, courts, judges. The cross enforced by the sword; the sword (or noose, or fire, or water) the enforcer of faith.

Things changed in England, of course, when King Henry VIII broke with Rome and established (in both senses) his new Church of England. But it was still Christendom. If anything, the fusion of church and state was stronger since king, not pope, now headed the church.

The Church of England was still a new thing in Pocahontas's day. She was born just fifty years after Henry VIII died. Streams of reform from the Continent were stirring in England. Though Henry's break with Rome was personal and political, it helped spark the English Reformation and later the rise of the Puritans and other reform movements.

Evangelical currents were churning the English Church. Exhibit number one was that great achievement, the *Book of Common Prayer*, first issued

---

1. See the discussion in Snyder and Scandrett, *Salvation Means Creation Healed,* chapters 1–2.

in 1549. Anglican reformers sought a *via media,* a middle path between Roman Catholicism and Continental Protestantism. They hoped to ground the church in the "Anglican triad" of Scripture, reason, and tradition.

In Europe, church and state had of course been firmly wedded centuries before, and they were not unwedded in England. The Church of England was the state church. If you were English, you were Anglican—or under suspicion if you weren't.

Various dissenting groups protested. The church should be a community of believers, a counterculture distinct from the state, with undivided loyalty to Jesus Christ, many said. Baptists got their start in England in the early 1600s, arguing for church-state separation, religious freedom, and liberty of conscience. The pioneering Baptist leader Roger Williams (c. 1603–1683) was Pocahontas's contemporary; George Fox (1624–1691), founder of the Society of Friends (Quakers), was born less than a decade after Pocahontas's death.

Baptists, Quakers, and other dissenting or "free church" groups would shortly make a big impact in America. But Virginia in the early 1600s was firmly Anglican. So far as Pocahontas could see, to be British meant to be part of the Church of England (however nominally). The kingdom of God and the British Empire were functionally one.[2]

This picture was vastly different from the church's first three centuries, when Christians firmly proclaimed that Jesus, not Caesar, was Lord and that his kingdom in nature and character were not of this world. It was unthinkable that the king or emperor could ever be head of the church!

So in the Pocahontas story, here was *the first distortion*—one that neither British colonists nor Pocahontas could clearly perceive.

CHRISTIAN COMMUNITY OR CIVIL SOCIETY?

Given the reigning state-church marriage, Anglicanism was of course woven into the fabric of the Virginia Colony. The church embodied the religious dimension of British existence in America, all intermixed with economics and politics. There was no separate Christian community, hence no way to distinguish Christian ethics and discipleship from British citizenship and loyalty to the crown.

2. Many theological and political struggles were of course going on, which can be framed as conflicting concepts of the kingdom of God. See Snyder, *Models of the Kingdom.*

Contrast this with New Testament teachings. Here the church is pictured as a community of disciples radically following Jesus. Christian community was the center of believers' lives. Christians were "members of the household of God," Christ Jesus himself "the cornerstone"; "a holy temple," "a dwelling place for God" (Eph 2:19–22). In contrast with surrounding society, the church was "a chosen race, a royal priesthood, a holy nation, God's own people," called to "proclaim the mighty acts" of the one who had now made them such a distinct people (1 Pet 2:9–10). The church was a one-another community based on mutual love and care—living in the world, yet as "aliens and exiles" (1 Pet 2:11).

Further, the New Testament church welcomed all believers as brothers and sisters, equal members of the same family—no longer slave or free, male or female, rich or poor, but all "one in Christ Jesus" (Gal 3:28). Even if this was imperfectly embodied, it was real enough to impress first-century pagans. Now in the seventeenth century, such radical community stood in sharp contrast to the laddered class structure of Anglican Christianity.

Pocahontas could in no way have seen the church in Virginia as such a radical community. Whatever Alexander Whitaker taught her about the church was filtered through official Anglican interpretations and reinforced by the on-the-ground realities of the Church of England in Virginia as Pocahontas experienced it.

Pocahontas had read the New Testament—how much, we don't know. Perhaps she came to perceive the contrasts between the early church and official Anglican Christianity in Virginia and later in London. She was more astute than people realized and saw more than she let on. She must have puzzled over the disparities between contemporary Anglicanism and the Christianity Alexander Whitaker taught her.

Pocahontas was open-hearted, and God's Spirit speaks to open hearts. In her heart of hearts, Pocahontas may have developed a more intimate communion with Jesus than anyone knew. It would not be surprising, given her inquisitive personality, her cultural perceptiveness, her seeking heart. She may have come to a deep, intimate love for Jesus and felt this reciprocated by the great Lover who laid down his life for his sheep, including those "not of this fold" (John 10:16). Once an Anglican, perhaps Pocahontas was also nurtured by the church's liturgy, sacraments, and *Book of Common Prayer* and grew in grace.

We don't really know. More likely, Pocahontas simply accepted the Anglican Church as the embodiment of what the Christian faith really should be. Centuries of layers of tradition obscured and partly distorted the reality of the good news of Jesus Christ.

HARMONY WITH CREATION OR WAR AGAINST NATURE?

The third distortion, if more subtle, is equally significant. Pocahontas was a child of the forest. She knew animals and plants and trees and rivers. She had an intimate practical (if not theoretical) knowledge of Virginia's ecology, which the British clearly lacked. She knew not only how to survive but thrive, living in harmony with creation.

In other words, Pocahontas knew life in harmony with the land as pictured and promised throughout the Old Testament.

Things were different in England. Enlightenment thought was shifting the accepted world view. Increasingly humans were pictured as struggling against nature, seeking to dominate and control wild threatening forces. Despite some countercurrents, this was the reigning world view carried by British explorers and colonists who sailed to America. It was the vision that accompanied and undergirded rising British power and would buttress emerging Western capitalism. The capstone came in 1776: Adam Smith's *Wealth of Nations*.

Man against nature, with its common parallel: civilized man against uncivilized savage.

Anglican Christians had little sense of what it meant to live in harmony with the created order, to prize creation—both to enjoy and to nurture "the garden" God planted. God's "everlasting covenant" with the earth (Genesis 9) and the biblical theme of living in caring harmony with the land, a stewardly relationship, was largely absent from British and Anglican sensibilities.

True, many English enjoyed gardens or tended small farms. They shared wisdom, accumulated over centuries, about the land and how to care for it. But by the 1600s this ancient wisdom was being eclipsed by rising urban and capitalist culture—currents that ushered in the Industrial Revolution in the late 1700s.

The unhappy result was filled with irony: When the Romantic Movement arose two centuries later, it valued "nature" for itself, but the culture largely lost the sense of stewardship. Enlightenment thought had replaced a personal God with human reason. Now Romanticism hymned the creature but lost sight of the Creator who lovingly had provided the natural world in covenant relationship with his people who were to enjoy, benefit from, and care for the land and its creatures. *Nature* became an *aesthetic* reality, not an *ecological* one. Romanticism appreciated and valued nature, but the sense of stewardly responsibility to the Creator had been lost.

Pocahontas however knew the land and its creatures. She understood them experientially and through the lens of the Powhatan religious world view.

This was not the biblical world view, of course. But the dominant Native American world view with its sensitivity to the created order was much closer to the biblical view in this respect than was the Enlightenment, even in its Christian forms, which increasingly dominated Europe.

Cherokee author Randy Woodley helps us here. In *Shalom and the Community of Creation: An Indigenous Vision*, Woodley shows that most Native American peoples had a deeper intuitive sense of what the Bible calls *shalom* than did Western Christians. *Shalom*: often translated "peace," but in the Old Testament carrying the deeper sense of well-being, proper relationship, and the flourishing of all life under the blessing of God.

Shalom, together with the themes of people, land, and covenant, is in fact a key Old Testament theme—a deeply ecological, holistic truth. As an essential strand in the biblical teaching of salvation, it colors how *peace, reconciliation,* and *community (koinonia)* are understood in the New Testament. Occurring more than 500 times in the Old Testament, *shalom* signifies peace and harmony in the broadest terms. As Woodley points out, *shalom* incorporates dimensions of "order, relationships, stewardship, beauty and rhythm," the whole picture of "the way God designed the universe to be."[3]

Woodley describes "a Native American harmony ethic," as he calls it, "a shared life-concept . . . related to well-being, or, to living and viewing life in harmony and balance"—a view "widespread among Native Americans." Woodley calls this the Harmony Way.[4]

Woodley argues, "In their nature as constructs, shalom and the Native American Harmony Way have much in common. Shalom, like Harmony Way, is made up of numerous notions and values, with the *whole* being much greater than the sum of its parts. They both set forth practical steps included within a vision for living. They both require specific action when the harmony or shalom is broken. They both have justice, restoration, and

---

3. Woodley, *Shalom,* 9–10. The words quoted are those of Terry McGonigal, in ibid., 10.

4. Ibid., xiii.

continuous right living as their goal. And, perhaps most importantly, they both originate as *the* right path for living, being viewed as a gift from the Creator."[5]

Pocahontas's passionate response to John Smith just weeks before she died, quoted in the previous chapter, clearly reflects this understanding of and commitment to the Harmony Way. And—importantly—this is the vision and these the values that Pocahontas could have contributed to Anglican Christianity, to its deepening and enriching, had she ever had the chance.

God's kingdom versus empire. Community versus social hierarchy and status. *Shalom* versus exploitation of the earth. These dynamics were at stake as Pocahontas embraced the Christian faith and tried to make sense of the good news of Jesus Christ.

But the gospel Pocahontas received and sincerely professed was a twisted version of the good news that Jesus taught and embodied. Pocahontas's faith seems to have been genuine and sincere. Perhaps it was deep. But it was severely compromised by the mixing of Christian faith with the expansionism, motives, and armed might of British empire.[6]

WILLIAM SYMONDS'S SERMON

Is this critique overdrawn? Well, consider the sermon of the Reverend William Symonds to the "Adventurers and Planters" headed for Virginia in 1609, which we looked at earlier. Symonds preached at Whitechapel on April 25 that year, with John Rolfe and many others present. (See chapter 9). Symonds's sermon embodies precisely the distortions we've just traced.

The service at which Symonds preached had a very practical purpose. When interest and investment in the Virginia venture dropped sharply after the string of depressing news from Jamestown, King James told Anglican clergy to promote the venture and to encourage potential colonists to sign up. They would be rewarded.

In his book *Religion and Empire*, Louis Wright elaborates:

5. Ibid., xv.

6. Susan Kingsbury, who carefully edited the records of the Virginia Company, noted the company's stated high purposes but added, "the theory that the chief motive of the enterprise was religious is not supported either by the spirit or by the data of the records" (Kingsbury, *Records of The Virginia Company*, 1:98).

Eager as were the ministers to commend English expansion into the New World, the burst of pulpit oratory in 1609 in praise of Virginia was not all spontaneous. Sir Thomas Smythe [Virginia Company treasurer and chief publicist] and his fellow officers were directly responsible. They chose certain popular ministers to preach before the shareholders and then printed their sermons as quickly as possible so that they might reach a wider audience. [In other words, state-sponsored propaganda.]

The choice for the first official sermon fell upon William Symonds, preacher at Saint Savior's, Southwark, and a former fellow of Magdalen College, Oxford, Symonds had confuted the papists and won a reputation for deep learning with the publication of *Pisgah Evangelica* (1605), his commentary on the Book of Revelation.[7]

Enthused support for the Virginia colony now poured forth from many Anglican pulpits. As Grace Steele Woodward notes, "The planting of a Protestant colony [in Virginia] was one of the most fervent wishes" of clergymen such as William Symonds, John Donne, and the Bishop of London, John King. Colonization could be an effective missionary strategy, at the same time staving off Roman Catholic incursions from France and Spain. For some time "English clergy had supported the idea" of abducting Indian children in order to raise them as Christians "largely because of their interest in converting the Indians."[8]

Symonds's sermon thus was typical, not unique. It breathes the spirit of many influential British leaders of his day. John Donne, dean of St. Paul's Cathedral, had similarly preached to the departing Virginia adventurers, "Your principal end is not gain, nor glory, but to gain souls to the glory of God."[9] Given the church-state alliance, every sermon was inescapably political.

Symonds himself had toyed with sailing off to Virginia. Did he really believe what he preached, or was he mainly at pains to stay on the king's good side? Either way, he was pushing a political agenda. Though a clergyman of Puritan leanings, he conformed to King James's order in 1606 that Anglican clergy must stick strictly to Church of England beliefs and practices.

---

7. Wright, *Religion and Empire*, 90.

8. Woodward, *Pocahontas*, 170, 152.

9. Fischer, *Albion's Seed*, 232. Donne was referring primarily to the Indians.

Symonds's sermon embodies the three distortions described above. Wright notes, "By a casuistry easy for a theologian, particularly one who had recently interpreted the prophecies of Revelation, Symonds transferred [the covenant] promise [in Genesis 12:1–3] from Abraham to the English." Symonds thus baptized a view that soon was "a cardinal point of doctrine among preachers and laymen alike—that the English were divinely appointed as another chosen people to establish themselves in the promised lands of the New World." America was "a Western Canaan reserved for England."[10] Thus for the Virginia colonists, as for their pious backers in London, "promised land" could be applied as easily to North America as it was to the standard imagery of heaven.

First: *Kingdom of God or British Empire?* In Symonds's mind, the two were practically one, at least so far as British interests in Virginia were concerned. Symonds's basic argument assumes that, since England is a Christian nation (given the union of church and state), biblical pictures and promises of the conquest of God's people over pagan nations can be applied directly to the British Empire. A replay of the book of Joshua would be legitimate. Symonds mines the Old Testament for support. His sermon directly equates Old Testament Israel with the British Empire.

Symonds' text is Genesis 12:1–3, God's call and covenant promise to Abraham: "Go from your country and your kindred and your father's house to the land that I will show you. I will make of you a great nation, and I will bless you, and make your name great, so that you will be a blessing. I will bless those who bless you, and the one who curses you I will curse; and in you all the families of the earth shall be blessed." So it shall be, Symonds says, with "the right noble and worthy Advancers of the Standard of Christ among the Gentiles, the Adventurers for the Plantation of Virginia." In time nations will bless them and be blessed by them.[11]

10. Wright, *Religion and Empire*, 91, 84. Wright notes, "From its foundation in 1606 until its dissolution in 1624, the Virginia Company employed preachers to deliver sermons before the shareholders on stated occasions. It printed these sermons at the expense of the company and distributed them widely. It also rewarded the preachers with payments in cash, and, in some instances, by giving them stock in the company. Dr. John Donne, dean of St. Paul's, was the most distinguished cleric in its pay, but there were many others almost as well known in their time. Moreover, among the shareholders themselves were many clergymen, some of them high in the church, who looked upon the Virginia Company as an enterprise especially ordained to carry out the divine plan. As a result, English pulpits rang with praise of the infant colony on the banks of the James" (87–88).

11. Symonds, "Sermon Preached at White-Chappel" (language modernized). All

There can be no doubt, Symonds boldly asserts, "that the Lord that called *Abraham* into another country also by the same holy hand calls you [the Virginia Adventurers] to carry the Gospel to a Nation that never heard of Christ."

Working through the Old Testament, Symonds identifies King Solomon as the "true type of Christ" and notes that Solomon was equipped with sword and arrows and was sent in God's name to do "dread deeds" (Ps 45:3–5).

Symonds explicitly identifies the British Empire and its king as authorized agents of the kingdom of God on earth. King James I embodies "the spirit of his great Ancestor, [Emperor] Constantine the pacifier of the world, and planter of the Gospel in places most remote."

Old Testament prophets get similar treatment. Symonds largely bypasses the New Testament, except to imply that the church established by Jesus Christ is now the rightful heir to this Old Testament understanding. Symonds uses heavy sarcasm to put down "Anabaptists" and others who disagree with this interpretation.

Second: *Christian community or hierarchical civil society?* Symonds actually says little about the church or Jesus' teachings. His assumption of church-state union meant that the present form of the Anglican Church was the unquestioned status quo in the homeland and would also be normative in Virginia. His sermon breathes not a whiff of church as counterculture or as a distinct community that lives by the teachings of Jesus in the power of the Spirit. The assumption rather is that what is, is what should be. This is God's will; God's hand.

Given this world view, Pocahontas under Alexander Whitaker's tutelage would have no way to comprehend New Testament Christian community. Neither would she have no way to perceive the kinship between New Testament ethics and what she was taught and experienced as a Powhatan.

Symonds assumes that British society with all its hierarchy, stratified classes, and exploitation, is truly Christian. This is how things are now (by God's good providence), whatever the situation might have been in the early church.

Symonds skips over the New Testament picture of the church as distinct community, a fellowship of Jesus' disciples living in conscious tension with the Roman Empire. Instead he directly equates British monarchy with

---

quotations following from Symonds come from this source.

Israel's Old Testament monarchy—with all that means for status, power, and social roles.

Result: What Pocahontas learned from the English about the Christian faith was really a superficially Christianized version of the old covenant, not the radical freshness and dynamism of the new covenant in Jesus' blood—the new people of God.

Third: *Harmony with creation or war against nature?* Pocahontas knew much more about biblical *shalom* than did the British—even though the British were the ones with the Scriptures and Pocahontas wouldn't have known the word *shalom*. The British had the Book of God, but Pocahontas had God's Book of Nature.[12]

Rev. Symonds's sermon embodies British views of the time. It was shaped by the early British Enlightenment, Britain's growing power, and its competition with other expanding European powers.

In Symonds's view, North America was "over there," across the Atlantic, just waiting and wanting to be exploited—by God's good providence. Abraham's call, and even Jesus' Great Commission, are cited in support. Jesus' commission in Matthew 28:19 was not for the first apostles only, Symonds suggests, but may be extended to contemporary England. Masterfully conflating the call of Abraham, Jesus' commission, and England's desire for new colonies, Symonds explains: "Seeing that, thanks be to God, we are thronged [in England] with multitudes; the Lord of hosts himself has given us the calling of his children to seek for room, and a place to dwell in."

Virginia was named for Queen Elizabeth, "The Virgin Queen." Elizabeth had died just six years earlier. To Symonds, now the land of Virginia was itself a "virgin" worthy to be "married" to virtuous England. Symonds prays, "Lord, finish this good work thou hast begun; and marry this land, a pure Virgin to thy Kingly son Christ Jesus; so shall thy name be magnified; and we shall have a Virgin or Maiden Britain [as] a comfortable addition to our Great Britain." Symonds's whole sermon is in fact about "Virgin Britain"—that is, the land of Virginia.

Symonds does confess one small problem. Virginia is already inhabited. Several opponents of colonization had raised this "scruple," pointing out that (in Symonds's words) the land the English were now calling

---

12. Western Christian theologians had spoken of the "Book of Nature," referring to God's self-disclosure in the created order, as parallel but subsidiary to the Bible. Among Protestants since the Reformation, the term was used by Jonathan Edwards (1703–1758) and John Wesley (1703–1791), among others.

Virginia "is possessed by owners that rule and govern it in their own right." So "with what conscience and equity can we thrust them, by violence, out of their inheritances?"

Symonds has a ready answer. First, in a rather contorted interpretation of Genesis, he argues that God wills his people to "replenish" and rule over *all* the earth. North America's native inhabitants however are not truly God's people, so they have no abiding right to the land.

Symonds points to Israel's armed conquest of Canaan under Joshua, and to the later Hebrew kings, David and Solomon. Symonds quotes Psalm 45:3–5, "Gird your sword on your thigh, O mighty one, in your glory and majesty. . . . Ride on victoriously for the cause of truth and to defend the right. . . . The peoples fall under you." With no sense of irony, Symonds applies this passage to British conquest in America. Messianic passages like Psalm 72:8 now apply to Great Britain: "May he have dominion from sea to sea, and from the River to the ends of the earth." Symonds also appropriates Jesus' words in Luke 14:23, "compel them to come in."

True, Symonds notes, it is impossible for the British to conquer other lands without "much lamentable effusion of blood," as some objectors had pointed out. But "if these objectors had any brains in their head," Symonds says modestly, they would see the vast "difference between a bloody invasion and the planting of a peaceable Colony in a waste country where the people" live in scattered small groups like herds of deer. In any case, such people are naked savages, slaves of the devil who practice child sacrifice, unlike those of "noble Saxon blood."

Anyway, the natives' weapons are primitive, no match for British arms, Symonds assures his hearers. And God will miraculously help. As he brought Israel out of Egypt, making "the raging waves of the sea to stand in heaps" like "strong walls," So God will miraculously aid the British adventurers. "God puts away all the ungodly of the earth like dross," says Symonds. Colonists, take courage!

Symonds concludes with this hopeful challenge to the new Virginia colonists, the "Adventurers and Planters": "Therefore, seeing we are content when the King calls us out to war, to go we know not where, nor under whom," with the single aim "to fight with a mighty enemy: Let us be cheerful to go to the place that God will show us to possess in peace and plenty, a land more like the Garden of Eden, which the Lord planted, then any part else of all the earth."

This is what John Rolfe and his companions heard as they were about to sail for Virginia. Pocahontas was still in her teens. She had befriended John Smith and was making occasional journeys back and forth between her Powhatan town of Werowocomoco and Jamestown, an emissary between Chief Powhatan and the English.

Symonds's sermon was not only an opportunistic and distorting use of the biblical gospel. He put the good news of God's kingdom to political, empire-building use. His sermon was in fact a massive *inversion* of sound biblical hermeneutics. Symonds actually turns numerous biblical texts on their heads.

For example, Symonds notes that in Old Testament days a captive Hebrew girl was God's instrument in curing the pagan general Naaman of his leprosy, through the prophet Elisha (2 Kgs 5). He then jumps to Paul's words in 1 Corinthians 1:27, "God chose what is weak in the world to shame the strong." Application: in Virginia the British can capture young Indians, raise them as Christians, and use them to evangelize their people. This inverts the meaning of both biblical texts, since it was God's people (Israel in the Old Testament and the vulnerable young church in the New) that was "weak," and the pagan and later Roman empires that were "strong."

One of the more glaring ironies of Symonds's linking Great Britain with Old Testament Israel was his skipping over Israel's prophets. Prophets from Isaiah to Malachi denounced Israel's unfaithfulness—its idolatries, injustices, and oppression of aliens and the poor. Few Englishmen who transferred to England the biblical promises made to Israel paid any attention to the warnings and denunciations pronounced by Israel's great prophets. The prophets repeatedly warned Israel that they would be God's people and enjoy peace, prosperity, and the land's abundance *only* if they were faithful to God's covenant. By "parity of reason" (one of John Wesley's phrases), transferring the promises requires transferring also the warnings. In fact the Old Testament is as full of promises of judgment as of blessing; of destruction as of flourishing.

Some Puritan and other British writers such as John Wesley did make this point, warning England of judgment. But these were largely ignored.

THE CONTINUING IRONY OF AMERICAN HISTORY

So irony piles upon irony like ice floes at the end of winter. Just four years later Pocahontas would be kidnapped by the British, and not for motives of evangelism. Within five years of hearing Symonds's sermon, John Rolfe, having survived the tempest of his disastrous Atlantic crossing and the death of his wife and daughter, would marry Pocahontas.

One wonders whether, later, Rolfe ever recalled or reflected on Symonds's words about the "pure Virgin" colony in America being married to England. Did he realize the symbolic potency of his own marriage?

Jamestown and the story of Pocahontas is a case study in how the gospel of Jesus Christ time and again gets twisted in the course of Christian history and missionary endeavor. Pocahontas casts a long shadow.

In his now classic work *The Irony of American History* (1952), Reinhold Niebuhr argued that American national identity is a blend of "the two great religious-moral traditions which informed our early life—New England Calvinism and Virginian Deism" (as expressed especially in the thought of Thomas Jefferson, 1743–1826). Niebuhr states that Calvinism, despite its pessimism about human nature, "in its conceptions of American destiny and its appreciation of American virtue finally arrived at conclusions strikingly similar to those of Deism."[13]

Niebuhr elaborates:

> Whether our nation interprets its spiritual heritage through Massachusetts or Virginia, we came into existence with the sense of being a "separated" nation, which God was using to make a new beginning for mankind. We had renounced the evils of European feudalism. We had escaped from the evils of European religious bigotry. We had found broad spaces for the satisfaction of human desire in place of the crowded Europe. Whether, as in the case of the New England theocrats, our forefathers thought of our "experiment" as primarily the creation of a new and purer church, or, as in the case of Jefferson and his coterie, they thought primarily of a new political community, they believed in either case that we had been called out by God to create a new humanity. We were God's "American Israel."[14] Our pretensions of innocency there-

---

13. Niebuhr, *Irony*, 24. See also Eddy, *Kingdom of God and the American Dream.*

14. The Puritan Edward Johnson wrote in 1650 that New England was the place "where the Lord would create a new heaven and a new earth, new churches and a new commonwealth together." In the 1780s Yale University President Ezra Stiles preached a sermon titled "The United States elevated to glory and honor" in which he described the new nation as "God's American Israel." Similarly the Jeffersonian poet Philip Freneau (1752–1832), though not an orthodox Christian, wrote that the United States would be "A new Jerusalem sent down from heaven [to] grace our happy earth" (Niebuhr, *Irony*, 25, 27).

fore heightened the whole concept of a virtuous humanity which characterizes the culture of our era [i.e., the 1950s]; and involve us in the ironic incongruity between our illusions and the realities which we experience. We find it almost as difficult as the communists to believe that anyone could think ill of us, since we are as persuaded as they that our society is so essentially virtuous that only malice could prompt criticism of any of our actions.[15]

This view is still remarkably prominent, perhaps dominant, in much of the United States and in her churches.

Niebuhr showed how New England Puritans saw their church as "purer than any church of Christendom." He noted, "Practically every Puritan tract contained the conviction that the Protestant Reformation reached its final culmination here [in America]. While the emphasis lay primarily upon the new purity [as in "Puritanism"] of the church, even the Puritans envisaged a new and perfect society." Jefferson's view, in contrast, "was not informed by the Biblical symbolism" of the Puritans, but was shaped rather by the European Enlightenment. Yet Jefferson felt that "nature's God had a very special purpose in founding" this new nation that had "broken with tyranny" and now had "wide economic opportunities" that "would prevent the emergence of those vices which characterized" an overcrowded Europe.[16]

Broken with tyranny? No vices? Pocahontas and many African slaves would surely have seen right through this!

Niebuhr puts his finger precisely on the sore spot of US history. The Virginia colonists and their descendants (with a few exceptions) could not see this. But Pocahontas and her father Chief Powhatan certainly could.[17]

But what of Pocahontas herself? Physically she died in 1617. Yet she acquired new and expanding life as myth. She died as historical actor and was reborn as useful metaphor. Her true identity was vague enough and pliable enough and short enough to energize and fertilize the flowering of mythic images. In the next chapters we look at the many faces of Pocahontas. Then we'll see Pocahontas in heaven and, finally, hear her speak.

15. Ibid., 24–25. Niebuhr also demolishes the potent myth that violence can purge away evil (11–16).

16. Ibid., 25–26. The words quoted are those of Niebuhr. Niebuhr fails to note however that the Puritan stream was present (though not as dominant) in Virginia as well, through people like Alexander Whitaker, John Rolfe, and others.

17. Niebuhr does not mention William Symonds's sermon, and of course Niebuhr was looking back 300 years, rather than ahead to Jamestown, as Symonds was, and so had a broader perspective.

Chapter Thirteen

Faces of Pocahontas
Justifying Myth

In his 2012 history of Yellowstone National Park, George Black speaks of the park's creation as "a quintessentially American story, of terrible things done in the name of high ideals, and of high ideals realized by dubious means."[1]

These words equally capture the story of Pocahontas.

Pocahontas has been *useful* in American history. A utility. Since her death she has appeared and reappeared in multiple guises and disguises, always for a purpose, always with a role to fill in the larger American story. She has been a Rorschach inkblot. People see what they want or are predisposed to see.

To James Paulding in his 1836 "Ode to Jamestown" Pocahontas was "The angel of the woodland shade, The miracle of God's own hand"; "Flower of the Forest, nature's pride."[2] One website lists over 140 "epithets bestowed on Pocahontas" from 1608 through 2003 ranging from Eve to entrepreneur, to Joan of Arc, Diplomat, Diana, Venus, angel sex, spotless virgin, and Buckskin Barbie.[3] Hundreds of visual images of Pocahontas inhabit the Internet.

1. Black, *Empire of Shadows*, x.

2. Quoted in Jenkins, "Three Centuries in the Development of the Pocahontas Story," 363.

3. Gallagher, "Epithets Bestowed on Pocahontas."

Seven key roles emerge, however, as we study the many portraits and images of Pocahontas (Matoaka, Rebecca Rolfe). These are roles Pocahontas has played and still plays—her varied faces. From John Smith's early accounts to the Disney films and the 2006 movie *The New World*, we see that Pocahontas has never really gone away.

Pocahontas is not a ghost. In multiple ways she continues to be a real actor in US history. But here's another irony: The real, living Pocahontas never fully knew how she was being used symbolically, even during her lifetime (though she had suspicions), nor how she would be used and manipulated over centuries to come.

These are the seven faces of Pocahontas, which we will explore in this and successive chapters: Legitimator, pornographic image, vicarious sacrifice, moral example, celebrity, true disciple, key actor in history.

LEGITIMATOR OF THE AMERICAN MYTH

Tour the US Capitol and you will see *The Baptism of Pocahontas,* by John Gadsby Chapman. The monumental canvas is one of eight heroic paintings circling the great Capitol Rotunda—historical paintings "portraying seminal moments in the birth and coming-of-age of the new nation," notes historian Robert Tilton.[4] Pocahontas is portrayed being baptized by Alexander Whitaker.

The Baptism of Pocahontas sends a clear message. Pocahontas is a hero of American history because she became a Christian, married a colonist, and mothered a progenitor of important Americans. More than this, she symbolizes reconciliation between Native America and the invading colonists. Yet clearly in a lopsided way: in the painting Pocahontas alone is kneeling, head bowed; the key British actors are standing; and the few other Indians present stand in the shadows or sit docilely on the floor.

Here is a picture of early American success and progress. Native Americans along the Atlantic seaboard have been brought under control as colonists built a new nation. A pattern has been set, a paradigm for America's westward expansion.

In *Pocahontas: The Evolution of an American Narrative,* Robert Tilton carefully examines Pocahontas's transformation from real person to myth in the centuries following her death. Comparing Pocahontas to the way Daniel Boone's life became the stuff of myth and legend, Tilton catalogs

4. Tilton, *Pocahontas,* 95.

the many visual and literary "incarnations of Pocahontas, the prototypical Indian princess"—depictions often representing "multiple and at times contradictory agendas."

Tilton notes that Pocahontas's "act of bravery in saving the life of Captain John Smith was recast and retold more often than any other American historical incident during the colonial and antebellum periods. The Pocahontas narrative provided literary and visual artists with a flexible discourse that came to be used to address a number of racial, political, and gender-related issues." The "thousands of individuals who have descended from Thomas Rolfe, and therefore from Pocahontas and John Rolfe, and ultimately from Powhatan and the hereditary rulers of America," have been carefully documented.[5]

Pocahontas's popularity continues. "Pocahontas's name and narrative are as multivalent today as in the nineteenth century," Tilton notes.[6] Much of "the power of the Pocahontas myth has been based on the multiplicity of correspondences available to the author who invokes the name of the heroine of Jamestown."[7] As evidence, Tilton includes not only many literary descriptions but some twenty-five visual portrayals, most of them depicting Smith's rescue.

So Pocahontas became an icon. In fact, she is depicted a second time in the Capitol Rotunda, in a sandstone relief above the west door. Entitled *The Preservation of Captain Smith by Pocahontas*, this 1825 work by Antonio Capellano shows Pocahontas rescuing Smith. Tilton notes, "Its inclusion in the Capitol at this early date makes clear that the rescue of Smith by Pocahontas had long been perceived as a crucial generative moment in the history of the United States."[8]

Together, these two Pocahontas portrayals in the US Capitol tell the saga of Indian-white relations. At first the Indians are hostile and dangerous. But key figures like Pocahontas bring reconciliation. Eventually the Indians are subdued and (according to the myth) integrated into the new nation. From the first, two options loomed for the Indians: peaceful integration on

5. Ibid., 1, 2.

6. When Elizabeth Warren was running for US Senate in Massachusetts in 2012, political enemies started calling her "Fauxcahontas" because of her references to her distant partial Native American ancestry. No explanation of the term was needed.

7. Tilton, *Pocahontas*, 2.

8. Ibid., 95. See Figure 5 (p. 100) in Tilton. This is one of four similar reliefs in the Capitol that show "various Indian-white interactions" (95).

the white man's terms (symbolized by Pocahontas's marriage and baptism), or forced submission, marginalization, or annihilation.

Pocahontas risked her life to save John Smith. But in later years (as history proved) few of the new white "Americans" would risk their lives to save the native peoples. In fact by the time Chapman's *Baptism of Pocahontas* was finished in 1839, Congress had passed the Indian Removal Act (1830). Tens of thousands of Cherokee and other Indians were forced west on the Trail of Tears to Oklahoma. Many died. Oklahoma is now a state, but originally it was promised as a permanent haven for native tribes.[9]

But the Capitol Rotunda depicts not the Trail of Tears, but rather, Pocahontas's baptism. This was history, of course. But more importantly, it fueled the myth of peaceful reconciliation with Native Americans and clearly signaled the Indians' subordinate status.

The Indians were both defeated and deracinated. *Deracinate* means to pull up by the roots—forced removal and alienation from one's native land. Over the next sixty years or so—from the Trail of Tears in 1838 to the Wounded Knee Massacre on December 29, 1890, at which more than 150 Lakota Sioux men, women, and children were killed by the US Cavalry[10]—America's native peoples were uprooted, deracinated, and often slaughtered. Many of course fought back. It was like the medieval Crusades, except that the American crusaders (often in the form of the US Cavalry) had superior arms. Indians were much less equipped for war than were medieval Muslim armies.

Due mainly to the John Smith rescue, Pocahontas quickly became a celebrity in American literature as well as visual art. William Warren Jenkins notes that "no single incident in the early American experience . . . has been more widely, more continuously, or more variously treated than the story of Pocahontas's rescue of Captain John Smith." Jenkins analyzed the various literary portrayals of Pocahontas in his 1977 dissertation, "Three Centuries in the Development of the Pocahontas Story in American Literature: 1608–1908." Quickly taking on mythic proportions, Pocahontas becomes in literary hands the "American Earth Mother" and "a symbol of the American soil—of the continent itself which invites exploration by the

---

9. Wallace, *Long, Bitter Trail*; Jahoda, *Trail of Tears*; Fassett, *Giving Our Hearts*, 44–45.

10. Brown, *Bury My Heart at Wounded Knee*; Hawk, "Indigenous Helpers," 117.

white man and in many ways served as an affirmation of the hopes and aspirations that are the American Dream."[11]

But as we have seen, an early version of this powerful myth was already in vogue at the very beginning of British exploration of America. Pocahontas gave the myth a face. She softened and humanized it: an incarnation.

Pocahontas has been the subject of a long string of plays, beginning with James Nelson Barker's operatic *The Indian Princess, or La Belle Savage* (pun intended) in 1808. In Barker's melodrama Pocahontas "speaks for the first time" from the American stage and thus "makes the first of her many appearances in the works of American playwrights who wrote between 1808 and 1908," notes Jenkins.[12] In the critical rescue scene, Pocahontas rushes to the execution block, clutches Smith's head to her breast and cries out: "White man thou shalt not die; or I will die with thee! My father, dost thou love thy daughter? Listen to her voice; look upon her tears; they ask for mercy to the captive. Is thy child dear to thee, my father? Thy child will die with the white man."[13]

No less a figure than the socialist entrepreneur and reformer Robert Dale Owen (1801–1877), who helped his father establish the New Harmony community in southern Indiana, wrote a Pocahontas play in 1837. His *Pocahontas: A Historical Drama* was seldom performed and never a success, but it's intriguing historically. Intended as factual portrayal, the drama mostly follows John Smith's accounts. Jenkins finds the play of poor quality, though its portrayal of Pocahontas and other Indians is its redeeming feature. "The very language that is used by his Indians seems to capture the rhythms of the native speech, and . . . even if this piece was not successful drama, it is certainly an excellent study in primitivism. Owen obviously had the primitivistic philosophy and the concept of the noble savage in mind."[14]

In the early 1840s Charlotte Barnes wrote *The Forest Princess, or Two Centuries Ago*, which, unlike most others, was produced first in England, in 1844. Only four years late did the play appear on a Philadelphia stage.[15]

Pocahontas farces and parodies were sure to come eventually, and this happened beginning in the 1850s with John Brougham's *Po-Ca-Hon-Tas,*

11. Jenkins, "Three Centuries," viii, xiv.

12. Ibid., 274.

13. Quoted in ibid., 283.

14. Ibid., 301.

15. Ibid., 303–4.

or The Noble Savage. Full of puns, comic scenes, satire, and contemporary references, the play was a big hit in New York. Similar dramas were to follow. Pocahontas plays and melodramas continued right on into the early twentieth century. Several appeared around the time of the Jamestown Tricentennial Exposition in 1906.[16]

In various guises, whether paintings, prose, or poems, Pocahontas became the legitimator of the American myth. But it was a myth. As history unfolded, Pocahontas's baptism and marriage proved *not* to be the way forward, even though the myth claimed otherwise.

Nevertheless, Pocahontas became the authenticator, the proof of the rightness of the American myth. The one who makes it legitimate. In the process she is also Mother of America, for she gives birth to the son of John Rolfe, whose many descendants and compatriots would increasingly dominate the young nation's economy, culture, and political processes. The myth would have been less powerful had Pocahontas not borne a male child.

At the hands of Vachel Lindsay, "The Prairie Troubadour," (1879–1931), Pocahontas becomes mother in a yet more symbolic sense. In his 1917 poem "Our Mother Pocahontas," Lindsay wrote,

> John Rolfe is not our ancestor.
> We rise from out the soul of her
> Held in native wonderland,
> While the sun's rays kissed her hand,
> In the springtime,
> In Virginia,
> Our Mother, Pocahontas.[17]

The influential American modernist poet Hart Crane (1899–1932) took the imagery further. In his 1930 epic poem "The Bridge, A Myth of America," Pocahontas comes to symbolize the fertile American land itself. She is now "our native clay . . . red, eternal flesh of Pocahontas." The continent itself is Pocahontas's prone body. Crane pictures a river flowing across the landscape like a snake and writes, "O Nights that brought me to her body bare. . . . I knew her body there, / Time like a serpent down her shoulder, dark, / And space, an eaglet's wing, laid on her hair."

In notes accompanying the poem, Crane explains that he saw Pocahontas as "the natural body of American fertility"—spread before Columbus "like a woman, ripe, waiting to be taken." For Hart the tragedy of

---

16. Ibid., 309–35.
17. Quoted in ibid., 403.

Pocahontas is part of the story: "she rose with maize—to die." Yet the nation should see "thy bride immortal in the maize!"[18]

Yet Crane was deeply ambivalent about this treatment of the land and its native peoples. "Nature gave way to control and exploitation just as the world of the Indian was to give way to control and exploitation," notes Genevieve Wachutka in her insightful essay, "Myth Making: Appropriation of Pocahontas in Hart Crane's *The Bridge*." In Crane's imagery the "connection between the fates of Nature and of 'the Indian' is figured in the female: the American land is rendered . . . as a body to be used, and the female who embodies that idea for Crane is the most famous Indian woman, Pocahontas." Crane realizes that "As the pioneers sought to tame the land[,] they exploited the Native American population, objectifying them in the same manner as they used women and the land," notes Wachutka. Thus these new pale-faced Americans "lost the continuity of a relationship with the land."[19]

Lindsay and Crane considered themselves quintessentially American writers. But here comes another huge irony. Probably neither poet ever heard of Rev. William Symonds or other early British promoters of Virginia colonization. Yet the same imagery had already surfaced there. The land is feminine; the colonizers are masculine; the conquest is thus at once justified, poetic, inevitable, glorious. As noted earlier, Rev. William Symonds had depicted Virginia as a "virgin" waiting to be "married" to England.

The irony is especially striking in the case of Hart Crane, who sought to write a narrative distinctly different from British and European models. But Crane was writing in the twentieth century when the nation's mistreatment of the land and its native inhabitants no longer appeared quite so romantic or virtuous. So now Pocahontas is mother in a more nuanced and mythic sense: not so much the Pocahontas of history, but now Earth Mother, or Mother Earth.

If George Washington is the Father of the Country, Pocahontas is Mother, in one guise or another.[20] She is in fact the first Miss America.

18. Ibid., 403–4. Columbus himself had used similar imagery. See also McClintock, *Imperial Leather,* 21–22.

19. Wachutka, "Myth Making," lines 25–29, 81–85.

20. Another irony of the Pocahontas story is that the last battle of the American Revolutionary War, in which George Washington with the help of the French finally defeated the British near the mouth of the York River, occurred only about ten miles from Powhatan's village of Werowocomoco, where Pocahontas lived when the British first met her and the site of the famous rescue of John Smith. The Yorktown battle took

PORNOGRAPHIC IMAGE

Camilla Townsend says flatly that "the traditional vision of Pocahontas is in essence a pornographic narrative."[21]

This is overstated. Yet there often is a voyeuristic cast to the whole tale of Pocahontas as she was seen through European and white American eyes. The great majority of portrayals of the young pre-Christian Pocahontas show her half naked, bare breasted, attractive, adventuresome, vigorous. This was true especially in the many versions of John Smith's rescue.

Other incidents from Pocahontas's life were rarely depicted. Relatively few drawings and paintings were made of her betrayal and kidnapping, her marriage to Rolfe, or her death.[22]

Eighteenth- and nineteenth-century pictures of Pocahontas do not show her in poses that today would be considered pornographic or seductive. There is little in the visual representations that is explicitly sexual or erotic. The essence of pornography however is the objectification of another person for one's own fulfillment, pleasure, or legitimation—whether that be sexual, psychological, or even spiritual.

In this sense many of the rescue scenes, in particular, may be described as pornographic. Mixing themes of sex, violence, conquest, and savagery in the rescue scenes made them so appealing that they were repeatedly painted, printed, and reprinted over the past 400 years.

Except in a couple of later sculptures, Pocahontas was never depicted nude. In these cases Pocahontas appears more as a classical Greek goddess, a kind of native Venus de Milo, than as the historic young Powhatan woman. But more than a hint of voyeurism is found in most of the pictures of the young Pocahontas, especially in the rescue scenes. The whole Pocahontas narrative from the beginning carried subliminal messages of sexuality, blended with imperialistic images of conquest. Maria Lyytinen points out that this has been typical of portrayals of Pocahontas and other "Indian princesses" in twentieth-century movies. The "Indian princess" typically "represented the colonizer's object of lustful desire; the exotic, sexual Other,

---

place in 1781, 164 years after Pocahontas's death.

21. Townsend, *Pocahontas,* 200n22.

22. Rasmussen and Tilton, *Pocahontas,* prepared for a Pocahontas exhibition, which contains numerous scenes from Pocahontas's life including her abduction, her baptism, her marriage, and her death.

or what Homi K. Bhabha calls a subject 'in the narrative economy of voyeurism and fetishism.'"[23]

Townsend notes that the London clergyman and travel writer Samuel Purchas, eager to meet the Indian celebrity when she arrived in England, "was predisposed to find the lovely Pocahontas fascinating. Before she herself had even been captured, he had called Virginia a 'virgin . . . not yet polluted with Spaniards' lust' and the colonists her 'wooers and suiters' bent on making her 'not a wanton minion, but an honest Christian wife.' Pocahontas was, then, the personification of his vision."[24]

Various writers had depicted America as an enticing woman—with the subliminal message of her waiting to be conquered. In the century leading up to Jamestown, "woodcuts had often represented America as a nearly naked Indian woman. Books and broadsides alike conveyed the idea that in taking an Indian woman, one took a continent, metaphorically speaking. Some authors [such as Sir Walter Raleigh even made the connection explicit]. . . . The vision of the conquest was enough to make a man's blood run warm."[25]

America was an exotic land to be exploited. Conquest, whether sexual or continental, can be erotic to adventuring men. The exotic quickly becomes the erotic.

This was the spirit of the age. So it is little surprise that, as Townsend writes, "John Smith loved the books that represented America as a forthcoming young and naked virgin."[26]

The idea of Queen Elizabeth as "the Virgin Queen" and the naming of a major part of North America for her played right into this psychology. The virgin land was waiting to be conquered! Townsend refers to Richard Hakluyt's 1588 book, *Principal Navigations, Voyages, Traffiques & Discoveries of the English Nation,* noting, "The English wanted to believe that the women [in Virginia] would be as welcoming as the Spanish had reported the Caribbean women to be, and Hakluyt offered his readers material to feed their hopes." John Smith and other explorers "embraced a notion of an explorer as a conqueror who strode with manly steps through lands of

23. Lyytinen, "Pocahontas Myth," 82.

24. Townsend, *Pocahontas,* 141.

25. Ibid., 26–27. Sir Walter Raleigh (c. 1554–1618) was a contemporary of Pocahontas and had led earlier unsuccessful efforts to found colonies in Virginia.

26. Ibid., 74. More generally, Townsend says "Smith seems to have liked racy stories about beautiful young island women being taken prisoner" (ibid., 26).

admirers, particularly admiring women. . . . The foreign women and the foreign lands wanted, even needed, these men."[27]

To portray land or the earth as feminine is of course ancient and archetypal. Nothing new here. In many cultures earth is portrayed as virgin, mother, or both, and often associated with agriculture. Think of fertility gods and fertility cults. In languages where nouns have gender, *earth* and *land* are often feminine. In the Bible, Israel, both land and people, are frequently depicted as feminine—nowhere more graphically than in the book of Hosea.

But in colonialism we are dealing with something different: Neither deification nor biblical covenant, but exploitation. As Lori Rowlett and others have pointed out, "Narratives of colonization . . . often evince a gender polarity in which the conquering culture (the one composing the story) gives itself characteristics which are considered masculine, while the colonized other is feminized." In harmony with this imagery, indigenous women are frequently "viewed as the embodiment of the forces of nature which must be brought under the civilizing control of men."[28] Here both women and the land are objectified, thus easily becoming victims of exploitation (which they purportedly secretly desire and so invite). Peter Hulme puts it this way: "Land is named as female as a passive counterpart to the massive thrust of male technology."[29] Christopher Columbus concluded that though the earth was round, its true shape was that of a pear or a woman's breast.[30]

Anne McClintock writes similarly, coining the term "porno-tropics" for the way (male) European explorers and writers portrayed newly discovered lands and peoples in the 1500s and 1600s. In her book *Imperial Leather: Race, Gender and Sexuality in the Colonial Context*, McClintock argues that colonialism is misread if not seen through the eyes of gender. She points to a very "long tradition of male travel as an erotics of ravishment." By the time of Pocahontas, "Africa and the Americas had become what can be called a porno-tropics for the European imagination—a fantastic magic lantern of the mind onto which Europe projected its forbidden sexual desires and fears."[31]

27. Ibid., 28, 29.
28. Rowlett, "Disney's Pocahontas," 66, 67.
29. Hulme, "Polytropic Man," 2:21. Cf. McClintock, *Imperial Leather*, 26.
30. Mann, *1493*, 15; McClintock, *Imperial Leather*, 22.
31. McClintock, *Imperial Leather*, 22.

Annette Kolodny explores such imagery in a 1975 study with the suggestive title *The Lay of the Land: Metaphor as Experience and History in American Life and Letters*.[32] Such imagery was already present in the earliest British accounts, Kolodny notes. In 1584 Arthur Barlowe "described the Indian women who greeted him and his men as uniformly beautiful, gracious, cheerful, and friendly"—much the way the British were awed by Tahitian women in the 1770s. Barlowe "initiated a habit of mind that came to see the Indian woman as a kind of emblem for a land" that was beautiful, bountiful, and inviting. Sir Walter Raleigh in 1595 pictured Guiana as "a country that has yet her maidenhood, never sacked, turned, nor wrought." In his 1609 poem "Nova Britannia" Robert Johnson wrote of Virginia's "valleys and plains streaming with sweet springs, like veins in a natural body."[33]

Early British explorers and promoters of colonization often used such "intentionally suggestive invitations" to encourage emigration to the New World. Yet such imagery inherently implied "a bold exercise of masculine power over the feminine—a feminine, moreover, that was being experienced as at once Mother and Virgin, with all the confusions possible between the two."[34]

Kolodny observes, "The excitement that greeted John Rolfe's marriage to Pocahontas, in April 1614, may have been due to the fact that it served, in some symbolic sense, as a kind of objective correlative for the possibility of Europeans' actually possessing the charms inherent in the virgin continent."[35] Many layers of meaning.

Here is "probably America's oldest and most cherished fantasy," Kolodny suggests: "a daily reality of harmony between man and nature based on an experience of the land as essentially feminine—that is, not simply the land as mother, but the land as woman, the total female principle of gratification—enclosing the individual in an environment of receptivity, repose, and painless and integral satisfaction." Kolodny believes that "at the deepest psychological level" the "single dominating metaphor" in America was "regression from the cares of adult life and a return to the

---

32. Kolodny, *Lay of the Land*.

33. Ibid., 5, 11 (sixteenth- and seventeenth-century English modernized). For historical comparison, see Moorehead, *Fatal Impact*.

34. Kolodny, *Lay of the Land*, 12, 22.

35. Ibid., 5.

primal warmth of womb or breast in a feminine landscape"—imagery not found in England's self-depiction.[36]

Pocahontas's arrival onstage at such an early phase of British colonization is notable in a couple of respects. England was ostensibly a Christian nation, so a Christian world view and ethics should have been at work, in a sense protecting Pocahontas. The earth is God's good creation, not our mother or a fertility goddess.

But this made no difference. Rather, this earth imagery becomes incarnate in an actual historical person. Pocahontas becomes virgin, mother, and earth, all in one. It works the other way, as well: all the powerful sensual images of the land as enticing virgin and fertile mother become *embodied*—first literally, then mythically—in an actual young Indian woman born around 1596.

It may be an intuition of such misuse of the true story of Pocahontas that explains the difference between English and native portrayals of the young Powhatan woman. At the hands of white authors, Pocahontas is a heroine. Yet we find "no Pocahontas figures when we examine novels written by American Indian authors," notes Tilton.[37] Maria Lyytinen makes the same point in her analysis of Monique Mojica's contemporary play, *Princess Pocahontas and the Blue Spots.*[38]

In neither of these symbolic incarnations—American myth legitimator and pornographic image—are we meeting the actual historical Matoaka. Pocahontas now represents—*becomes*—something other than what she really was. In these first two images of Pocahontas, history has become myth.

36. Ibid., 4, 6.

37. Tilton, *Pocahontas,* 180.

38. Lyytinen, "Pocahontas Myth," 78–87.

Chapter Fourteen

_____

Faces of Pocahontas
Virgin Mother

R eal people can be exploited both positively and negatively. As legitimator, Pocahontas is heroine. But she has been incarnated also as vicarious sacrifice, moral example, and true disciple. In some depictions she
becomes "the mother of us all" yet also "Virgin Queen"—images that meld
Queen Elizabeth I and the Virgin Mary.

VICARIOUS SACRIFICE

Like Custer, Pocahontas "died for our sins."[39] Was she then a kind of sacrifice? Child sacrifice? Pocahontas, redeemer?

Jared Sparks in his 1839 book *Lives of Alexander Wilson and Captain
John Smith* described Pocahontas's rescue of Smith this way: "Pocahontas,
the King's favorite daughter—at that time a child of twelve or thirteen years

---

39. Deloria, *Custer Died for Your Sins*. Deloria's title comes from a bumper sticker
popular in the 1960s. Deloria discusses this in his chapter "Indian Humor," 146–67. He
notes, "The most popular and enduring subject of Indian humor is, of course, General
Custer. There are probably more jokes about Custer than there were participants in the
battle" in which Custer died (148). Deloria was raised an Episcopal Christian but later
became disillusioned due to what he saw of Christian treatment of Indians. "Indian people have always been confused at the public stance of the Christian churches," he wrote.
"The churches preached peace for years yet have always endorsed the wars in which the
nation has been engaged" (113).

of age—finding that her piteous entreaties to save the life of Smith were unavailing, rushed forward, clasped his head in her arms, and laid her own upon it, determined either to save his life, or share his fate. Her generous and heroic conduct touched her father's iron heart, and the life of the captive was spared."

Sparks adds, "The account of this beautiful and most touching scene, familiar as it is to every one, can hardly be read with unmoistened eyes." He concludes, "We could almost as reasonably expect an angel to have come down from heaven, and rescued the captive, as that his deliverer should have sprung from the bosom of Powhatan's family." Surely Pocahontas deserves "the eternal gratitude of the inhabitants of this country; for the fate of the colony may be said to have hung upon the arms of Smith's executioners."[40]

The overtones here of Jesus' incarnation and vicarious self-sacrifice are striking, though probably unintentional. Pocahontas laid down her life for her friend. She appeased her father's wrath.[41]

Sparks's language is remarkably similar to that of some Christian theological accounts of Christ's atonement. Here Pocahontas appears as a kind of female Savior, Christa. In reality Pocahontas was of course spared. Like biblical Queen Esther, she did not die. Yet Pocahontas's premature death in England just ten years later—her voyage to England perhaps another form of incarnation and *via dolorosa*—likely would not have happened had she not befriended John Smith in 1607.

If the English and the colonists—the ancestors and progenitors of the new nation—sinned in their treatment of the Native Americans, then yes, Pocahontas died for our sins.

Pocahontas often reappears as a kind of savior and redeemer in American history. Her rescue of John Smith, the most oft-repeated depiction of Pocahontas, is an icon of the American myth. Her Christian baptism and marriage to John Rolfe allowed later writers to co-opt the story, making it our own. The Indian Pocahontas becomes incarnate as part of America's new chosen race.

40. Sparks, *Lives of Alexander Wilson and Captain John Smith*, xvi.

41. Despite the obvious and essential differences between Jesus and Pocahontas, the parallels are striking. Both Jesus and Pocahontas led exemplary lives; were betrayed by a presumed friend; served in a sense as cultural bridges; appreciated and were at home with (not exploiters of) the created order; offered themselves voluntarily on behalf of others; were descendants of a king; died young; and died as a kind of sacrifice. Jesus of course was unique as the incarnate Son of God, Messiah, and Savior; and Jesus was a Hebrew single man whereas Pocahontas was a married Gentile woman.

So Pocahontas becomes also one of America's Founding Mothers. In 1861 John Esten Cooke—a Virginian and Confederate officer who later wrote biographies of Robert E. Lee and Stonewall Jackson—published a poem in *Harper's New Monthly Magazine* titled "A Dream of the Cavaliers," celebrating Virginia's founders. Cooke describes Pocahontas's heroic rescue of John Smith:

> She comes! — like a fawn in the forest,
>   With a bearing mild and meek,
> The blood of a line of chieftains
>   Rich in her golden cheek.
>
> With the tender, fluttering bosom,
>   And the rounded shoulders, bare—
> The folds of her mantle waving
>   In the breath of the idle air.
>
> With a crown of nodding feathers
>   Set round with glimmering pearls;
> And the light of the dreamy sunshine
>   Asleep in her raven curls!
>
> Our own dear Pocahontas!
>   The Virgin Queen of the West—
> With the heart of a Christian hero
>   In a timid maiden's breast!
>
> You have heard the moving story
>   Of the days of long ago,
> How the tender girlish bosom
>   Shrunk not from the deadly blow:
>
> How the valiant son of England,
>   In the woodland drear and wild,
> Was saved from the savage war-club
>   By the courage of a child.
>
> And now in the light of glory
>   The noble figures stand—
> The founder of Virginia,
>   And the pride of the Southern land![42]

42. Cooke, "Dream of the Cavaliers," 252–54. Cf. Tilton, *Pocahontas*, 168.

Now—as the US Civil War was about to explode—Pocahontas appears as the pride of the South and "the Virgin Queen of the West"—an American counterpart to Elizabeth, the Virgin Queen of England, far away to the east. So as vicarious sacrifice, also, Pocahontas becomes the legitimator of the American myth—and now also a partisan for the South.

Cooke later wrote *My Lady Pocahontas* (1885), which has been described as "perhaps the best novel" about her[43] (and there are many). The book purports to be "A True Relation of Virginia. Writ by Anas Todkill, Puritan and Pilgrim. With Notes by John Esten Cooke." Todkill was a real person and an early associate in Virginia of John Smith who left some writings. So he serves as a convenient foil for Cooke.

Cooke first pictures Pocahontas as "the angel" emerging from the woods "with her wild train of attendants." He writes, "The maid comes toward us, stepping with a pretty and proud gait, like a fawn. Her hair was black and straight, but scarce seen for the broad white plume in it. Now I knew that my Captain [Smith] had spoken truth of her face and form, for scarce have I in England seen maid so beautiful. She comes putting down each little foot, covered with bead moccasins, light but firm, and smiling out of black eyes."[44]

In Cooke's version, Pocahontas and Smith fall head over moccasins in love. "Had a Christian man fallen in love with a heathen girl?" Yes, and "I could see that the maid had lost her heart to the young soldier."[45] (Fade to Disney!)

When Smith later disappears however, and Pocahontas believes he is dead, she gradually gives her heart to John Rolfe, after he comes on the scene.

Cooke, in the voice of one or another of his characters, describes Pocahontas as "next under God, . . . the instrument" for saving Jamestown "from death, famine, and utter confusion" and thus a true "exemplar" for all who will follow.[46]

Striking a note that many writers would echo, Cooke writes, "What I marvelled at most was the child and the woman mixed in her."[47]

---

43. Rasmussen and Tilton, *Pocahontas*, 41.
44. Cooke, *My Lady Pocahontas*, 32.
45. Ibid., 33.
46. Ibid., 34.
47. Ibid., 36.

Cooke has Anas Todkill also fall in love with Pocahontas. Like Smith, Todkill is captured by Indians and then rescued by Pocahontas. So the smitten Todkill writes, "And so I, who had laughed at Smith for calling the blessed maiden his guardian angel, now bowed down before her, and though no vain and foolish Papist, but a good Puritan of Puritans, made her my Saint Pokahontas."[48]

But there's more to come. The novel's most dramatic scene is near the end, when Pocahontas goes to England. Queen Anne invites Pocahontas to attend "a Virginia play" at the Globe Theatre. The play is Shakespeare's *The Tempest*. Pocahontas, who "speaks good English now," agrees to attend.[49]

On the set evening, "nigh sunset," Pocahontas and John Rolfe find themselves with the queen in a special box overlooking the stage. As the play progresses, the spectators watch Prospero, his daughter Miranda, the wild Caliban, as well as Ariel, "an airy spirit," and the other characters.

Suddenly Pocahontas "turneth a little white, and her bosom under her ruff rises and falls like two waves, and she catcheth her breath." What is it?

Pocahontas has heard Caliban say that Prospero calls his beautiful daughter Miranda his "nonpareil." The very thing Smith had called her in Virginia! Now, in the theatre, "the name strikes her sudden and woful [sic] as she hears it in the play."[50] Pocahontas begins to see her own story unfold onstage, the words killing her softly.

As the play ends, Pocahontas notices that straight across from her, in a similar box, a curtain has opened. Looking intently, she sees in the shadows William Shakespeare himself, seated with another man. She is shocked to see it is Captain John Smith! She turns "white as her smock, and trembles a little, her eyes fixed on Smith." She whispers to Anas Todkill, "He is not dead, you see; it was a lie they told! He is not dead! He is not dead!"[51]

Smith now in turn sees Pocahontas and looks at her "with a long, still gaze." Pocahontas realizes Smith had come to the play to see *her*, knowing she would be attending. In Cooke's telling, Smith and Shakespeare are friends, and Shakespeare had learned of Pocahontas, the *nonpareil*, from Smith. A clever twist.

---

48. Ibid., 53.

49. Ibid., 160.

50. Ibid., 167–68. See Shakespeare, *The Tempest*, 53 (Act III, Scene 2). As a noun *nonpareil* means someone with no equal; unparalleled or incomparable.

51. Cooke, *My Lady Pocahontas*, 168–69.

Cooke's novel goes on to recount Smith's final conversation with Pocahontas, shortly before her death. "I thought to wed my little Princess," Smith tells Todkill, "but 'tis vain now, and here is the end." For good measure, Smith predicts that later some people will doubt his account of his rescue at Pocahontas's hands, saying "I made up this story."[52]

Cooke ends his novel with a short account of "How my Lady Pokahontas passed in Peace." At the end Pocahontas "looks up and joins her two white hands together." She whispers, "Blessed Jesus, thou wilt have me!" Then "comes a sudden stillness. My Lady is ended."[53]

My Lady Pocahontas is a romance, not a morality play. Pocahontas is not explicitly portrayed as a sacrifice. Yet the overtones of selflessness and self-giving are clear enough. At the end she falls "into a great melancholy" over Smith. Had it not been for her Christian faith she would have "pined away" for him, "and so ended." "But her faith kept her from despairing," Cooke writes, "and she would talk always of going back to Virginia. Her own people were to be converted, and she would be God's instrument"— but tragically "that great business fell in her grave."[54]

MORAL EXAMPLE

Pocahontas thus stands as an example of strength, character, endurance, patience, caring, and self-giving. Many American writers have celebrated these virtues.

Of course the question of the morality of marrying a native, a "savage"—even a converted one—was troublesome from the beginning. John Rolfe himself wrestled with this when he fell in love with Pocahontas. For some, intermarriage with natives was the path to assimilation and evangelism. To others, it was an abomination. In his 1609 sermon, which Rolfe apparently heard, William Symonds sternly warned against it: God's people "must not marry nor give in marriage to the heathen, that are uncircumcised. The breaking of this rule, may break the neck of all good success on this voyage."[55] Tilton notes, "Symonds here makes one of the earliest cases for the power of racial purity, which he believed would ensure the prosperity of the Virginia colony. Such expressions of the fear of [intermarriage],

52. Ibid., 179–81.
53. Ibid., 189.
54. Ibid., 188.
55. Quoted in Tilton, *Pocahontas,* 13.

as well as of any type of 'unnatural mixing,' become a constant feature of colonial and early American thought."[56]

But Pocahontas converted to Christianity and so in effect became English. Instead of a temptress, she becomes a moral icon. As a Native American, she becomes an example of what all natives should do. As a faithful Christian wife, she becomes a model of submissive moral virtue.

In fact the British were of two minds. To some, the marriage of Pocahontas was "a model that, to the detriment of both Indians and whites, had not been followed," unfortunately, from the beginning. Yet it was "proof that a merging of the two peoples and cultures was, or at least had been, possible." If such intermarriage "had been reenacted on a larger scale, then perhaps the continual animosity between the races . . . might have been averted." Thus Pocahontas's Christian marriage came to be seen as "the great archetype of Indian-white conjugal union."[57]

Opposition to any intermarriage with natives was strong from the beginning, however. It would only grow over time, especially once African slaves entered the equation. In the days of slavery the dicey question of racial mixing, intermarriage, and "miscegenation"—the mixing or inter-breeding of different races, whether within or outside marriage—became a burning but often embarrassing topic. Virginia specifically outlawed inter-racial marriage in 1662, and in 1691 amended the law to make explicit that this included marriage with Indians.[58]

But the dominant narrative has been Pocahontas as model and moral exemplar. John Chamberlayne Pickett's words in 1947 are typical: "In all history and in all romance it would be difficult to find a more perfect character than Pocahontas; and taking her as she has come down to us, it appears to me to be impossible to say wherein it could have been improved."[59]

Thus Pocahontas was romanticized and celebrated as a virtuous hero-ine and mother of America.

Rayna Green explores the contradictory nature of the many Poca-hontas images in her essay, "The Pocahontas Perplex: The Image of Indian Women in American Culture." Green shows how Pocahontas became "a

56. Tilton, *Pocahontas*, 13.

57. Ibid., 12. The phrase "the great archetype of Indian-white conjugal union" is from Bernard W. Sheehan, quoted by Tilton.

58. Ibid., 14–15. Tilton devotes his first chapter to "Miscegenation and the Poca-hontas Narrative in Colonial and Federalist America." His last chapter deals with "The Figure of Pocahontas in Sectionalist Propaganda."

59. Quoted in ibid., 1.

model for the national understanding of Indian women"—appearing not only in stories and art but also as a sales gimmick for cigars, perfume, and other products, and "as the figurehead for American warships and clippers." Yet in popular imagination she stands side by side with a contrasting image, the Indian squaw, an "anti-Pocahontas," less attractive, "darker, negatively viewed."[60]

Green also makes a connection between Pocahontas and classical European culture. Beginning with Pocahontas, "the Indian woman began her symbolic, many-faceted life as a Mother figure—exotic, powerful, dangerous, and beautiful—and as a representative of American liberty and European classical virtue translated into New World terms." Green points to the similarities between statues of Pocahontas and classical images of Greek, Roman, and early Renaissance women.[61]

When we reflect on Pocahontas as a person and a Christian, rather than as legitimator of America's history, we do in fact find much to admire. She is legitimately a moral example when seen not as justifier of British and later US rule in America, but rather as a remarkable woman who tried to make sense of the Powhatan and English cultures and their interrelationships, and of the Christian faith.

TRUE DISCIPLE

As we have seen, Pocahontas's Christian conversion seems genuine. Her faith must have been deep, even if her comprehension of Jesus Christ and the fullness of the gospel was limited.

Pocahontas appears in history as a true disciple of Jesus Christ. She adopted the faith and practices of Christianity. She claimed Jesus Christ as her Lord and Savior. Most importantly —in contrast of many of those around her, among both the Powhatan and the English—her character and actions exhibit nothing contrary to the spirit of Jesus Christ.

In Pocahontas's character we see a stellar blend of selflessness and self-possession. Of self-giving for the sake of others, and yet confident self-determination. Like Jesus in the Gospel of John, we see Pocahontas as the object or victim of others' actions, actions well intended or mal-intended. Yet we sense that at a deep level, she remains in charge. Her adaptability

60. Green, R. "Pocahontas Perplex," 698–700.

61. Ibid., 700–715.

came from strength, not weakness. She never seems to have lost her sense of herself, or her Powhatan identity, or later her Christian commitment.

Pocahontas certainly was not passive. Repeatedly, strategically, she took initiative, even among the English, shaping circumstances as she could. Even when forced into submission, her heart was steadfast and her will unbowed.

It could be said of her as it was of Jesus: "When he was abused, he did not return abuse; when he suffered, he did not threaten; but he entrusted himself to the one who judges justly" (1 Pet 2:23).

Unlike most of her English contemporaries, Pocahontas also hints at a discipleship grounded in appreciation for the land, in sensitivity to plants and animals and the quality of *shalom*. We wish we knew just how much of the native Harmony Way she brought into her marriage and her new faith, and what she would have taught her son and other possible future children and grandchildren.

In her blend of self-identity and self-giving; in her understanding of the land and its living creatures as gifts from the Creator to be appreciated and nurtured; in her relationships with other people and with strange cultural practices; in her concern for her own people and their welfare, Pocahontas modeled the life of a true disciple.

The Harmony Way.

These are all winsome images. In art, books, and national imagination, Pocahontas emerges as vicarious sacrifice, moral example, true disciple. Mother of America.

But we have yet to come to terms with Pocahontas, *celebrity*.

Chapter Fifteen

Faces of Pocahontas

Disney Celebrity

In the twentieth century, Pocahontas served as legitimator of the American myth by reemerging on the celebrity stage. Despite the ups and downs of 400 years of history, Pocahontas remains famous. Inherently powerful, her story still survives the changing fads and fashions of entertainment.

So now we focus on Pocahontas's most famous face: up-to-date celebrity. Then we must return finally to her actual role as shaper of American history.

MODERN CELEBRITY

This is Pocahontas's big starring role today: celebrity entertainer.

Disney released its children's romance *Pocahontas* in 1995—their first animated feature based on a historical figure. This was followed by a straight-to-video sequel in 1998, *Pocahontas II: Journey to a New World.*

Early in the first movie, blond John Smith and statuesque Pocahontas, equally tall, fall in love. Pocahontas and John Smith: Barbie and Ken in period costume. After a few words in her native Algonquin, Pocahontas magically switches to hip twentieth-century English.

In the film the British colonizers and the native Powhatans equally view each other as "Savages! Savages!" (in one song). Pocahontas and Smith work desperately to head off impending war. Smith is captured, but saved from death by Pocahontas's bravery. He is wounded, however, by a stray English bullet and must return to England, leaving his beloved Pocahontas behind.

The movie closes with a romantic kiss, then waved good-byes as Smith's ship sails off to England and Pocahontas stands lonely on a precipice.

By ending the story with Smith's departure for England, the movie neatly avoids having to deal with the awkward fact of Pocahontas's conversion, and her kidnapping. There are no references at all to Christianity—though plenty to native beliefs. A childlike version of Native American spirituality permeates the movie.

Pocahontas is guided by Grandmother Willow. "What is my path?" Pocahontas asks. Grandmother Willow replies, "All around you are spirits. If you listen, they will guide you." Again, later, "Let the spirits of the earth guide you." So they do. To the English, however, "the earth is just a dead thing you can claim," as one song has it.

The earth—rivers, forests, mountains—is huge in *Pocahontas*. Oddly however, the colors are unnatural. Earth tones and native greenery give way to bright oranges, purples, blues, and other colors that actually obscure the reality and naturalness of the earth.

Maria Lyytinen notes that Disney's *Pocahontas*, "despite arising almost two hundred years after [several earlier] plays, does not differ much from nineteenth-century Pocahontas fictions in terms of story line and approach."[1] Lori Rowlett adds, "Disney's film contains many errors of fact. Pocahontas would have been only about twelve years old when Smith was in Jamestown, not a well-developed woman. . . . Pocahontas was made to look more Asian than Native American, which indicates that perhaps the Disney personnel thought that one 'other' was more or less the same as any 'other' . . . . Disney's artist used various models in creating the cartoon Pocahontas, including one from the Philippines."[2]

Disney deals in fantasy, of course, so we really don't expect any bother with history. And yet *Pocahontas* the movie safely inoculates small children from ever taking the fascinatingly real Pocahontas seriously as an influential historical figure. Certainly not as a Christian. History itself, and the earth, are fantasy.

1. Lyytinen, "Pocahontas Myth," 83.
2. Rowlett, "Disney's Pocahontas," 70.

Every movie carries a message. Especially ones with visual images and romances. In this sense the Disney film is actually anti-Christian, for they purposely omit central facts and so falsify, misinform, and by default carry an anti-Christian-faith bias.

Worldwide, *Pocahontas* has grossed about $350 million for Disney.[3]

The sequel *Pocahontas II: Journey to a New World* purports to tell the rest of the story. Actually it is even more a fantasy than the original. The title is clever however, for here the "New World" is England, not America—a brave new world to Pocahontas.

In this Revised Disney Version, Pocahontas's kidnapping, conversion, marriage, and death are again all omitted. A new narrative is invented. Pocahontas, still unmarried, volunteers to travel with John Rolfe to England as an ambassador of peace. Prior to this Pocahontas again consults Grandmother Willow, who tells her, "Only the spirit within can guide you. Listen to the spirit within."

Pocahontas dons English dress only in London (not in Virginia) in order to attend the "Hunt Ball," Disney's version of the court masque. Soon she encounters John Smith, whom she thought was dead (that much is accurate). And now Smith and Rolfe become superheroes, together rescuing Pocahontas from the Tower of London where she's been wrongfully imprisoned due to the evil scheming of Captain Ratcliffe. An all-out English attack on the Powhatan Indians threatens, but is averted due to the bravado of Rolfe and Smith.

Pocahontas's heart is torn between her two superheroes, but she is won over by Rolfe's kindness and good manners. At the end of the movie she gives up Smith and returns with Rolfe to America to live happily ever after. Pocahontas and Rolfe sing, "We'll build a bridge of love between two worlds!"

Pocahontas was never, of course, imprisoned in the Tower of London. At this time she was Mrs. Rebecca Rolfe and had a son. But the most blatant betrayal of history is Pocahontas's return to Virginia, when in fact she died in England.

In sum, viewers of *Pocahontas II* never know that she married John Rolfe; that she had a son; that she was a celebrity, not a captive, in London; and that she never returned to her homeland, due to her premature death in England. The film has no Christian symbolism whatsoever, so viewers are also unaware of her Christian conversion.

3. Box Office Mojo, "Pocahontas," lines 1–10.

Again, such distortions might be meaningless if Pocahontas were fictional—if she were not an actual historical person, a real actor in history whose influence still shapes US self-identity and self-understanding. Since she *was* an influential historical person, how she is viewed today is still consequential.

Earlier film versions of the Pocahontas story also dealt more in fantasy than history. A good example is the 1953 MGM movie, *Captain Smith and Pocahontas*. Starring Jody Lawrence as Pocahontas, Anthony Dexter as John Smith, and Robert Clarke as John Rolfe, the movie presents itself from the beginning as "A Legend" with fictitious characters and events.[4] But the source of the story is of course the real Pocahontas.

In this version, Pocahontas is already a mature woman when she meets John Smith. Rather than being captured by Powhatan warriors, Smith is led in peace to Chief Powhatan's town. There an Indian warrior, Opechanco,[5] convinces the chief that the English are a threat and Smith must die.

What follows is another version of the famous rescue scene. Pocahontas rushes forward to save Smith. In this version, however, rescuing Smith means Pocahontas is bound by tribal law to marry him.

Pocahontas and Smith wed in an Indian ceremony—not for love, but to secure the peace. Pocahontas explains, "The Great Spirit does not like killing." Her motives are altruistic, and Smith himself recognizes that the union will bring peace between the Indians and the English.

Once married, Smith and Pocahontas gradually fall in love. But soon Smith is seriously injured in a gunpowder explosion and returns to England, leaving John Rolfe to look after Pocahontas and help guide the English settlement at Jamestown.

At the end of the movie a conversation back in London between Smith and King James explains that Pocahontas and Rolfe have now wed, and all is well in Virginia.

In this movie Pocahontas longs to see London, but remains in Virginia. However, by leaving Rolfe and Pocahontas happily wed in Jamestown, the film opens the possibility of a later voyage and of and Pocahontas's final days in England. The movie's last scene shows a fictional statue of Pocahontas in London with the legend, "Pocahontas, 1595–1617—A Great Lady—A Princess of Her People."[6]

4. The movie was directed by Levi Landers.

5. Loosely based on Opechancanough, Chief Powhatan's half brother and successor.

6. The Pocahontas statue in the movie resembles but is different from the actual

The movie thus mixes fact and fantasy to tell a new version of the Pocahontas story. There is no hint of Christian faith or Pocahontas's conversion. The movie is full of gender and cultural stereotypes; the Powhatan Indians are dressed like Plains Indians rather than actual Powhatans. Chief Powhatan sports a large, long feathered headdress.

Captain Smith and Pocahontas is thus simply another link in the long chain of stories that use actual history to create myths.

The 2006 movie *The New World,* directed by Terrence Malick, is the most recent Hollywood version of Pocahontas. The movie stars Q'orianka Kilcher (who is of partial native descent) as Pocahontas.[7] John Smith (Colin Farrell) and John Rolfe (Christian Bale) figure prominently in the movie, and the venerable Christopher Plummer appears as Captain Newport. (In the movie he manages to keep both arms.)

The New World is a dreamy, slow-moving romantic fantasy, beautiful in its photography.[8] Unlike the Disney films, it covers the whole story of Pocahontas, including her baptism, marriage, and death. It gets many details right. But overall it shows hardly any more regard for history than does Disney. The first part of the movie, up to John Smith's return to England, seems based more on Disney's *Pocahontas* than on historical accounts. Even some of the scenes look like those in Disney, except here played by real people.

Overall, with facts and events rearranged, *The New World* reflects the sentimental romances of the 1800s more than firsthand accounts from the 1600s. Pocahontas struggles with a divided heart, torn between love for both John Smith and John Rolfe.

One oddity is the absence of Alexander Whitaker. He is mentioned, but in the movie he dies before the captive Pocahontas arrives at Jamestown—and Pocahontas moves into his vacant room! As a result of this discrepancy, Pocahontas's baptism and marriage are performed by Christopher Plummer (Captain Newport); Whitaker is not involved. Without Whitaker, perhaps the most transforming moment in the whole story disappears.

Pocahontas statue at St. George's Church, Gravesend, England, where Pocahontas was buried—which is a replica of the William Ordway Partridge statue of Pocahontas in Jamestown.

7. Her father was a Quechua Indian from Peru.

8. In an interview in which he didn't seem very enthusiastic about the movie, Christopher Plummer said the director wanted the whole movie to have a dreamlike quality (interview included on the movie's DVD.)

Ironically the movie's director, Terrence Malick, stressed his insistence on "authenticity" in presenting the story. This "authenticity" extends to artifacts, dress, food, behavior—but tellingly, not to historical facts and sequences!

The film's redeeming feature is young Q'orianka Kilcher as Pocahontas. Miss Kilcher gives viewers a sense of what it must have been like to be the young Indian woman. This despite the fact that ten years of Pocahontas's life are conflated to just a couple. Q'orianka remarkably resembles Pocahontas as drawn from life by Simon Van de Passe—right down to the natural slight cleft in her chin and the dark eyes.

Pocahontas's faith postconversion is pictured here as a mix of Christian and native (or New Age) beliefs. Pocahontas often prays to "Mother," a sort of spirit-blend of her own deceased mother and Mother Earth.

In an interview with Christian writer Camerin Courtney, Q'orianka Kilcher (fourteen at the time of filming) said she really identified with Pocahontas. Her New Agey interpretation underplays Pocahontas's Christian faith, but in other respects Kilcher mostly gets it right. "I fell in love with her," says Kilcher, "because she was a visionary of peace far ahead of her time. She was able to dream of two very different worlds coexisting and collaborating together in peace."[9]

Kilcher also catches something of what it must have been like for Pocahontas to adapt to English ways. "The first time I tried on my English wardrobe," she says, "I had them tie my corset extra tight and give me shoes a size too small in order to feel how constrained I imagine Pocahontas must have felt. I went home that night and cried because I felt like a caged bird, like the freedom was torn away."[10]

Pocahontas's actual transition was not quite that abrupt—and she was after all in love with John Rolfe. Even so, it must have been a very wrenching change.

The key thing that gets lost in this and nearly all the versions of the Pocahontas story is her relationship with Jesus Christ, and how that fits integrally into her real historical significance. Though *The New World* portrays Pocahontas's conversion sympathetically, the integrity and full meaning of her baptism and Christian faith are obscured.

The 2009 movie *Avatar*, though ostensibly an epic sci-fi movie about a faraway planet named Pandora, actually looks like a retelling of the

9. Courtney, "Pocahontas," para. 17.

10. Ibid., "Being Pocahontas," para. 8.

Pocahontas story. The parallels are striking. Daniel Hawk terms the movie "a variation on America's national narrative of westward expansion and empire-building, whereby invaders with advanced technology drive out indigenous peoples and occupy their lands."[11] *Avatar*'s two main characters, the human Jake Sully and the attractive young native Na'vi woman Neytiri, reenact the roles of John Smith (same initials) and Pocahontas. Jake, now in the form of his high-tech avatar body, is rescued by Neytiri and initiated into Na'vi society. The native religion also parallels the nature religion found in *The New World* and Disney's *Pocahontas*.

So the mythmaking continues. In 2013 Simon Winchester published *The Men Who United the States*, a lively account of the "Explorers, Inventors, Eccentrics, and Mavericks" who gave us "One Nation, Indivisible." Though not men, Pocahontas and Sacajawea get mentions.

Winchester essentially perpetuates the Pocahontas myth. Pocahontas is "the chief's beautiful teenage daughter" who saves John Smith by "laying her own head upon" his. Thus she becomes "the noblest of all the noble savages" whose "genes have since been spread liberally through a vast swath" of American society, "from the Jeffersons to the Reagans."[12] Winchester calls America's native peoples "the locals" who were "often not unreasonably hostile" to European encroachments.[13]

KEY ACTOR IN HISTORY

Pocahontas's various roles and guises can hide her most important role. She was not a myth; she was real—"a real and complicated woman with her own plans, goals, and ideas," as Camilla Townsend rightly says.[14]

As a real Powhatan young woman, daughter of a Grand Chief, Pocahontas was a key actor in American history. Further, as a woman, she could see things that were hidden from her own kinsmen as well as from her English acquaintances.

---

11. Hawk, "*Avatar* in Three Dimensions," 1–2. A number of observers have noted and commented on the similarities (and contrasts) between the movie and the Pocahontas narrative, as a Google search will show.

12. Winchester, *Men Who United*, 167–68. Recounting the Lewis and Clark Expedition, Winchester tells of the "heavily pregnant fifteen-year-old Shoshone girl named Sacajawea" who served as the expedition's guide and translator (49).

13. Ibid., 165, 166.

14. Townsend, *Pocahontas*, xi.

Most Americans probably know that Pocahontas was a real person. The dramatic painting of Pocahontas's baptism that today embellishes the Capitol Rotunda wouldn't exist if Pocahontas had not actually lived, liaised with the English, and eventually married John Rolfe. But Pocahontas's most important role as a real person and historical actor is easily obscured by the flowering of myths following her death.

Pocahontas's historical significance becomes clear when we imagine Jamestown or the adventures of John Smith without her. Without Pocahontas's interventions it is very likely that:

John Smith would have lost his life among the Powhatan Indians.

Jamestown would have been wiped out in 1609 or 1610.

The Powhatan would have become totally hostile.

One of two things would have happened in England. Either Jamestown's many critics would have won, and Virginia colonization would have been abandoned or postponed. Or, more likely, in reprisal for Jamestown the British would have invaded with increased force and violence and would have largely annihilated the natives. As she did 166 years later when her American colonies rebelled, England might have sent 400 warships and 40,000 armed soldiers and sailors to settle the score once and for all.

In either case, repercussions in England would have been profound.

What did Pocahontas *actually* do? She tried to understand the English. She was curious and insightful, a quick learner. She developed an affection for John Smith long before she ever met John Rolfe. She was an emissary and at times a reconciler between the Powhatan and the English. She was a key player in keeping Jamestown from starving to death. She maintained great dignity when betrayed and captured by the English. She learned how to bridge cultures. She responded warmly to John Rolfe's love, but saw through British pretensions.

She was a help to Rolfe and sincerely adopted his Christian faith. She in effect became British without abandoning her Powhatan loyalty, identity, and passion. Her behavior in England, and especially her final outburst at John Smith, suggest that she continued to see herself, within her limited sphere of influence, as a mediator between her people and the British invaders. She accepted with grace the many decisions and roles that were forced upon her, yet never lost her poise or sense of identity and self-respect.

She married the first successful tobacco entrepreneur in America and bore a son whose descendants would become key players in the expanding American drama.

What struggles and tears and questions and ponderings and second-guessings went on during night hours when John was asleep we can only guess. Perhaps she learned simply to leave everything, time and again, in Jesus' hands.

For all these reasons Pocahontas—Mrs. John Rolfe—is one of the most remarkable and influential real actors in history. She is part of that stream of remarkable, courageous young women who made a historic difference for good in strongly male-dominant and male-dominated societies through the centuries.

What would have happened if Pocahontas had survived the foul London air and returned safely to Jamestown?

She would have taken her place as part of English colonial society, no doubt, but with a special role as mediator between the English and her own Powhatan people. She might well have proved the key to peaceful relationships with the Indians, at least in Virginia. If so the terrible massacre of the English by the Powhatans a few years later likely would never have happened. On the morning of Friday, March 22, 1622, Opechancanough, Chief Powhatan's youngest brother and successor, led a well-coordinated surprise attack on most of the British settlements up and down the James River. As many as 400 men, women, and children were slaughtered—nearly a third of the total white population.[15]

Just days earlier Opechancanough had assured the settlers that peace was now so firm "that the sky should fall sooner than it should be violated on his part." The English now understood the awful irony of his words.[16]

Old Chief Powhatan knew nothing of this, for he had died in the Virginia woods in April 1618, about a year after hearing of Pocahontas's death.[17] John Rolfe seems to have escaped the massacre, though he died the same year, probably shortly before the Powhatan attack. In 1619 he married Jane Pierce, the daughter of successful Virginia colonists, and to them Thomas Rolfe's half-sister, Elizabeth, was born in 1620.[18]

At the time of the massacre, young Thomas Rolfe was still safely in England. He returned to Virginia in 1635, at age twenty. He found himself

---

15. Haile, ed., *Jamestown Narratives*, 50–51. Price, *Love and Hate*, 206–10, gives details.

16. Anderson, *History*, 1:275.

17. Price, *Love and Hate*, 185.

18. See Kupperman, *Jamestown Project*, 311.

the owner of huge tracts of land inherited from his grandfather, Chief Powhatan, as well as master of his father's estate and holdings.[19]

But what if Pocahontas had survived? With Pocahontas as mediator, might a lasting peace between Native Americans and colonists have been established—perhaps a model for future relations with the Indians? Possibly. But patterns of violence were already set. Intertribal hostilities and warfare continued, as well. This, plus the certainty of thousands more English arriving and more settlements being established, made a peaceful outcome unlikely.

And what of Pocahontas's Christian influence? Had she returned to Virginia, would she have gotten inside the Bible—begun reading the Word with her Powhatan eyes, rather than with English eyes? Would she have gotten her mind inside the Sermon on the Mount, for instance, or read of the new community Jesus began where there is no longer Jew or Greek, slave or free, male or female, but rather unity in Christ (Gal 3:28)?

We don't know. As with Abraham Lincoln's tragic assassination, we are left wondering what might have been.

For the American myth, however, Pocahontas's death was convenient. With Pocahontas's passing it is as though someone sang "Let the myth-making begin!" But Pocahontas died both as a Powhatan loyal to her people and land, and as a Christian seeking to do what was right and just.

This is certain: Pocahontas was a key actor in history. This is, most of all, the true face of Pocahontas.

REPRISE

The true story of Pocahontas is both historical and archetypal. This combination of real history and potent myth gives Pocahontas enduring power. Stories about a young girl or woman rescuing an adventuresome stranger from death at the hands of her own people show up in many cultures of the world, as various authors have noted. Pocahontas fits this pattern.

Pocahontas herself, both as myth and as a flesh-and-blood Native American, virtually begs for comparison with other young women—women

---

19. Woodward, *Pocahontas,* 190. Thomas married an Englishwoman, Jane Poythress, a union from which "descended seven successive generations of educators, ministers, statesmen, and lawmakers," including the influential US Congressman (later Senator) John Randolph of Roanoke (Woodward, *Pocahontas,* 191).

who in a world dominated by men were key actors in history while maintaining their integrity and virtue.

In her own time, Pocahontas was identified with and in a sense reincarnated as the biblical Rebecca (Rebekah), who left her own family to become the wife of the patriarch Isaac (Gen 22–24). She was like Naaman's unnamed Hebrew slave girl, cited in William Symonds's sermon, who brokered her master's healing (2 Kgs 5).

Pocahontas can be compared with many heroic female figures in the Bible and throughout history. Ruth certainly, in the Old Testament, who left her people and her gods to marry a Hebrew and become part of God's chosen people, an ancestor of Jesus. The bold prophetess Deborah, who helped deliver Israel from her enemies and thus "arose as a mother in Israel" (Judg 5:7). Or in a different way Queen Esther, who risked her life to save her people.

Images of Pocahontas as "virgin" and "Mother" have obvious resonances with the Virgin Mary. In other ways Pocahontas appears as a sort of Mary Magdalene.

In Western history, Joan of Arc and Sacajawea invite comparison at varying levels. Joan of Arc (1412–1431), "The Maid of Orleans," two centuries before Pocahontas, forfeited her life by following God's call and seeking to save her people, dying at the stake at the age of nineteen.

Sacajawea, Shoshone Indian guide on the Lewis and Clark expedition from 1804 to 1806, was only sixteen and pregnant when she and her French Canadian husband, Toussaint Charbonneau, began accompanying Lewis and Clark. Sacajawea traveled thousands of miles with the expedition, from North Dakota to the Pacific, and likely died in 1812, at age twenty-four.[20]

In his brief biography of Sacajawea, based mainly on the Lewis and Clark journals, Kenneth Thomasma notes, "Her negotiation skills, translation abilities, awareness of Indian culture, familiarity with the territory and its flora and fauna, and her almost daily provision of roots, berries, and herbs made her a respected" and virtually indispensable member of the expedition. Much of Thomasma's description of Sacajawea could be said equally of Pocahontas. "As the young girl grew, her mother expertly and carefully taught her daughter to find and preserve food, make clothing, construct shelters, care for children, and pack for travel to distant hunting grounds."[21]

---

20. Black, *Empire of Shadows*, 2.

21. Thomasma, *Truth about Sacajawea*, 1, 9. Some accounts say she lived a long life.

Daniel Hawk points out other parallels between Sacajawea and Pocahontas. In many cultural conquest narratives where one people takes over the lands of another, an "indigenous helper" appears who welcomes the invaders and eases their acceptance by the native inhabitants. In this sense both Pocahontas and Sacajawea parallel Rahab in the biblical book of Joshua. Indigenous helpers "welcome the invader and announce the disappearance of the indigenous peoples and the land's reordering through conquest and occupation," thus facilitating "the transformation of indigenous land into the invader's homeland." So finally "the land [is] remade in the image of the invader."[22]

A recent novel about Sacajawea imagines the Shoshone woman saying of the white explorers, "They write in their journals. But they do not know the land. They give the animals names that do not belong to them. That do not say who they are."[23]

We may celebrate the heroes of war, politics, and patriotism, but history has often been molded, changed for the better, by vulnerable but strong young women at the margins of power who through courage and force of character molded the behavior of others. We see the thread running right through from Rebekah in the Old Testament, to Mary in the New, on to Pocahontas and others. Right up to fifteen-year-old Elizabeth Eckford of Little Rock, Arkansas, who on September 4, 1957 braved a taunting mob to integrate Central High School. "Go home, nigger! Go back to Africa!" someone shouted. But local news photographer Will Counts was on hand and snapped the iconic photo of Elizabeth before the jeering crowd that would change history.

Elizabeth was supposed to have been joined by eight other black teens—the Little Rock Nine—but she hadn't gotten the key phone message. Her family had no phone.[24]

Howard, *Sacajawea*, examines the evidence (175–92).

22. Hawk, "Indigenous Helpers," 115. Hawk points out that "Wanton slaughter and devastating warfare [as in the biblical book of Joshua] also marked colonial and federal campaigns against indigenous nations, in every region and at every phase of conflict, bracketed by massacres at Mystic Fort [of a Pequot Indian village by the Pilgrims in Massachusetts] in 1637 and Wounded Knee in 1890" (ibid., 117). See similarly Rowlett, "Disney's Pocahontas," 66–75.

23. Glancy, *Stone Heart*, 25. Cited in Donaldson, "Red Woman, White Dreams," 528.

24. Tougas, *Little Rock Girl*, 4–10.

And so on to today, to the remarkable schoolgirl Malala Yousafzai of Pakistan, who recovered from a vicious Taliban attack in October 2012 to become a reformer and activist for the rights of girls and women—and winner of the 2014 Nobel Peace Prize.

Such stories remind us of something we know intuitively. Women often see things differently from men. In the American interaction between Indians and whites, women had a different viewpoint. In her study of pioneer women's diaries, Lillian Schlissel noted that white women more often described the Indians as "helpful guides and purveyors of services" than as enemies—though they did of course fear the Indians. Schlissel adds that "women, in the naturalness of their telling, offer a new perception of the relations between the emigrants and the Indians. Having no special stake in asserting their bravery, . . . the women correct the historical record as they write of the daily exchanges by which the Indians were part of life on the road."[25]

In fact at a deep level, pioneering white women had much in common with their native sisters—more than with their own husbands or male colleagues at some points. And vice versa. Similarly, white men often were more like their native male adversaries that they were like their own wives—and vice versa.[26]

This is part of the beauty and mystery and dilemma of Pocahontas. She saw and understood what others didn't, and moreso than they knew.

The story of Pocahontas, whether as myth or history, reminds us also of the power of the story itself. Although we have traced the myths and twisting paths of the saga through 400 years of history, the central concern of this book is in fact Pocahontas herself—the real red-blooded DNA person—and her relationship to Jesus Christ as she experienced him.

This means we have to focus on Pocahontas *the Christian*, the disciple. For this is what she was, even though this central fact is cut from most tellings. Few versions of the story even mention her Christian faith. If it is mentioned, her baptism is treated as an anachronism—merely a tiny link in the chain of her life's story, not especially important.

But our focus is Pocahontas the Powhatan young woman who decided to become a Christian and, as near as we can tell, sought to live out that

25. Schlissel, *Women's Diaries*, 14–15.

26. I don't deal with them in this book, but narratives of captured white women's interactions with native women, and captured Indian women's interactions with white women, often show this.

faith. In the process we learn much about church and mission in seventeenth-century England and colonial America, and the continuing echoes today.

This is the story. Yet there is more to tell—the story not only of Pocahontas, but of the scores of Indian tribes across North America that had their own epic encounters with the ever expanding white population.

Chapter Sixteen

The Long, Bitter Trail

To most twentieth century Americans, the legacy of slavery was serious business, the legacy of conquest was not. . . . The subject of slavery was the domain of serious scholars and the occasion of sober national reflection; the subject of conquest was the domain of mass entertainment and the occasion of light-hearted national escapism. An element of regret for "what we did to the Indians" has entered the picture, but the dominant feature of conquest remained "adventure." Children happily played "cowboys and Indians" but stopped short of "masters and slaves." — Historian Patricia Limerick[1]

There is scarcely a square foot of land in all North America that was not unethically taken from its native inhabitants—whether by deceit, violence, habitat destruction, broken promises, or outright extermination. For Native Americans, the years from Pocahontas's death in 1617 to the Wounded Knee massacre in 1890—and especially the critical decades from 1830 to 1890—were indeed a "long, bitter trail," to use anthropologist Anthony F. C. Wallace's words.[2]

1. Limerick, *Legacy of Conquest,* 17–18.
2. Wallace, *Long, Bitter Trail.* Wallace was referring mainly to the Trail of Tears at the beginning of this period; I am applying it more broadly.

That's the way the West was "won."

In the centuries following its founding, the United States gradually pushed its borders farther and farther west. The Northwest Ordinance of 1787, involving what are now Michigan, Wisconsin, Minnesota, Illinois, Indiana, and Ohio, "expressly declare[d] that the Indians' property shall never be taken except by purchase, or in wars duly authorized by Congress," noted clergyman Henry Whipple. But this was honored more in the breach than in the practice.[3] The same pattern continued for more than a century.

Even earlier, in the Revolutionary period, violent precedents were set. In the Ohio Country, ninety Lenape Indians were systematically massacred by a detachment of Continental Army militiamen from Pennsylvania. It was early 1782, and the Revolutionary War was essentially over—but on the Ohio frontier British and Continental forces still fought for control, using Native surrogates. The Continental soldiers came upon a Lenape town and accused the inhabitants of having murdered white colonists. The soldiers killed them all, two at a time—twenty-nine men, twenty-seven women, and thirty-four children and infants.

In fact, these Lenape were peaceful Christians who had been won to faith in Jesus Christ through the Moravian missionaries David and Susan Zeisberger and John and Sara Heckewelder, who established Gnadenhütten (Cabins of Grace), one of the earliest Christian settlements in Ohio.[4]

A major expansion of the United States came with the Louisiana Purchase of 1803. This agreement with Napoleon, which added 828,000 square miles to the country at a cost of about 40 cents per acre, was supposed to have safeguarded Indian rights—but did not.[5]

Well before the Louisiana Purchase, the United States was already expanding westward. A ragged but steady wave of settlers, adventurers, explorers, prospectors, miners, and hunters kept pushing west. Military control soon followed as hundreds of US Army forts sprang up everywhere from the Appalachians to the Rockies. White Americans and immigrants from Europe kept moving farther and farther west, through the forests and across the prairies and mountains. Pioneer wagon trains by the score and then railroads sped the expansion even as they destroyed Indian hunting

3. Whipple, *Lights and Shadows*, 48.

4. Olmstead, *David Zeisberger*, 325–35; Hawk, "Foreword," in Wildman, *Sign Language*, 12–14.

5. Wildman, *Sign Language*, 48–49. Cf. Debo, *History of the Indians*, 89; Wallace, *Long, Bitter Trail*, 26–27, 32.

grounds. Some Indians were mystified. Some were angered. Many became dispirited. Yet native leaders saw clearly what was happening. They coped as best they could—whether by flight, violence, or accommodation.

By 1890 the white population controlled the continent, Atlantic to Pacific, Canada to Mexico. For all practical purposes, the Indians had vanished. The "vanishing Indian" and "vanishing race" became clichés.[6] Robert Warrior commented in 1989, "The indigenous people of this hemisphere have endured a subjugation now one hundred years longer than the sojourn of Israel in Egypt."[7]

HOW THE WEST WAS OVERRUN

Through the years, the US Army found a variety of ways to fashion a final solution to the Indian problem, depending on local circumstances. Sometimes it was open warfare, especially on the prairies with Indians who now had ponies and rifles. Sometimes it was through total devastation of Indian villages—burning teepees and buffalo robes and anything else combustible; breaking holes in earthenware pots, so the Indians would starve.

Several times it was outright massacres of men, women, and children. Such assaults might come in retaliation for Indian attacks on settlers or Indian agencies. Often, however, those slaughtered were not the same Indians, or even the same tribes, as those who launched the attacks.

The mass killing of buffalo, though a flourishing business, was also understood as a good way to finish off the Indians.[8]

Over centuries treaty-breaking was carried out—partly by intent, partly by deceit, partly by bureaucratic corruption or incompetence. A typical example of deceit involved the Winnebagos of Michigan and Wisconsin. In 1837 a Winnebago delegation went to Washington to negotiate a treaty. In the nation's capital they were pressured into vacating land in Wisconsin only recently granted them and moving farther west into an area of Iowa already inhabited by other tribes. The Winnebago were assured they had eight years to make the move. Later they discovered the treaty specified

6 See Dippie, *Vanishing American*.

7. Warrior, "Canaanites, Cowboys, and Indians," 8.

8. Though technically bison, the term *buffalo* is so widely used that it is employed here.

only eight months. An interpreter revealed that he had been instructed to trick the Winnebago delegates.[9]

Treaty-making with Indians was from the start an imposition. Indians repeatedly ceded land over while they had no concept of private property or legal ownership. They simply recognized they had no survivable option other than to abandon lands they had long considered free and sacred, and to move to restricted or "reserved" areas defined by the whites.

It was not a question, in other words, of exchange of legal property ownership or "real estate." It was a case of sheer expulsion from ancestral lands through the pretense of a legal framework. In most cases the US government, through surveys and maps, knew just how much land was involved, whereas the Indians had only a more general sense of the land's extent.

Treaties usually promised annual cash payments for many years in exchange for huge tracts of land and Indian confinement on reservations. But promised annuities often arrived late, or not at all. When the cash did come, the Indians found that white traders claimed most of it for things Indians had allegedly bought on credit, or for damages. More than once, Indians were left nearly destitute as harsh northern winters arrived. This kind of mistreatment sometimes sparked Indian uprisings or attacks—which of course then brought severe white retaliation.

The "winning" of the Great Plains took several decades, from the 1840s to 1890. But the conquering and displacement of native populations followed the pattern already set east of the Mississippi and in the Michigan, Wisconsin, and Minnesota territories in the years leading up to statehood, roughly 1805 to 1850.[10]

THE PEOPLES OF THE LAKES

The opening of the Erie Canal in 1825 swung "wide the gates for emigrants from the east" into the Great Lakes region. By 1830 whites vastly outnumbered Indians, who probably totaled less than 100,000, compared with 1.7 million white residents.[11]

---

9. Editors of Time-Life Books, *People of the Lakes*, 161.

10. Michigan was officially a "territory" from 1805 until statehood in 1837, as was Wisconsin (which initially included what later became Minnesota) from 1836 to statehood in 1848, and Minnesota, from 1849 until statehood in 1858.

11. Editors of Time-Life Books, *People of the Lakes*, 159.

Between 1795 and 1842, seventeen treaties were made with native tribes through which all of Michigan was ceded to the US government—from the Treaty of Greenville, Ohio, in 1795 and the Treaty of Detroit in 1807, to the Treaty of LaPointe, Wisconsin Territory, in 1842. These involved primarily the Chippewa (Ojibwa), Potawatomi, and Ottawa peoples, but also others.[12]

As early as 1819, Michigan territorial Governor Lewis Cass pressured Ojibwa leaders into a treaty ceding a large swath of central Michigan to the United States. The book *People of the Lakes* notes: "For persuasive effect, Cass brought along a company of U.S. Army troops and a shipment of 'presents' that included nearly 200 gallons of liquor. When the assembled Ojibwas refused to come to terms, traders and interpreters at the council offered individual chiefs inducements of goods, guns, and alcohol to bring them around" (an approach that was becoming common practice in the treaty-making business). The Ojibwas signed over about six million acres and were restricted to a reservation of only about 100,000 acres.[13]

Today high school sports teams in Manistee, Michigan, are called the Manistee Chippewas.

Charles DeLand, in his 1903 history of Michigan's Jackson County, described the removal of the Potawatomi people in southern Michigan:

> In 1839 and 1840 the general government effected the removal of most of the Pottawattomies to the reservation set apart for them near Green Bay, Wisconsin. The Fourth United States Infantry . . . and four companies of the Second United States Cavalry, . . . came to Jackson . . . and began to gather up the Indians. About fifteen hundred were collected and the Indians were escorted to Detroit and embarked on boats to Green Bay. In the fall of 1840 there was another round-up, and all but a few scattering bands were removed. . . . The removal of the red men abated a great nuisance to the settlers, though they were not considered dangerous. . . . But they were . . . a great nuisance and the people were rejoiced to be rid of them.[14]

One witness to this forced removal was Lydia Lane, wife of the publisher for the Methodist Episcopal Church, George Lane. In September, 1840, Mrs. Lane was traveling with her husband, visiting Methodist annual

---

12. LeBeau, *Rethinking Michigan*, 195–96.

13. Editors of Time-Life Books, *People of the Lakes*, 160.

14. DeLand, *History of Jackson County*, 53.

conferences. In a letter to her niece Ellen Stowe in New York City, Lydia described a visit to a US Army encampment near Marshall, Michigan, where she saw firsthand the Indian removal. She wrote, "The commanding officer came out and invited us within their lines, we had an opportunity of viewing their tents and seeing the Indian families they are collecting. They have orders to gather all the Pottowattimy [sic] Indians, and remove them from the state of Michigan. Poor creatures they are unwilling to be removed and I do not wonder, for this was their father's land, and is also their home, which they will love with an everlasting love."[15]

Lydia Lane looked upon the Potawatomi as a mother and a compassionate Christian. She is one example of the many Christian workers and missionaries throughout the centuries of Indian exploitation who voiced concern and in some cases protested or intervened.

Another was Episcopal Bishop Henry Whipple in Minnesota.

BISHOP WHIPPLE OF MINNESOTA

Henry Benjamin Whipple (1822–1901), the first Episcopal bishop of Minnesota, left a remarkable 576-page autobiography, *Lights and Shadows of a Long Episcopate*, which gives keen insights into Native American and white settler conflicts in Minnesota during and following the US Civil War.[16]

Going to Minnesota from Chicago in 1859, Bishop Whipple soon found himself in the middle of Indian issues. Gustav Niebuhr's 2014 book *Lincoln's Bishop: A President, a Priest, and the Fate of 300 Dakota Sioux Warriors* focuses on these issues and especially the so-called Dakota War of 1862.[17]

Henry Whipple was born in far upstate New York. He married and became an Episcopal priest. His talents were recognized early, and he was recruited to do pioneer mission work in Chicago, especially among railroad workers. Earlier Whipple spent a year at Oberlin College in Ohio, where his uncle taught mathematics. Whipple wrote that "The Rev. Charles Finney, president of the college, was a remarkable man. His kindness and

15. Letter, Mrs. Lydia Lane to Ellen Stowe, Sept. 2, 1840. Cited in Snyder, *Populist Saints*, 53. Ellen Stowe, then a teenager, later became the wife of Benjamin T. Roberts, principal founder of the Free Methodist Church.

16. Whipple, *Lights and Shadows*.

17. Niebuhr, *Lincoln's Bishop*. See also Oehler, *Great Sioux Uprising*, especially 212–13.

consideration toward me I shall never forget, and his loving interest in my career gave him a sacred place in my memory."[18]

Whipple had success in Chicago, building a vibrant congregation. His ministry embodied a transforming, Christ-centered gospel.

To his surprise, Whipple was elected the first Episcopal bishop of Minnesota in 1859, at the age of thirty-seven. He served in that capacity for over forty years, until his death in 1901.

Taking up his duties in Minnesota, Whipple found himself confronted by conflicts between Native Americans and the growing tide of white settlers—as well as the US military, which became the prime agent for pushing the Indians farther and farther off their lands and onto small, often barren reservations. A man of great cultural sensitivity, Whipple quickly developed a keen love for the native peoples. He initiated successful mission work among the Dakota Sioux and other tribes.

Then came the Dakota War of 1862—right at the height of the US Civil War. A band of Dakota Sioux killed about 800 white settlers, including whole families. The perpetrators were a renegade group of young Dakota warriors who were incensed not so much by the settlers themselves as by the US government's failure to honor treaties made, leaving many of the Indians destitute.

The US Cavalry intervened. Hundreds of Indians—most of whom had nothing to do with the violence—were rounded up. After hasty trials more than 300 Dakota Sioux were condemned to death by hanging.

Bishop Whipple was aghast—both at the trials and at the widespread thirst for revenge against *all* Indians. He wrote articles and preached sermons explaining the circumstances leading to the outbreak of violence. His key role however was in appealing directly to President Abraham Lincoln.

Whipple traveled to Washington, DC and secured an interview with the president. To his credit, Lincoln, though nearly overwhelmed by Civil War responsibilities, requested a record of the trials. Niebuhr writes, "On December 6 [1862] Lincoln said that he had reviewed the trial records and found evidence in only thirty-nine cases that would warrant capital punishment." It is clear, Niebuhr says, that Lincoln "had come down on mercy's side. He would spare 87 percent of the convicted Dakotas."[19]

Lincoln's verdict upset whites in Minnesota. But Whipple supported and defended it. He continued advocating for Indian rights, and

18. Whipple, *Lights and Shadows*, 4.
19. Niebuhr, *Lincoln's Bishop*, 162, 163.

in particular for reform of the US Department of Indian Affairs, which he criticized as corrupt and incompetent.

Meanwhile in Minnesota, authorities in 1863 placed a bounty on Indian scalps after some starving Ojibwas turned to violence. The *St. Paul Pioneer Press* announced: "Good News for Indian Hunters—The Indian-hunting trade is likely to prove a profitable investment to our hunters and scouts in the Big Woods, the Commander-in-Chief having increased the bounty for each top-knot of a 'bloody heathen' to $200."[20]

Bishop Whipple had his own blind spots and prejudices, of course. But in the 400-year dreary, often bloody history of American Indians being forced from their native lands and way of life, Whipple represents that small parade of Christians who stand as conscientious exceptions. There were many others: Earlier, William Penn in Pennsylvania; Christian missionaries who protested injustices at the time of Congress's Indian Removal Act of 1830; and others, both earlier and later. Regarding the 1862 Sioux uprising and the white backlash, C. M. Oehler writes: "Only the missionaries held out hope for the future."[21]

Meanwhile the Department (later Bureau) of Indian Affairs remained largely immune to reform. When Ulysses S. Grant came to the US presidency he tried appointing genuine Christians as Indian agents. His so-called "Quaker Policy" brought improvements here and there. Yet, as Ralph Andrist notes, "before [Grant's] term ended . . . both his Secretary of the Interior and Secretary of War [were] forced out of office because of corruption in connection with Indian affairs." The hard fact remained that "no Quaker Policy or other reform . . . was going to save the Indian as long as he stood in the way of Western pioneers."[22]

"CALL UP THE CAVALRY!"

As the US frontier spread further west across the Great Plains, the Army established dozens more bases to protect settlers and the scores of pioneer wagon trains rocking along the Oregon, Santa Fe, and Smoky Hill trails. The many Indian tribes scattered across the Great Plains sometimes fought to protect their homes, families, and habitats.

20. Editors of Time-Life Books, *People of the Lakes*, 164.

21. Oehler, *Great Sioux Uprising*, 212.

22. Andrist, *Long Death*, 159.

Fort Riley, along the Smoky Hill Trail about two hundred miles west of Kansas City, was established in 1853. It is still an active Army base and the site of the US Cavalry Museum and the former home of General George Armstrong Custer.

One of the Cavalry Museum's displays focuses on "Indian Engagements of the West, 1857–1890"—that is, the Indian Wars that began as pioneers moved west and ended only with the massacre at Wounded Knee, South Dakota, in December, 1890. Over those four decades, multiplied numbers of plains tribes were attacked and either killed or forced onto tiny reservations where life was unsustainable.

Ralph Andrist's remarkable study *The Long Death: The Last Days of the Plains Indians* covers in detail this period of the Indian Wars—the half century leading up to 1890 during which Plains Indians were all but annihilated.

The Long Death is painful reading, for it's full of blood and massacres, misunderstandings and broken treaties. One section of the book explains "The Techniques of Treaty-Breaking."

The larger story goes back to the 1830 Indian Removal Act passed by Congress—really, in fact, all the way back to Jamestown in 1607 and Pocahontas. After 1830 the American government relentlessly forced all eastern tribes onto reservations. Then most of these tribes were pushed farther west across the Mississippi. The Plains Indians were in turn driven even farther west.

As hundreds of wagon trains carried white settlers across the Great Plains toward the West Coast, the Indians were pressed still harder. Huge buffalo herds were wiped out. Repeatedly treaties were made and broken. Skirmishes continued for decades—Indians attacking wagon trains; US Cavalry striking back, bloodily destroying Indian villages, including women and children. Young Indian warriors destroyed white homesteads, sometimes committing atrocities, prompting retaliation by US forces, sparking further Indian attacks. Scalps were collected and proudly displayed on both sides.

We still live with the clichés: "circle the wagons," "call up the cavalry," "the only good Indian is a dead Indian," "Custer's last stand."[23]

---

23. The 1876 Battle of the Little Bighorn in what is now Montana, in which Custer died, and the many mistakes and miscalculations leading up to it, are thoroughly covered in Andrist, *Long Death,* 239–300. See also Van de Water, *Glory-Hunter;* Wert, *Custer.*

Army leaders struggling to pacify the West were often outspoken about their strategy and intentions. Generals made famous by the US Civil War, such as William Tecumseh Sherman and Philip H. Sheridan, said the Indians must be eliminated entirely. Others voiced similar sentiments, if more obliquely.

When Ulysses S. Grant became president in 1869, Sherman succeeded him as Army commanding general. Sheridan in turn succeeded Sherman as a key commander in the Indian Wars. After a military defeat at the hands of Sioux warriors in 1866 Sherman said, "We must act with vindictive earnestness against the Sioux, even to their extermination, men, women and children. Nothing else will reach the root of this case." In later battles with a small band of Modoc Indians along the California-Oregon border, Sherman instructed the Army commander involved: "You will be fully justified in their utter extermination."[24]

Similarly in late 1879 Colorado Governor Frederick Pitkin was quoted as saying of the White River Utes, "My idea is that, unless removed by the government, they must necessarily be exterminated."[25] As usual, the underlying issue was land.

Andrist notes that by the 1870s "the Army had learned that the best way to fight Indians was to go after them, coldly and ruthlessly, with the main purpose of wiping out everything they possessed." An example was the killing of 1,400 Indian horses and mules after a conflict in northern Texas in 1875. Soldiers methodically destroyed teepees, arrows, dried meat, tanned hides, buffalo robes, and cooking kettles, burning everything that would burn, "great coils of greasy smoke" rising above the canyon where the village had been.[26]

Meanwhile, in Washington, DC, the US Congress passed a series of laws that further eroded Indian rights. Most far-reaching was the Dawes Act of 1887. The law authorized the US President to allocate Indian reservation land to individual Indian owners—who could in turn sell it.[27] Thom Fassett writes, "In 1887, Indian tribes collectively owned about 140 million acres of land. The net effect of [the Dawes Act] was to allow over 90 million acres of land to pass to non-Indian ownership within forty-five years. So-

24. Andrist, *Long Death*, 124, 227.

25. Ibid., 331.

26. Ibid., 195.

27. Rynkiewich, "Mission in an Age of Imperialism," 8; Fassett, *Giving Our Hearts*, 63–64.

called 'surplus' Indian land [not allocated to individual Indians or Indian families] was sold off or opened to land rush races with emigrants staking their claims for both survival and profit."[28]

END OF THE INDIAN WARS

The defeat of the Indians and the pacification of the Great Plains was vastly accelerated by the arrival of the railroads in the 1860s. The Union Pacific pushed west from Omaha in 1865. Four years later, on May 10, 1869, it joined up with the Central Pacific, expanding eastward from San Francisco. This first transcontinental railroad was soon followed by others, quickly spawning hundreds of branch lines.

The railroads and the telegraph worsened life for the Indians. In fact, for virtually every development that white Americans called progress, the Indians experienced as new techniques of oppression and dispossession.

The railroads sped up the destruction of the Great Plains' surging buffalo herds. Mass slaughter of buffalo began in the 1870s. The Plains Indians quickly "saw their way of life threatened as nothing that had happened so far had threatened it."[29]

Buffalo hunting became organized and highly profitable, once eastern tanneries discovered how to turn the hides into usable leather.[30] Soon a buffalo-hide rush was on. "Once it was systematized, the killing of buffalo for hides was a pathetically businesslike operation in which the beast had not the slightest chance," notes Andrist. Teams of hunters fanned out over the plains. Experienced and skilled hunters could slaughter 100 or more buffalo a day, keeping four or five skinners busy, morning to night.[31]

The resulting scene of scattered white buffalo skeletons made clear the scale of the slaughter. "Parts of Kansas that had been carpeted with grazing buffalo a season [earlier] were now great expanses of bones." In fact many a settler arriving in the early 1870s got through the first year or two by gathering and selling bison bones—a first "cash crop." Settlers carted the bones to nearby railway stations to be shipped back east to fertilizer plants and also to sugar refineries, which used them for carbon. "Huge ricks of

28. Fassett, *Giving Our Hearts*, 64.

29. Andrist, *Long Death*, 177.

30. Gwynne, *Empire*, 258–62. The killing of buffalo also became an organized and profitable sport, with trains dedicated exclusively to this purpose.

31. Andrist, *Long Death*, 181.

bones were piled along railroad sidings (one 12 ft. high, almost 12 ft. wide at the base, and ½ mile long was reported at Granada, Colorado)." Some freight trains "carried nothing but bones, and the Santa Fe alone hauled seven million tons of them in 1874" in "a sad commerce that continued for many seasons," Andrist reports.[32]

When it was all over, ten million buffalo were gone.

This combination of settler expansion, treaty making and breaking, military action, and habitat destruction brought the era of Indian North America to an end.[33]

Andrist summarizes:

> The entire [Great Plains] had been solemnly pledged to the Indians by the government in the years before 1840, to have and to hold forever. Even though the promise of the United States to Indian tribes had been proved worthless again and again, there were special circumstances that made many sincere men believe that here in the West, for the first time, an Indian treaty would actually be honored. But nothing was different. The usual encroachments by frontiersmen soon began, and steadily increased until the hardest-pressed tribes lashed back. Before long, the bright flames of open war were flickering up and down the plains, not to be completely extinguished for almost thirty years.[34]

Ironically, during most of this period eastern whites considered the Great Plains worthless—a "Great Desert." The goal was to cross it and reach more promising land in California and Oregon—and then the mountains, once gold was found.

So by 1890 "the Indian wars of the plains were ended, and with them the long struggle of the American Indians, from the Atlantic to the Pacific, to preserve some portion of their ancestral lands and tribal ways."[35] The remaining Indians were confined to reservations.

One of the great Indian chiefs, Satanta of the Kiowa, said: "I don't want to settle. I love to roam over the prairies. . . . These soldiers cut down my

---

32. Ibid., 182.

33. Vine Deloria documents the ways "pacification" and treaty breaking were practiced toward the end of this period in the Pacific Northwest (*Indians of the Pacific Northwest*).

34. Andrist, *Long Death*, 2.

35. Ibid., 1.

timber; they kill my buffalo; and when I see that it feels as if my heart would burst with sorrow."[36]

But it wasn't just Sioux and Kiowa, Chippewa and Potawatomi who were forced from their lands. It was also Pequot, Cherokee, Massachusett, Hopi, Kansa, Lenape (Delaware), Iowa, Osage, Creek, Choctaw, Chickasaw, Cowlitz, Wallawalla, Mashpee, Nisqually, Seminole, Crow, Omaha, Fox, Sauk, Arapaho, Comanche, Ponca, Cheyenne, Apache, Pawnee, Nez Percé, Mandan, Monacans, Arikara, Miami, Navajo, Hidatsa, Assiniboine, Blackfeet, Shoshone, Atsina, Quinault, Quileute, Chehali, Chinook, Winnebago, Ute, Oto, Snake, Penobscot, Bannock, Wampanoag, Powhatan, Peoria, Lakota, Chickahominy, Iroquois, Tonkawa, Wichita, Caddo, Modoc, Klamath, Santee, Yankton, Yakima, Yamacraw, Yamasee, Yuchi, Oglala, Makah, Brule, and many, many others.[37]

By 1900, most of the solemn treaties of the previous 200 years had become dead letters. Fassett notes that from 1776 to 1871 "the United States and Indian nations entered into well over four hundred legal agreements that were recognized as covenants between sovereign nation powers according to the Constitution, Article VI, Section 2."[38] As the twentieth century dawned, most of these had been so compromised as to be meaningless—nothing but dead historical artifacts.

It is a long story, but it began in the days of Pocahontas and of Plymouth Rock. The story had played out already in the so-called King Philip's War of 1676, in the vicinity of Plymouth, Massachusetts—one of the earliest conflicts between the English and Native Americans. As the Puritans increasingly encroached on their lands, Wampanoag warriors attacked, bringing a Puritan counteroffensive. The key Wampanoag leader was Metacomet, known to the English as King Philip.

---

36. Ibid., 146.

37. Indian tribal names are difficult to sort out since some are French, Spanish, or English transliterations of native names, some are descriptive or derogatory names given by whites, and some are regional subgroups of larger tribal groups. Indians that the whites called Sioux called themselves Dakota, meaning "allies." Andrist calls "Sioux" "an etymological monstrosity," the truncated form of a French form of a Chippewa word meaning "little snake" (which was the Chippewa designation for their enemies the Dakota). The large Sioux nation used the names Dakota, Nakota, and Lakota to designate respectively their eastern prairie tribes, the tribes known to whites as the Yankton, and the western Teton Sioux (Andrist, *Long Death*, 265).

38. Fassett, *Giving Our Hearts*, 42. Fassett traces the story on through the twentieth century, up to 2008 (48–125).

The war brought Metacomet's death on August 12, 1676. He had warned his compatriots earlier, "Brothers, these people from the unknown world will cut down our groves, spoil our hunting and planting grounds, and drive us and our children from the graves of our fathers, and our council fires, and enslave our women and children."[39]

But to the Puritans, the Indians were enemies—both theirs and God's. Robert Warrior notes, "Many Puritan preachers were fond of referring to Native Americans as Amelkites [sic] and Canaanites—in other words, people who, if they would not be converted, were worthy of annihilation." It is easy to understand, says Warrior, "how America's self-image as a 'chosen people' had provided a rhetoric to mystify domination."[40]

In his account of King Philip's War, Increase Mather noted that the Puritans had earlier captured and imprisoned Metacomet's wife and son. Mather wrote, "Thus hath God brought that grand Enemy into great misery before he quite destroy him. It must needs be bitter as death to him, to loose [sic] his Wife and only Son (for the Indians are marvelous fond and affectionate towards their Children)."[41]

So the conquest spread from east to west. As the Indian Wars were winding down nearly 300 years later, the language of "winning the West" became common currency and unexamined myth. Young Theodore Roosevelt, still in his thirties, set the pattern with his four-volume *The Winning of the West,* published between 1889 and 1896. Roosevelt pictured a new race emerging—*Americans*—white America, the latest embodiment of the fit displacing the unfit.[42]

Roosevelt decried all "sentimental nonsense" about "taking the Indians' land." In fact the western Indians "never had any real ownership in it at all." Mostly the Indians roamed about, following herds of game; they could claim no rights to the land itself. Indian and white settlers should be treated "the same way," Roosevelt said. Give each Indian "his little claim"; if he refuses it, "then let him share the fate of the thousands of white hunters and trappers who have lived on the game that the settlement of the country

39. Calloway, *First Peoples,* 128.

40. Warrior, "Canaanites, Cowboys, and Indians," 7.

41. Calloway, *First Peoples,* 126.

42. Morris, *Rise of Theodore Roosevelt,* 387–88; Goodwin, *Bully Pulpit,* 129. *The Winning of the West* was one of Roosevelt's most major and influential works.

has exterminated, and let him, like these whites, who will not work, perish from the face of the earth which he cumbers."[43]

This is how the West was won.

43. Roosevelt, *Memories of the American Frontier*, 40–41.

Chapter Seventeen

_____

Pocahontas in Heaven

Pocahontas died in 1617. What happened next? Can we imagine Pocahontas in heaven?

We can visualize Pocahontas experiencing heaven in two quite different ways. One reflects the traditional Christian conception, which Pocahontas would have learned from Alexander Whitaker. The other is the vision of creation healed, the full biblical promise.

POCAHONTAS: THE BEATIFIC VISION

Pocahontas's spirit left her body on March 21, 1617, in Gravesend, England. Instantly Pocahontas knew she was in God's presence. Brilliant light; a sense of angels hovering, a feeling of flying away from earth.

Whether her spirit had slept for many, many years before entering the immediate presence of God, or whether her physical death brought her instantly into paradise, she couldn't tell. The question never came to mind. Now, Pocahontas knew, she was living in a new, endless reality, a realm where space and time were no more.

Pocahontas sensed she was drawing near the brilliant throne of the Lord God, the Ever-Living One. What seemed to be clouds colored by the rising sun began to fade, melting away. The light was dazzling, yet not fearsome. Now she saw a great throne, and seated there was the Lord God, the Almighty.

Her impressions were of light, and color, and brilliance, and joy, and love. The sparkling light looked like a spray of bright jewels. All around was a wonderful luminous, glowing rainbow.

Pocahontas knew she was in the awesome presence of the holy triune God—the very presence of the Father, the Holy Spirit, and Jesus Christ. Many other spirits were present all around. The great throne was encircled by other thrones, and glorious beings dressed in white, crowned with golden crowns, were seated there.

Light, color, more light, and a sense of awe, yet of joy and peace. Sounds like those of a great choir, accompanied by a timpani of rumbling thunder. Somehow Pocahontas sensed that God's very Spirit was around and above and within her, and Jesus was her comfort.

Flaming, flying creatures were all about. Pocahontas didn't know what they were, but they seemed to be angels. She had the impression of moving wings and myriad seeing eyes. The air was full of the sound of praise from millions of voices, and she understood the song: "Holy, holy, holy, is the Lord God the Almighty, who was and is and is to come."

The song praised God for the glorious work of creation and salvation. The song praised Jesus Christ, the One who was slain and now lives forever. The song continued: "To the one seated on the throne and to the Lamb be blessing and honor and glory and might forever and ever!" It seemed to rise from every creature, every voice in all creation (Rev 5:13).

Looking around, Pocahontas now saw a great multitude of people, way beyond counting. She could see they came from many different tribes and peoples. They raised their hands and voices in praise to God. Pocahontas quickly and gladly joined in. She found herself singing, "Hallelujah! Salvation and glory and power to our God! Hallelujah! For the Lord our God, the Almighty One, reigns forever and ever" (Rev 19:1, 6).

Gradually the sea of faces became clearer, and Pocahontas began to recognize some people. There was her son Thomas! There was her beloved husband John! Now she recognized some of her own kinsmen, many Powhatan who had come to know Jesus Christ as Savior. She felt a bond of love and communion with each and all.

And together they all joined in praising Almighty God forever and ever. A great and mighty choir of praise.

Perhaps this was Pocahontas's experience.

Or maybe not. Maybe we have it wrong. Perhaps rather it was like this:

POCAHONTAS: CREATION HEALED

When Pocahontas's spirit left her body on March 21, 1617, she saw light and felt herself in the immediate presence of God. At first all she could see was light in brilliant colors, and she heard music. She didn't know whether her spirit had slept for many, many years as her body lay in the Gravesend cemetery, or whether her physical death had brought her instantly into paradise. The question never came to mind. Now she was living in wide dimensions of reality where space and time no longer mattered.

Pocahontas watched fascinated as the brilliant light resolved gradually into rainbow colors—brilliant blues and greens and yellows; softer shades, changing; shining cloud-like mists dissolving into a new emerging reality. And Jesus was there. She had sensed his presence from the first instant. Now she began to see his form. His face shone like the sun, and his clothes were dazzling white. And it seemed his Spirit was all around, and within her.

She had a feeling of air and space, vastness. But the colors started to change, and she began to see what looked like a blue haze. Then the haze began melting away, and she could see blue skies above and blue, gentle ocean waves below. She seemed to be moving forward, sky above, waves below. Now birds appeared in the sky, white and black and brown, like gulls.

Pocahontas looked ahead and thought she saw trees, and a shoreline. She was moving closer. She seemed to float above the water.

Yes, she could see clearly now—the shore, trees, a vast forest, rocks, sand, grass, ferns and flowers. The shore shone with God's glory.

It all looked new, and yet familiar. These were trees and flowers she knew. As she drew nearer, she recognized the place.

This was home, the place of her birth—Tsenacomoco, the land the English had called Virginia.

Now she was walking along the shore. She reached down and picked up a handful of damp sand, let it run gently through her fingers. Some grains stuck to her skin. She looked around at the trees. Oaks, birches, some pines and hickories—she remembered all their Powhatan names. Nuts were growing large on the hickories; acorns on the oaks.

Something moved along the ground at the edge of the trees. It was a fat raccoon, and it showed no fear. Pocahontas walked closer and laughed as she saw the raccoon glance her way, then waddle by and move on.

Pocahontas knew she was not alone. She could sense people around her. Her husband John and son Thomas ran up to her, with big hugs. How

Thomas had grown! But she knew him instantly. Now others were joining them.

"Who are these?" Pocahontas asked John.

"Grandchildren! Great grandchildren!" John smiled back. "Let me introduce them . . ."

A little later as Pocahontas started walking into the forest, she saw that Jesus was now ahead of her, standing there, Jesus alone, leaning against a great oak, his hand flat against the rough bark. He was looking directly at her. His quiet expression and eyes seemed to say, "Welcome home! Do not be afraid!"

Now they were walking together through the forest and into an open meadow in the cool of the day. Pocahontas, John, Thomas, others, walking slowly with Jesus. Tiny child's hands grasped hers. Pocahontas felt the grass under her feet. The slanting rays of the sun caught orange, yellow, and multicolored butterflies and dragonflies hovering above the grasses and flowers.

"Come," Jesus said. He led them on. Now they heard the sound of singing. As they walked it grew louder, sounding like a great choir.

They passed again through a stand of trees, filled with birds and squirrels, and saw other living creatures. Some large elk passed slowly—a huge buck, and some does and fawns. Beautiful, stately, unhurried.

Pocahontas could see they were approaching a large clearing. The singing grew louder. She saw the clearing was full of people. Who were they? Some Powhatan, she recognized. Also English, and some dressed in clothing and costumes she didn't know. She saw Indians of other tribes, including Susquehannock and Monacan, once mortal enemies of the Powhatan.

A great multitude of people. Men, women, children. Different, but all singing the same song. All singing praise to Jesus, the unparalleled Savior, Healer, and Re-creator. Light shone all about, and God in all his glory—Father, Son, and Holy Spirit—was praised, and she heard the sound of the rushing of mighty waters. Animals—she saw a bear and a panther—were standing or walking about, seemingly attentive to the music.

Pocahontas and her family joined in the music, gladly yet almost involuntarily.

But after some time Jesus led them farther into the woods, and along the river. Soon Pocahontas saw that this was the Pamunkey River, the river the English call York, the very river on whose shores she had played as a child. Children even now were playing in the shallow water at the river's edge, a mix of children—some black, some white, some of other hues. They were laughing and splashing.

Farther on Pocahontas saw a young woman standing under a huge Shagbark hickory. She was doing something; Pocahontas couldn't see what. The woman reminded her of herself years and years ago. Pocahontas drew nearer and saw that the woman was painting a beautiful picture of the trees and flowers at the sunlit edge of a meadow.

Walking farther, Pocahontas saw a mixed group of adults, men and women, sitting about in a circle, though some were standing. They seemed engaged in intense conversation, stretching their minds and wits.

Suddenly—pondering all she had just seen—words arose in Pocahontas's mind. She recalled a passage from Isaiah:

> The wolf shall live with the lamb,
>   the leopard shall lie down with the kid,
>   the calf and the lion and the fatling together,
>   and a little child shall lead them.
> The cow and the bear shall graze,
>   their young shall lie down together;
>   and the lion shall eat straw like the ox.
> The nursing child shall play over the hole of the asp,
>   and the weaned child shall put its hand on the adder's den.
> They will not hurt or destroy
>   on all my holy mountain;
>   for the earth will be full of the knowledge of the Lord
>   as the waters cover the sea (Isa 11:6–9).

As Pocahontas and Jesus and the others walked on, another Scripture came to mind. Alexander Whitaker had pointed it out to her long, long ago: "They shall all sit under their own vines and under their own fig trees, and no one shall make them afraid; for the mouth of the Lord of hosts has spoken" (Mic 4:4). "That's a picture of God's kingdom promises fulfilled," Rev. Whitaker had said.

They walked on in silence. Then Jesus said, "This is the new earth and heaven. I am making all things new, as promised."

Jesus continued, "You remember what you were taught from the Scriptures. It was necessary that I should suffer and then enter into my glory." Then beginning with Moses and all the prophets, Jesus interpreted to Pocahontas all the things about himself in all the Scriptures.

Jesus said to Pocahontas, "Touch me and see. I am not a ghost, not a mere spirit! I have flesh and bones, as you can see."

"It is just as I said at the beginning," Jesus continued. "Everything written about me in the law of Moses, the prophets, and the Psalms has now been fulfilled. I had to suffer and to rise again from the dead, so that repentance and forgiveness of sins could be proclaimed in my name to every nation on earth. Now I've come back to live on earth, just as I promised.

"You see there is plenty of room here," Jesus said. "If it were not so, I would have told you. I have prepared a place for you, just as I said. No one need steal another's land or name now, Matoaka."

Pocahontas stopped, stunned. "You spoke my real name!"

"Yes, of course. Your old name, your secret name, Matoaka, restored. Healed. Now it's your New Name. No one will ever take it from you.

"I am pleased with you, Matoaka, and I know your name. Before you were formed in the womb I knew you. Before you were born I had a purpose for you.

"I have loved you with an everlasting love," he said. "I was faithful to you when you didn't know it."

Pocahontas thought. "And I have loved you, hardly knowing you, since John Rolfe and Mr. Whitaker first showed me your love," she said.

Jesus smiled. "I call all my sheep by name, and lead them in pleasant paths," he said. "I give names as well to all the stars and planets and plants and birds and butterflies, and the whales in the sea. Until now you have seen dimly, as in a looking glass, or at a distance. Now you will know fully, just as I fully know you."

Pocahontas felt her mind wondrously opening to new vistas of truth and glory. She recalled the words from long ago: "Now we see in a mirror, dimly, but then we will see face to face. Now I know only in part; then I will know fully, even as I have been fully known." Joy overwhelmed her, yet completely satisfied her deepest soul.

As Pocahontas walked on through creation restored, she thought again of Jesus words: "See, I make all things new."[1]

---

1. In addition to Scriptures verses specifically cited in this chapter, see Ps 23; Isa 54:48, 61:2; Jer 1:4–5, 31:3; Luke 24:25–47; John 10, 15; 1 Cor 13; Rev 2:17, 3:12, 21–22.

Chapter Eighteen

Pocahontas Speaks

Throughout this book, Pocahontas is mostly mute. Rarely has she spoken, and then sparingly. Her longest speech on record was her passionate outburst to John Smith in their final encounter just weeks before she died.

What would Pocahontas say now? What does she have to tell the world, and especially her descendants and admirers in America?

Certainly she would echo the words of the aged Lakota holy man Black Elk (c. 1863–1950), looking back on the historic 1890 Wounded Knee massacre:

> I did not know then how much was ended. When I look back now from this high hill of my old age, I can still see the butchered women and children lying heaped and scattered all along the crooked gulch as plain as when I saw them with eyes still young. And I can see that something else died there in the bloody mud, and was buried in the blizzard. A people's dream died there. It was a beautiful dream . . . The nation's hoop is broken and scattered. There is no centre any longer, and the sacred tree is dead.[1]

Pocahontas would say words something like these, and much else. We know this because of the few recorded words we *do* have from her, and because of her evidently keen cultural insight.

So let us, at last, listen to Pocahontas.

1. Wilson, *Earth Shall Weep*, xviii.

From her unique vantage point as a Native American who came to understand the British probably better than any other First Nations person—better even than themselves—Pocahontas saw and understood much. As a woman, she perceived things hidden to her compatriots, as well as to her English acquaintances. From the beginning it was clear she had unusual, if not uncanny, insight into cultural dynamics and differences.

Today Pocahontas still has much to say to contemporary Americans, as well as to her own people and the Christian Church.

Some won't listen, of course. We hear the voices: "That was long ago. A different time. History has moved on. Yes, there were tragic chapters in the early British and American encounters with native peoples, but now we're in a different age. We have made *progress*. We must focus on today's issues and problems, not burden ourselves with the past; be history's hostages. We're Americans! Not chained to yesterday."

To these, to all, Pocahontas speaks. Though we have few of her actual words, her life and example speak eloquently.[2]

LISTEN TO POCAHONTAS

I long thought John Smith was dead. Everyone at Jamestown said so. Why did they lie? When I got to England, I learned the truth.

Now I must speak *my* truth.

I told John, my husband, many things in private. He didn't really understand. He loved me, but he couldn't really understand.

And of course, I am *only a woman*. Yet he loved me and respected me and spoke tender words.

Many things I would have taught our son Thomas. Especially if we had returned to Virginia, to Tsenacomoco. I would have taught him about plants and fish, about flowers and medicines and butterflies. Showed him the roots and berries that make you sick and the ones that make you well, as my mother taught me. I would have taught him to love and protect all things living—birds of the air, whales of the sea, the lonely wayfaring albatross.

We would have walked under the vast night sky, and I would have pointed out the clusters of stars and their meaning while we listened for the owl and heard the night wind whisper in the trees.

2. Putting words in a historical character's mouth is at best a dubious enterprise, of course. What I present here is a summary of the message of Pocahontas's life and legacy, set in first-person singular. I believe Pocahontas does indeed still "speak" in these terms.

I would have taught him to love the Powhatan, *his own people*. Not just the English. To understand, be a bridge, as I once was. To love peace; be a peacemaker. A builder of harmony.

Of course I would have taught him about Jesus, and how to understand the Bible.

I would have, but it was not to be. That was long ago.

We can't go back. We must go forward. *Yet the past is still here.* It is still with us. Not to be forgotten. It does not go away.

I know what people say. History is gone. It is dead. Ages flow on like a river. We can't go back. Ancient wrongs cannot be righted. We must live in the present.

But *I* say: *History does not work that way.*

My land changed when I was just a girl. . . . England came to America.

America! Not even a native name. Not from the soil. Yet it's the name known to all the world, your common and spoken and "proper" name as a nation. You white people even stole many of our sacred tribal names for your states and rivers and lakes and cities. Massachusetts, Dakota, Minnesota, Miami, Mississippi, Manhattan, Chicago, Peoria, and many, many more.

You invented songs like "This is My Country" and "This land is your land, this land is my land." You named sports teams "Indians" and "Braves" and "Redskins"!

Mr. Whitaker taught me about the Bible and the love of Jesus. So did my husband John. But then my thoughts grew puzzled. John and Mr. Whitaker showed me love, the love they talked about. The love of God and good news from Jesus.

But I watched the lives of the white people of Jamestown and Henrico. They said they were good Christians. I saw them at the Eucharist. Some really were good Christians, kind and loving and just. But others, most of them . . .

It seemed a puzzle and a contradiction. Foremost—where was the love and the truth and the justice? Why did they kill my people, treat them cruelly, with deception? Why did they burn our crops and destroy our homes? I know my people struck back when they felt threatened. Sometimes they were cruel, yes. But *you* said you came to live in peace and harmony. You came in the name of a Christian king.

I found that few lived like Jesus. Few practiced the good news Mr. Whitaker taught.

Many of the English showed love for their own people but had no love or understanding for mine. Many were not truthful.

Your countrymen lie much.

Now they are *my* countrymen!

I studied the Creed. I read the Bible. I prayed and meditated. I had dreams and visions. I saw *three great sins*, but no repentance or atonement. Sins not even admitted.

I see the extinguishing of my people. I see genocide across the land. Many tribes and people. Wherever white men and women went, death followed. Disease was a fellow traveler. Nine of every ten of our people died. Solemn promises were made and unkept. Weeping women and little children. Many lamps extinguished. Darkness.

You stole our land; cut down our forests. You marched us west. My people. You promised new land, but it was barren and hard. Too small for the ranging wild animals. Not our land. No roots of our ancestors. No flowing rivers.

Do your people know what they have done? Where is repentance? Where is atonement? Where is restoration?

Then you brought slavery like we had never known. You unloaded black people, many of them ill, like limp sacks of coal from cramped, dirty ships. Many, many thousands! Ship after bloody ship. People from Africa—uprooted, confused, dispirited, angry, homeless. You made them animals. You bred them and bought and sold them and stole their babies and worked them to the ground. You broke up their tribes and poisoned their meaning. You made them sing their songs, and your songs, strange songs in a strange land.

You needed slaves, you thought, because our people were gone, and the work was hard.

Do your people know what they have done? Where is repentance? Where is atonement? Where is reparation?

You raped the land. You forced back the forest coverings and burned the prairies. You upset the music of the land and fouled the streams. You took away the homes of the birds and animals and flowers, our friends.

Now you have many pets, but no real animal friends.

You did not learn the music of nature; how to keep harmony.

You saw the wide earth as a wild-eyed enemy. You trampled down the soil that fed you and stomped the herbs and stopped the rivers that nourished you. You did not see that you needed them; that if the land dies, you die.

You killed the animals to fill your purse. You sent their warm coats far away. You killed the source of your own life.

Do your people know what they have done? Where is repentance? Where is atonement? Where is restitution?

Three great sins: Killing our people; staining the earth with the blood of slaves; and raping our land.

But to these I add a *fourth great sin*. Really it's the first. You sought gold above all else. You came to get rich. Nothing else mattered. So you killed the people, took the land, fouled the waters, killed the animals, and brought slaves in chains. Three great sins. No! Four great sins, *unatoned*. Quickly forgotten.

Where was your conscience?

And the sickness remains.

I could see it. I saw it coming.

Yes, your countrymen, our countrymen, lie much.

But now I rest. The words of Matoaka are finished.

Chapter Nineteen

The Uses of Pocahontas
and the Four Sins

We began examining native people's issues with Jamestown 1607 and the Pocahontas story. But as we lift our eyes above the Appalachians, over the Midwest, across the Great Plains and over the Rockies, all the way to the Pacific, what do we see? The same story over and over and over.

A story America has romanticized and sanitized, rather than coming to terms with it historically or ethically. We still call sports teams Redskins and Braves and Apaches.

Mostly the Pocahontas story, like many Old Testament stories, has been used in one of two ways: to justify national existence and expansion, or simply as a romantic tale showing how fascinating the nation's birth was. In such mythic uses of Pocahontas the contrasting stories of Jamestown and Plymouth were blended into the larger American myth. So we saw.

But when we pause to look at the real Pocahontas in light of the biblical gospel, Christian mission, and US history, questions arise.

Have American Christians ever come to terms with the self-serving myth of the United States as God's chosen people, a city on a hill, a light to the nations?

In the history of many nations we find similar pretensions and at times misappropriation of Scripture. But I am most familiar with the American myth.

In the Bible, images of "specialness" and divine election are never used to justify nationalism or patriotism or "destiny," manifest or otherwise. Israel's prophets eloquently make this clear. Consider for example Ezekiel, chapters 17–24, God's denunciation of Israel's pretensions.

On this point the Word speaks especially to the US situation. Viewed biblically, the real Pocahontas turns the American myth on its head. Especially it exposes the four cancerous American sins Pocahontas exposes—sins never really acknowledged, let alone atoned for.

STEALING THE LAND

Pocahontas speaks first of the stealing of native lands and the genocide of native peoples—America's original sin. Though well known and fully documented, this sin's moral meaning *has never been faced*. The scattered impoverished Indian reservations sprinkled helter-skelter across the landscape, plus the underclass of Native Americans in many large US cities, bear contemporary witness.

HUMAN SLAVERY

Then genocide led to slavery. From British plantations, African slavery was only a short bloody step. The first African slaves to reach North American shores arrived in Jamestown in 1619, not long after Pocahontas had died. The slaves beat the Pilgrims by two years.

The institution of hereditary slavery took quick root. Later it helped enthrone King Cotton. After the dying off of 90 percent of the native population in the 1500s, there simply weren't enough natives for back-breaking plantation work. Compelling slaves made compelling economic sense.

David Price notes the irony: The ship that brought the first captive African woman to Virginia in 1619 "was the same *Treasurer* that had brought Pocahontas to Jamestown in captivity" just a few years earlier.[1]

From Virginia, slavery inexorably spread. Jimmy Carter explains what happened further south: "Georgia had begun its early colonial existence in 1733 by rejecting fervently the concept of slavery, but this ideal yielded twenty years later to the influence of large landowners along the Atlantic coast who saw their neighbors in the Carolinas getting rich from rice,

---

1. Price, *Love and Hate*, 196.

silk, indigo, and cotton produced by the slave labor imported from Africa. Within a few decades after being legalized, slaves made up two-thirds of a plantation family's total wealth, with about one-half the remainder coming from the land they worked."[2]

RAPE OF THE LAND

Pocahontas speaks thirdly of the rape of the land. *Rape* is not too strong. North America was once clothed with rich forests, verdant plains, pristine rivers that nourished millions of species, and a flourishing ecology. But the colonial fantasy of conquest soon became national reality.

Later the Land Ordinance of 1785, passed by the Continental Congress, and the subsequent Indian Removal Act of 1830 and the Homestead Act of 1862 enabled the systematic dispossession of native lands as surveyors measured out the territory in six-mile-square townships whose straight lines often can still be seen in the grid of county and state roads across much of the United States.[3]

True, today large tracts of North America have been set aside as parks and wilderness. But myriad trees, plants, birds, fish, and animals died away and others face extinction in coming years. They won't return.[4]

THE RACE FOR RICHES

Three great sins, but really four. The constant race for riches, which the Bible so warns of, permeated all else. Gold is god and the dollar rules and quiets the conscience in the face of genocide, terracide, and human enslavement.

Repeatedly the US government in various guises made solemn treaties with native peoples. But one word could void all treaties, cancel all rights, and blast all ethical and moral sentiments—and that word was *gold*. Once pronounced, a land-grabbing, gold-grubbing free-for-all began.

From the beginning, the quest was for gold. Where literal gold was not found, other forms of wealth were: furs, buffalo hides, timber, river

2. Carter, *Hour Before Daylight*, 18–19.

3. Kukla, *Wilderness So Immense*, 51; Winchester, *Men Who United*, 10–16.

4. Some species may eventually be "recreated" through manipulation of preserved genetic material from extinct species. But even if this proves viable, at its best it would fall far short of restoring lost ecosystems and ecological niches.

commerce, Indian girls, and of course the land itself. The promise or prospect of riches trumps all else.

Yet deep down we know that people and the earth must come before profits. Otherwise the profit motive turns into a death wish.

Most Americans, including Christians, still have not learned to live in harmony with the earth. We have not learned *shalom*. We do not know the meaning of the land and how to thrive on and with it rather than bleaching it with poisons and paving it over with malls, parking lots, and sprawling highways. We do not understand that the land is much more than just a necessary bother, a commodity to be used in unsustainable industrial food production.

The land plays its own key role in the drama.

In 1962 Philip Young published a remarkable essay: "The Mother of Us All: Pocahontas Reconsidered." After examining the various images and faces of Pocahontas as we have done here, Young concludes: "Pocahontas is the archetypal sacrifice to respectability in America—a victim of what has been from the beginning our overwhelming anxiety to housebreak all things in nature, until wilderness and wildness be reduced to a few state parks and a few wild oats."[5]

Young's interpretation is that in giving herself to save John Smith but then not marrying him—rather, becoming separated and alienated from him—Pocahontas becomes the North American continent itself (the "virgin" land, Virginia and all that lay farther west). She gave herself to save the new nation. But for its part the nation fails to "marry," husband, nurture, protect, and care for the land—the natural environment with all its living things, both human and not.

So the story remains unfinished, hanging. Neither the land nor its peoples have been healed.

So Pocahontas becomes at once a national heroine and a strategic myth. All the more so when she gave herself a second time (after abduction!) to the colonists in her baptism and her marriage to John Rolfe. Pocahontas becomes the first Christian, the first American, the mother of us all.

But if we truly love Jesus and if we would love Pocahontas as Jesus did—the real flesh and blood DNA winsome Powhatan Pocahontas—we will still seek even now holistic and complete redemption: the "reconciliation of all things" that Jesus promised and provides.

---

5. Young, "Mother of Us All," 13–33 (quotation, 32).

The most impressive thing about Pocahontas, really, is her remarkable self-determination. Her sense of self and her resolve within the limits imposed on her to chart her own course; make up her own mind; choose wisely between looming alternatives. She seems to have done so not out of self-regard only, but out of concern for the world around her; the good of others.

How much this traced to Powhatan identity and "solidarity," and how much to her newfound Christian faith, we don't know. My own feeling is that in her mischievousness Pocahontas was inherently good-hearted; that because of this she responded positively to John Rolfe's interest and character; and that she was thus predisposed (by grace) to hear and receive the good news of Jesus Christ.

Whatever good Pocahontas received from her Christian instruction, and to whatever degree that good touched her heart and conscience, we also can't fully know. Not yet. Certainly the benefit she received from her new faith reinforced all that was already good and others-minded in her. Puritans would have seen all this as early signs of sovereign grace at work.

Pocahontas knew very well that she was living in a *man's* world—both among the English and with her own people. Her circle of real freedom was squeezed small, a corset not her own. She knew that all the key decisions shaping her life would be made by men.

That was a given; the way the world worked. But within those constraints she found a measure of freedom to be herself—either to push the boundaries or to turn them to her advantage if possible. Even her mischievousness suggests a capacity to see things simultaneously from both hers and others' perspectives.

Pocahontas's charisma won freedoms often denied other women, Indian or English. But as her short life shows, her freedom was bittersweet. It came at a cost.

John Smith and John Rolfe were by far the most admirable of all the English who played key roles with the Indians. Admirable and also capable, showing some cultural respect and understanding.

Both learned a lot from Pocahontas. How much Smith learned from Pocahontas and from his efforts to understand the Indians is suggested by his concluding words in *Description of New England*. "We are not born for ourselves," he wrote, "but to help each other."[6]

---

6. John Smith, *Description of New England* (1616), quoted in Price, *Love and Hate*, 232 (language modernized).

Chapter Twenty

Takeaways

What It All Means

The story of Jesus and Pocahontas is a story of joy and pain; of ecstasy and agony. Yet also a story of hope.

The Pocahontas story is woven into the tapestry of American history, for good and ill. Over and over Pocahontas appears in the tales of how the United States came to be; what it is; how the West was won.[1]

With an eye on global Christian mission, in this final chapter I summarize five key takeaways of the whole story. These speak directly to the global church of Jesus Christ today, illuminating issues of gospel and culture. They touch all nations and peoples in the wide earth.

After noting these takeaways, we will look finally at abiding issues of Native American policy in the United States and how these apply to the global church.

---

1. See L'Amour, *How the West Was Won*, based on the screenplay by James R. Webb. The novel begins, "The shining land lay open—ready for conquest," and speaks of the rivers that flowed through a "dangerous but unawakened land where riches awaited" (1). Louis L'Amour (1908–1988) was born in Jamestown, South Dakota. His scores of novels helped shape popular images of the American West. Among many other honors, he was awarded the Medal of Freedom by President Ronald Reagan in 1984.

FIRST TAKEAWAY: CULTURE

The story of Pocahontas is a story about culture—a clash of cultures and civilizations. It is an especially instructive example because it's far enough past that we have some distance, some perspective—yet near enough to make us uncomfortable.

From beginning to end, from creation to new creation and beyond, the Christian story is the story of culture. The significance of this is often missed. It's overlooked in our own lives, very often, and in the history of church and mission.

By *culture* I mean all the ways human beings interact with each other, with their physical environment, and with the unseen environment.

Culture is first of all physical objects and ecologies, because on these all human life rests. Every cultural artifact comes first from the earth. It is made of physical things—objects and living creatures found in the specific environments where humans live. Wood, rocks, shells, paint, glass, ants, worms, eagles, microbes, whatever.

Cultural artifacts, physical or not, are then built from the symbols and thoughts and music that arise from human engagement with such physical things.

Consider music, for example. In *The Great Animal Orchestra*, Bernie Krause describes the myriad sounds arising from creation—from the air, land, and waters. "The planet itself teems with a vigorous resonance that is as complete and expansive as it is delicately balanced. Every place, with its vast populations of plants and animals, becomes a concert hall, and everywhere a unique orchestra performs an unmatched symphony." Listen, and you will hear "the tuning of the great animal orchestra, a revelation of the acoustic harmony of the wild. . . . It is likely that the origins of every piece of music we enjoy and word we speak come, at some point, from this collective voice."[2]

Earthly culture is physical-thing dependent. This is why it varies with weather, terrain, and available food and building materials. Is there anything more cultural than food? Yet music is close behind.

We easily forget the *physicality* of culture. Say "culture" and we think of art and ideas and orchestras, or science and philosophies and customs—not dirt. But culture mostly rises from the earth.

2. Krause, *Great Animal Orchestra*, 9–10.

Physical things like hills and fruit and rocks and animals become the raw material of language, which builds up analogies and metaphors and ideas, which shape thought and stories, which grow into literature, music, dance, spirituality, and more, and thus over time arise as culture. Take away material things and the "natural" world, and culture collapses.

Culture grows like a tree; sings like a bird; rolls like thunder; uses tools like hoes and violins all made from the stuff nature provides. From the earth.

The physical, material side of culture is so omnipresent however that it disappears from view. The physical becomes invisible. Yet it never *really* disappears. Which is why it is always present in the gospel and in church and in mission, just as it is present from the first to the last page of Scripture—from "Let there be light" to "tree of life."

In our reading of Scripture the visible easily becomes invisible. We get so used to sheep, fig trees, sandals, fish, and so forth that we stop really *seeing* them. Looking for the invisible, we miss the visible. It's really a form of dualism. So we think Jesus' parables teach only *spiritual* lessons, have only heavenly meanings.

Pocahontas reminds us that Christian mission always happens within one or many cultures. So we'd better get used to it. We need to figure out how to work with culture, not against it—and within culture, seek to cooperate with the Spirit's work of bringing all things into conformity to Jesus Christ. Not to ignore culture; not to commodify; not to exploit nor dominate. But to appreciate, redeem, enjoy, enrich.

SECOND TAKEAWAY: CELEBRATION!

We can celebrate the beautiful if tragic life of Pocahontas—her courage and character; her faith and her spunky spontaneity. Her insights and her ability to speak without words. The way she turned two world's values upside down.

With her we can celebrate the love of John Rolfe and the faithfulness of Alexander Whitaker. John Smith, despite his many flaws, we may celebrate for his attempt to understand hostile native cultures, for his tenderness with Pocahontas, and for the ways he gradually changed. Socially in England he was nearly a nobody. Perhaps for that reason he was prepared to empathize with Pocahontas and seek understanding.

Smith has been vilified for his embellishments and for his violence in a violent time. Or contrariwise he has been celebrated for the wrong things—an intrepid but self-justifying explorer. Yet he was touched by Pocahontas and made better.

Above all, we may celebrate Pocahontas's faith, hazy and clouded as it perhaps was at first, and her love for Jesus, and his for her.

THIRD TAKEAWAY: LEARNING NATIVE PEOPLES

The story of Pocahontas, like the story of England and America generally, has been one-sided in its telling. Thanks to the research of recent decades we are learning more about Powhatan life and culture. Like all culture, Native American and First Nations cultures have their own mix of light and shadows. But understanding native cultures and especially their connection with the land helps us see America's story more in the round, with more truth.

Learning Native American cultures will teach us how vast and varied the North American peoples have been. Indians did not all look alike. They varied in values and views of right and wrong. Some were relatively peaceful; others more warlike. Some were nomadic or migratory; others were more settled. Some practiced agriculture; others did not. Some had better health and nutrition than others. Climate, terrain, a varying range of natural resources, and other ecological factors played roles.

Native Americans changed greatly over time as they acquired the bow and arrow, then horses (from the Spanish) and guns (from the French, English, and then white Americans). They changed through vast networks of trade across much of the continent.

Traveling far up the Missouri River in 1833–34, the German prince and adventurer Alexander Maximilian noted that the Mandan people strategically settled along the upper Missouri "became prosperous middlemen in a vast trade network that linked tribes as far away as Canada, the Pacific Coast, and the Southwest."[3] Far-flung trade networks across North America had existed for centuries.

---

3. Freedman, *Indian Winter*, 20–21. One key example: the Yellowstone River flows into the Missouri, which empties into the Mississippi, which flows to the Gulf of Mexico—part of the vast North American river system that also extends east as far as Pennsylvania.

In short, American Indians had much in common and much that distinguished them from each other. The same is true with all large cultural groupings worldwide.

This is a reality the body of Christ faces everywhere. As never before and for many reasons, the Christian church is coming to understand itself as inescapably embedded in culture—many and varied cultures. And coming to know what that means for mission and discipleship. We are beginning—only just starting, perhaps—to learn from each other as the body of Christ becomes ever more a mixed multitude from every nation and tribe and tongue and nation.

FOURTH TAKEAWAY: LAND

This is the fourth but also first takeaway. Early British explorers stood amazed at the beauty and bounty of North America's coastlands. They described them in glowing, fascinated terms—then later in more nuanced ways. But *they were never concerned about the land itself, for its own sake.* Only for their own sake. Glory, conquest, riches, exploitation, expropriation—more often than not, allegedly for God's glory.

Today we pay the price. The Jamestown settlers were unable to learn from Pocahontas and the Powhatan people how to respect and care for the land. Many English died as a result.

Worldwide, many are still dying because we do not know and respect the land. Not knowing the land and its ecology, we do not know that poisoning the land is poisoning ourselves, and especially the world's poor.

We live in the twenty-first century, not the seventeenth. But those former days are still with us—not least in the person of Pocahontas.

FIFTH TAKEAWAY: WARNING!

Pocahontas is the cautionary tale of cautionary tales. We see her impact over centuries, right to today. As history, as myth, and as an inseparable mix of the two.

She warns us, wherever in the world we live, about national myths and idolatries. All the ways we sugarcoat history and whitewash the past; conveniently sanitize the bad and sanctify or celebrate the good. The key warning for the church is to seek first the kingdom of God and be clear how that undermines ideologies of race and nation and religion and theories of politics and economics.

Pocahontas can't literally speak today. But people like Cherokee Randy Woodley can.

Woodley calls for "waking up from the American Dream." This national metanarrative, Woodley says, "accompanied by notions of equality for all, has been used to smooth over historically inconvenient truths and awkward facts of tragedy that have befallen America's indigenous peoples at the willing hands of America's settler population." He adds,

> The truth is, the country that most Americans hold so dear is mostly stolen property. Part of the purpose of the American Dream's familiar narrative is to create a "pseudo-place." The pseudo-place of social location is held in place of the real land. The social location acts as a placeholder for real land. In turn, the placeholder of social location deeply influences an American theology of the land.
>
> The American Dream is actually a false premise based on the success of relatively few people, held up as a carrot for the masses. In truth, an American Dream based on the misery of others caters to a selfish, consumer-driven mentality that values wealth and personal gain over justice and peace.

The hard truth, Woodley says, is that the United States, despite a large Christian population, "was never built on Christian morality. . . . America is a far cry from being a 'Christian nation' or even a nation built upon Christian principles."[4]

"Some American Christian historians" admit this, Woodley notes. But they insist that pious New Englanders had a different vision "focused on godly ideals." Yet Woodley rightly points out that all "three original colonies—Jamestown, Plymouth, and Massachusetts Bay—assumed by proof in their founding charters that the land they sought already belonged to the English king, regardless of whether or not it was already occupied by Native tribes. Whatever the colonists' Christian goals, they all began their work by asserting their fundamental superiority over the Native inhabitants of North America. In this way, the very foundation of America and the American Dream was built on a mentality of theft, imperialism, and supposed superiority."[5]

4. Woodley, *Shalom*, 131.
5. Ibid., 131–32.

So it continues. Our national narrative supports "an American myth of progress via an overarching strand of thought that claims America, while prone to mistakes in earlier years, has somehow self-corrected by 'allowing' civil rights for women and minorities." This is whitewash slapped on with the broad brushes of the dominant. "The American myth of progress skims over injustices that most Americans would severely critique if they were perpetuated by any other nation, that is, any nation outside the historic Euro-western colonial mentality."[6]

What right did the whites have to call the ongoing dispossession of the Indians "progress" and later celebrate "how the West was won"?

ATONEMENT? REPARATION?

The Pawnee scholar Walter Echo-Hawk takes up this theme and pushes it further, into the sphere of compensation and reparation. Citing historian Patricia Limerick's comment that the conquest of native peoples and their lands is merely "the domain of mass entertainment" and "light-hearted national escapism," Echo-Hawk asks: Why this moral myopia? And what is its ethical meaning today?

Echo-Hawk explores this question in his book *In the Light of Justice: The Rise of Human Rights in Native America and the United Nations Declaration on the Rights of Indigenous Peoples*. Using the UN Declaration on the Rights of Indigenous Peoples as his tool, Echo-Hawk dissolves the collective amnesia that places this question outside serious discourse.

The United States has "been baffled about the 'Indian problem'" ever since colonial days, notes Echo-Hawk. In response it developed a dualistic legal framework that put Indian rights in a separate category outside considerations of justice or human rights. "The language of human rights is familiar. However, Americans have not engaged in serious discourse about the human rights of American Indians." Echo-Hawk finds this "puzzling," given Americans' fundamental commitment to "justice for all."[7]

How could the United States justify the infamous Indian Removal Act of 1830 (to take one of the worst examples) that led to the Trail of Tears? The Chief Justice of the Tennessee Supreme Court put it this way: "Our claim is based on the right to coerce obedience [from Native Americans]. The claim may be denounced by the moralist. We answer, it is the law of

6. Ibid., 132.

7. Echo-Hawk, *In the Light of Justice*, 7.

the land. Without its assertion and vigorous execution, this continent never could have been inhabited by our ancestors. To abandon [this doctrine now would be] to assert that they were unjust usurpers, and that we, succeeding to their usurped authority and void claims to possess and govern the country, should in all honesty abandon it, return to Europe, and let the subdued parts again become a wilderness and hunting ground."[8]

Clearly a double standard. Americans celebrate "the equality principle" enshrined in their founding documents, but "we cannot reconcile the double-standard in our shoddy treatment of Native Americans with equality principles that [apply to] everyone else."[9]

And yet, Echo-Hawk argues, still today "We can make amends to Native America, and discourse is the first step." This means discussing reparation. Legally, "the remedial concept of *reparation* is defined as 'the act of making amends' for a wrong that has been committed. It includes any 'measure aimed at restoring a person and/or a community of a loss, harm or damage suffered consequent to an action or omission.' It is *an act of atonement* that repairs damage, heals an injury, and allows both the victim and the wrongdoer to go forward in good faith once justice has been restored and all of the injurious consequences of the wrong have been wiped clean."[10]

"At its essence," Echo-Hawk notes, "the goal of every legal system is reparation. Indeed, the moment when adequate reparations are actually granted to an injured party is the very moment when justice crystallizes; and in that moment, justice is realized."[11]

The proper term today for the cumulative impact on native peoples of "the many ignoble acts of dispossession, violence, forcible removal, systematic discrimination, destruction of culture and habitat, and enforced assimilation," notes Echo-Hawk, is *genocide*.[12]

"We have courageously made amends [to a degree] for historical wrongs committed against slaves, blacks, and other immigrant groups. There is no reason to run swiftly from appropriate acts of atonement for the

---

8. *State v. Foreman*, 16 Tenn. 256, 266 (1835), quoted in Echo-Hawk, *In the Light of Justice*, 19.

9. Echo-Hawk, *In the Light of Justice*, 19.

10. Ibid., 10, quoting from *Black's Law Dictionary* (2010), 1107, and the *Oxford English Dictionary* (emphasis added).

11. Ibid., 11. See also Harvey, *Whiteness and Morality*, chapter 4, "The Imperative of Reparations," 141–72.

12. Echo-Hawk, *In the Light of Justice*, 19.

legacy of conquest." Rather we must "confront the fact that our core values were seriously degraded by the exploitation of Native Americans."[13]

What of those who argue that "we are not responsible for the sins of our fathers"—that it is "*unfair* to ask innocent people, who personally committed no wrong, to repair harm done to Native Americans when they had no part in committing the harm, and it is *unfair* to apply today's standards to past conduct"?

Echo-Hawk's answer is that "present generations are responsible for the past, because it shapes the present. When harm from past wrongs is still seen and felt today, our complicity in perpetuating the lasting injury cannot be ignored." In fact, "Many historical abuses of Native Americans were illegal or immoral at the time they were committed, violated existing norms, or were committed at a time when equality and fundamental human rights were the order of the day for non-indigenous peoples."[14]

Echo-Hawk adds that "the lapse of time" is no "equitable defense that bars restorative justice when: (1) victims were unable to secure redress in settler courts, (2) wrongdoers unjustly enriched themselves through privilege gained by suppression or other abuses at Native American expense, or (3) past abuses created socio-economic disparities still seen today. In these instances, unjust enrichment cannot be ignored." There is no "statute of limitations" on such massive unrequited abuses.[15]

In sum, Echo-Hawk says, "It is not unfair to ask descendants to atone for the wrongs of their ancestors. What is *actually* unfair is to turn a blind eye to unjust enrichment, manifest injustice, or human suffering in Native American communities, when fairness and good conscience demand reparation and appropriate legal safeguards to protect against the repetition of continuation of the harm."[16]

Echo-Hawk does not appeal to Scripture. But we may ponder Jesus' words. When tempted to think of the US as an especially godly nation, or view it as God's new Israel or a city on a hill, we may want to pause and hear Jesus again: "This generation [will] be charged with the blood of all the prophets shed since the foundation of the world, from the blood of Abel to the blood of Zechariah, who perished between the altar and the sanctuary. Yes, I tell you, it will be charged against this generation" (Luke 11:50–51).

13. Ibid., 21.

14. Ibid., 254–55 (emphasis original).

15. Ibid., 255.

16. Ibid., 256 (emphasis original).

Jesus was speaking about Israel in his day, of course. Yet he was expressing a fundamental biblical theme. The Bible is full of the sense of generational responsibility and the need for atonement.

Can a nation learn repentance? Can God bless America, or the American church, without deep, humbling repentance?

Can we learn the difference between blessing, biblically understood, and material prosperity or successful careers?

Some see signs of a rethinking, maybe an awakening, in the United States concerning native peoples. The positive if somewhat confused images of "Indians" in movies like *The Lone Ranger* (2013, where Johnny Depp plays Tonto), may be a sign. Growing controversy over "Redskins" as the name for sports teams may be another.[17] In his discussion of the movie *Avatar,* Daniel Hawk comments that "*Avatar's* dignifying portrayal of indigenous people . . . suggests that American society is in the midst of a similar rethinking." Perhaps "America's present preoccupation with alien invasion motifs" as exemplified in *Avatar* and other films hints at some deep shift "going on in the American national psyche."[18]

Meanwhile in 2014 the City Council in Seattle, Washington, unanimously voted to designate the second Monday in October as Indigenous Peoples' Day, downplaying Columbus Day.[19]

THE UGLY MISSIONARY?

Is the Pocahontas story from beginning to end an indictment of global Christian missions? Is this the story of ugly missionaries once again exploiting native peoples?

No. In missionaries such as Alexander Whitaker we see church-state assumptions that seriously compromised the intended Christian mission in America and elsewhere. Yet Whitaker emerges as a man of stellar character, commitment, and genuine compassion. He and the majority of his Anglican colleagues did much more good than harm. William Littleton

---

17. In October 2013, students in a Philadelphia high school touched off a free-speech debate and legal case when the student newspaper said it would no longer use "the 'R' word" (Redskins, the school's mascot) in its pages. Similar debates have occurred elsewhere, and attitudes appear to be shifting. See Fields, "Philadelphia Students and School Administrators Clash Over Redskins Name."

18. Hawk, "*Avatar* in Three Dimensions," 1, 4, 8.

19. Beekman, "Native Americans cheer."

concluded his study of Whitaker, "His fame lies in the fact that he happened to be in Virginia at a given time. Perhaps that is his secret and his greatness, that he 'happened' to be serving as best he knew how in a place where less courageous souls dared not go, at a time when less committed men chose to settle amid the folds of security and draw their lines in pleasant places."[20]

The history of global Protestant missions since Jamestown is highly complex, with its lights and shadows. But on balance, the story is a positive one.

Recent research documents the huge, if often unintended, positive impact that Protestant missionaries have had over time. Extensive studies conducted by Robert Woodberry and his colleagues confirm this. As summarized in *Christianity Today,* "Areas where Protestant missionaries had a significant presence in the past are on average more economically developed today, with comparatively better health, lower infant mortality, lower corruption, greater literacy, higher educational attainment (especially for women), and more robust membership in nongovernmental associations."[21]

This is significant. But although it may be the global picture on average, it leaves many important questions unanswered. Woodberry himself points out that these results pertain only to missionaries who were not government sponsored. "Protestant clergy financed by the state, as well as Catholic missionaries prior to the 1960s, had no comparable effect in the areas where they worked," notes the *Christianity Today* report by Andrea Palpant Dilley.[22] Many factors are in play and color the results in particular cases.

Woodberry's upbeat research results on Christian missions does not give the church license to downplay the blemishes and tragedies. Yes, the United States and Canada have benefited hugely from the influence of the gospel and of Christian missionaries. But time after time the good has been compromised by the evil—particularly the four great sins highlighted in chapter nineteen.

How much greater today would be the American nations had they understood and respected native peoples and lands! To this day, neither are deeply understood. The good news calls us to a more comprehensive

20. Littleton, "Alexander Whitaker," 348.

21. Dilley, "World the Missionaries Made," 35–41.

22. Ibid., 40. Woodberry reports his research in detail in Woodberry, "Missionary Roots of Liberal Democracy."

experience of reconciliation so that the church looks more like the kingdom of God. Miroslav Volf is surely right: "There can be no redemption unless the truth about the world is told and justice is done. To treat sin as if it were not there, when in fact it is there, amounts to living as if the world were redeemed when in fact it is not. The claim to redemption has degenerated into an empty ideology, and a dangerous one at that."[23]

FINAL WORD

We can't go back; unwind the past. "What ifs" don't count now. But the future still lies mostly open. If we can't right wrongs, we can admit them, make amends and reparations where possible, and on that basis seek a new fidelity and the renewed work of the Spirit.

The burden of this book is much larger than questions of justice and reparations, important as they are. This book concerns cultures, Christian mission, and Jesus' good news. An immense range of issues is wrapped up in the story of Jesus and Pocahontas.

The largest, most central, and most pressing issue is the interplay of *gospel*, *culture*, and *land*. How gospel, culture, and land interact in the divine economy and ecology of salvation—and how God's human creatures respond.

The five takeaways above are an open door. If we learn carefully from the book of history, the Book of Nature, and above all the Word of God transcribed in the Bible and incarnate in Jesus Christ by the Spirit, we can anticipate a time of renewed gospel witness that will nourish the nations and peoples and cultures of the world as never before.

We must not forget either history or the land. This Pocahontas reminds us. Within all the complexities of her story, the most haunting words are those she spoke in her last encounter with John Smith: "Your countrymen lie much."

The church's mission today: Tell and live the truth about Jesus, the land, and God's work in history.

23. Volf, *Exclusion and Embrace*, 294.

Sources and Acknowledgements

SOURCES

Of the many sources now available on Jamestown, Pocahontas, and related topics, five proved especially useful for this project: *The True Story of Pocahontas: The Other Side of History,* by Linwood "Little Bear" Custalow and Angela L. "Silver Star" Daniel (2007), *Pocahontas, Powhatan, Opechancanough: Three Lives Changed by Jamestown,* by the Virginia anthropologist Helen C. Rountree (2005), *Pocahontas and the Powhatan Dilemma,* by Camilla Townsend (2004), *Love and Hate in Jamestown: John Smith, Pocahontas, and the Heart of a New Nation,* by David A. Price (2003), and *Jamestown Narratives: Eyewitness Accounts of the Virginia Colony—The First Decade: 1607–1617,* edited by Edward Wright Haile (1998, 2001). This last volume is a 946-page collection of original source material, much of it largely unknown or neglected for more than 200 years.

In recent years we have been learning much more about highly significant ecological factors that were critical in the period covered here. These are explored by Charles C. Mann in his books *1491: New Revelations of the Americas Before Columbus* (2005) and *1493: Uncovering the New World Columbus Created* (2011). Mann explains the "Columbian Exchange" through which earth's eastern and western hemispheres impacted each other ecologically—the unintended and largely unknown consequences of colonialism. Acknowledging such ecological factors enables us to develop a much better rounded picture of Pocahontas and her world than would have been possible twenty or thirty years ago.

Of the basic facts there is little doubt, for the history of the Jamestown settlement is well documented. There are however occasional discrepancies in dates and the interpretation of events (as noted). Most of these are minor, and I've generally accepted the dates as given in the most reliable sources.

Pocahontas's birth year is variously given as 1595, 1596, 1597, and 1598, for example. Rountree suggests 1596 as the most likely year of Pocahontas's birth, and I have used that date.

English spellings of Indian names and terms varied widely, and still do. I have generally followed the spellings as given in Rountree, due to the anthropological sensitivity of her study. In quoting seventeenth-century sources, I have usually modernized the language in order to facilitate understanding.

TERMINOLOGY

Since terms and names for things often convey stereotypes, I have sought to avoid words that Native Americans find paternalistic. Accordingly I use sparingly or not at all terms such as "Indian village" (rather than "town"), "braves," "princess," "squaw," and "Big Chief." Similarly the term "Indian maiden," which as Randy Woodley says "is the image of the romanticized Indian on steroids" who often dies a tragic death "because she could not be with her star-crossed lover." Instead I use the term "young woman."

ACKNOWLEDGEMENTS

This book had its genesis in a visit my wife Janice and I made to Colonial Williamsburg at Christmas time, 2005. Side trips to Yorktown and especially Jamestown whetted our appetite to know more. So we made a return trip to Jamestown and environs in 2013, also visiting the site of Henrico and the "falls" of the James River at Richmond. Janice has been my constant companion throughout this journey, and the book owes much to her interest, encouragement, and perceptive questions. Thank you!

The Virginia Historical Society in Richmond is a rich source of information and documents on the history of Jamestown and of Colonial Virginia generally. I especially thank John McClure, Reference Department Manager at the Virginia Historical Society Library, for valuable research assistance. Thanks also to folks at The Library of Virginia, Richmond, for their assistance in locating relevant archival materials.

The staff of the B. L. Fisher Library at Asbury Theological Seminary were ever helpful, particularly in assisting with interlibrary loans of books and journals.

Sources and Acknowledgements

Professor Randy Woodley read an early draft of the manuscript and provided detailed feedback that saved me from many embarrassing mistakes. I also received valuable insight from several folks who read and critiqued the manuscript—in particular Marvelle Vannest, Bryan Wisdom, Jerilyn Snyder Winstead, Kathy Callahan Howell, Elaine Heath, Daniel Hawk, and Jeremy Wheelock. Some of these offered very detailed feedback that helped me improve the manuscript. I happily and gratefully acknowledge their help. Thanks also to John "Ike" Owen and Michael Rynkiewich for some helpful insights at a critical time.

I also thank the members of our Tuesday night Home Fellowship for their constant interest, encouragement, and prayers: Marcia Burgess, Cathy Stonehouse, Ron and Nancy Johns, Warren and Marguerite Brude, Earle and Dottie Bowen, Skip and Darlene Elliott, and Jonathan and Irene Raymond.

Thanks also to Japanese-born Hiroko Cook, venerable widow of Chippewa Chief Wabeness White Bird, of Houghton Lake, Michigan, for several fascinating conversations in July, 2014, which deepened my understanding of and sensitivity to Native American issues. Susan Carter Payne, descendant of a Monacan Indian, kindly gave permission to use her photo of the Pocahontas statue at Jamestown—thank you!

I am thankful also to Rodney Clapp, himself an author, for his careful editing of the manuscript.

Whatever errors or misunderstandings remain in the book are of course my own responsibility, and I will correct them as readers give feedback.

Bibliography

Abrams, Ann Uhry. *The Pilgrims and Pocahontas: Rival Myths of American Origin.* Boulder, CO: Westview, 1999.

Adams, Robert M., ed. *Ben Jonson's Plays and Masques.* New York: W. W. Norton and Company, 1979.

Allen, Paula Gunn. *Pocahontas: Medicine Woman, Spy, Entrepreneur, Diplomat.* New York: HarperCollins, 2003.

Ancient Planters of Virginia. "A Brief Declaration." In *Jamestown Narratives*, edited by Edward Wright Haile, 891–911. Champlain, VA: RoundHouse, 1998.

Anderson, James S. M. *The History of the Church of England in the Colonies and Foreign Dependencies of the British Empire.* 3 vols. 2nd ed. London: Rivingtons, 1856.

Andrist, Ralph K. *The Long Death: The Last Days of the Plains Indians.* New York: Collier, 1964.

Archer, Gabriel. "A relation of the discovery of our river from James Fort into the main, made by Captain Christopher Newport, and sincerely written and observed by a gentleman of the colony" (1607). In *Jamestown Narratives*, edited by Edward Wright Haile, 101–18. Champlain, VA: RoundHouse, 1998.

Argall, Samuel. "Letter to Hawes, June 1613." In *Jamestown Narratives*, edited by Edward Wright Haile, 752–56. Champlain, VA: RoundHouse, 1998.

Bailyn, Bernard. *The Barbarous Years: The Peopling of British North America: the Conflict of Civilizations, 1600–1675.* New York: Alfred A. Knopf, 2012.

Baltzer, Charles. *Henry F. Farny.* Cincinnati: Indian Hill Historical Museum Association, 1975.

Barbour, Philip L. *Pocahontas and Her World.* Boston: Houghton Mifflin, 1970.

Bate, Jonathan. "Introduction." In *The Tempest*, by William Shakespeare, vii–xx. New York: The Modern Library, 2008.

Beekman, Daniel. "Native Americans cheer Indigenous Peoples' Day." *The Seattle Times*, October 7, 2014.

Berkofer, Robert F., Jr. *The White Man's Indian: Images of the American Indian from Columbus to the Present.* New York: Vintage, 1979.

Black, George. *Empire of Shadows: The Epic Story of Yellowstone.* New York: St. Martin's, 2012.

Black Elk, Nicholas. *Black Elk Speaks: Being the Life Story of a Holy Man of the Oglala Sioux.* As told through John G. Neihardt. Lincoln, NE: University of Nebraska Press, 2000.

BIBLIOGRAPHY

Box Office Mojo. "Pocahontas." http://www.boxofficemojo.com/movies/?id=pocahontas. htm.

Brazil, Robert Sean. "More Virginia Propaganda and a Sonnets Link." http://1609chronology .blogspot.com/2009/04/more-virginia-propaganda-strange.html.

Brown, Alexander, ed. *The Genesis of the United States*. 2 vols. Boston: Houghton, Mifflin and Co., 1890.

Brown, Dee. *Bury My Heart at Wounded Knee: An Indian History of the American West*. New York: Bantam, 1972.

Brown, Stuart E., Jr., Lorraine F. Myers, and Eileen M. Chappel. *Pocahontas' Descendants*. Berryville, VA: Pocahontas Foundation, 1985.

Burton, Lewis W. *Annals of Henrico Parish, Diocese of Virginia, and especially of St. John's Church, the Present Mother Church of the Parish, from 1611 to 1884*. Richmond, VA: Williams Printing, 1904.

Calloway, Colin C. *First Peoples: A Documentary Survey of American Indian History*. Boston, MA: Bedford/St. Martin's, 1999.

Calvin, John. *Institutes of the Christian Religion*. 2 vols. Translated by Henry Beveridge. Grand Rapids: Eerdmans, 1972, 1975.

Carroll, John M., ed. *Custer's Chief of Scouts: The Reminiscences of Charles A. Varnum*. Lincoln, NE: University of Nebraska Press, 1987.

Carter, Jimmy. *An Hour Before Daylight: Memories of a Rural Boyhood*. New York: Simon and Schuster, 2001.

Cincinnati Art Museum. *Henry F. Farny, 1847–1916*. Cincinnati: Cincinnati Art Museum, 1965.

Cleland, Charles E. *Rites of Conquest: The History and Culture of Michigan's Native Americans*. Ann Arbor, MI: University of Michigan Press, 1992.

Cooke, John Esten. "A Dream of the Cavaliers." *Harper's New Monthly Magazine* 32, 128 (January 1861) 252–54.

———. *My Lady Pocahontas*. Boston: Houghton Mifflin, 1885.

Courtney, Camerin. "Being Pocahontas." Christianity Today Online (January 17, 2006). http://www.christianitytoday.com/ct/2006/januaryweb-only/qoriankakilcher.html.

———. "Pocahontas: Girl, Interpreted." Christianity Today Online (January 17, 2006). http://www.christianitytoday.com/ct/2006/januaryweb-only/pocahontas.html.

Crane, Hart. "Powhatan's Daughter," from "The Bridge." Online: http://digital.lib.lehigh. edu/trial/pocahontas/pdf/2071.

Crosby, Alfred W., Jr. *The Columbian Exchange: Biological and Cultural Consequences of 1492*. Westport, CT: Greenwood, 1972.

———. *Ecological Imperialism: The Biological Expansion of Europe, 900–1900*. Cambridge, UK: Cambridge University Press, 1986.

Culliford, S. G. *William Strachey, 1572–1621*. Charlottesville, VA: University Press of Virginia, 1965.

Custalow, Linwood "Little Bear," and Angela L. Daniel "Silver Star." *The True Story of Pocahontas: The Other Side of History From the Sacred History of the Mattaponi Reservation People*. Golden, CO: Fulcrum, 2007.

Dale, Thomas. "Letter to Winwood, 3 June 1616." In *Jamestown Narratives*, edited by Edward Wright Haile, 878–79. Champlain, VA: RoundHouse, 1998.

Darwin, John. *Unfinished Empire: The Global Expansion of Britain*. New York: Bloomsbury, 2012.

Deans, Bob. *The River Where America Began: A Journey Along the James.* Lanham, MD: Rowman and Littlefield, 2007.

Debo, Angie. *A History of the Indians of the United States.* Norman, OK: University of Oklahoma Press, 1970, 1984.

DeLand, Charles V. *History of Jackson County, Michigan.* Logansport, IN: B. F. Bowen, 1903.

Deloria, Vine, Jr. *Custer Died for Your Sins: An Indian Manifesto.* Norman, OK: University of Oklahoma Press, 1969.

———. *Indians of the Pacific Northwest From the Coming of the White Man to the Present Day.* Golden, CO: Fulcrum, 2012.

Dilley, Andrea Palpant. "The World the Missionaries Made." *Christianity Today* 58:1 (January/February 2014) 35–41.

Dippie, Brian W. *The Vanishing American: White Attitudes and U.S. Indian Policy.* Lawrence, KS: University of Kansas Press, 1982.

Dolin, Eric Jay. *Fur, Fortune, and Empire: The Epic History of the Fur Trade in America.* New York: W. W. Norton, 2010.

Donaldson, Laura E. "Red Woman, White Dreams: Searching for Sacagawea." *Feminist Studies* 32:3 (2006) 523–33.

Drury, Thomas Wortley. *How We Got Our Prayer Book.* London: Nisbet and Co., 1955.

Echo-Hawk, Walter R. *In the Light of Justice: The Rise of Human Rights in Native America and the United Nations Declaration of the Rights of Indigenous Peoples.* Golden, CO: Fulcrum, 2013.

Eddy, Sherwood. *The Kingdom of God and the American Dream: The Religious and Secular Ideals of American History.* New York: Harper and Brothers, 1941.

Editors of Time-Life Books. *People of the Lakes.* Alexandria, VA: Time-Life, 1994.

Faery, Rebecca Blevins. *Cartographies of Desire: Captivity, Race, and Sex in the Shaping of an American Nation.* Norman, OK: University of Oklahoma Press, 1999.

Fassett, Thom White Wolf. *Giving Our Hearts Away: Native American Survival.* New York: Women's Division, General Board of Global Ministries, United Methodist Church, 2008.

Ferguson, Niall. *Civilization: The West and the Rest.* New York: Penguin, 2011.

Fields, Liz. "Philadelphia Students and School Administrators Clash Over Redskins Name." http://abcnews.go.com/US/philadelphia-students-school-administrators-clash -redskins/story?id=20913350.

Fischer, David Hackett. *Albion's Seed: Four British Folkways in America.* New York: Oxford University Press, 1989.

Freedman, Russell. *An Indian Winter: Paintings and Drawings by Karl Bodmer.* New York: Scholastic, 1994.

Fritz, Jean. *The Double Life of Pocahontas.* New York: Penguin, 1987.

Gallagher, Edward. "Epithets Bestowed on Pocahontas." http://digital.lib.lehigh.edu/trial/ pocahontas/epithets.php.

Glancy, Diane. *Stone Heart: A Novel of Sacagawea.* New York: Overlook, 2003.

Gleach, Frederic W. *Powhatan's World and Colonial Virginia: A Conflict of Cultures.* Lincoln, NE: University of Nebraska Press, 1997.

Glover, Lorri, and Daniel Blake Smith. *The Shipwreck That Saved Jamestown: The Sea Venture Castaways and the Fate of America.* New York: Henry Holt, 2008.

Goodwin, Doris Kearns. *The Bully Pulpit: Theodore Roosevelt, William Howard Taft, and the Golden Age of Journalism.* New York: Simon and Schuster, 2013.

Goodwin, Edward Lewis. *The Colonial Church in Virginia*. Milwaukee: Morehouse, 1927.

Governor and Council in Virginia. "Letter to the Virginia Company of London, 7 July 1610." In *Jamestown Narratives*, edited by Edward Wright Haile, 454–64. Champlain, VA: RoundHouse, 1998.

Gray, Robert. *A Good Speed to Virginia*. London: Felix Kingston, 1609. http://1609chronology.blogspot.com/2009/04/more-virginia-propaganda-strange.html.

Green, Ian. *The Christian's ABC: Catechisms and Catechizing in England c. 1530–1740*. New York: Oxford University Press, 1996.

Green, Rayna. "The Pocahontas Perplex: The Image of Indian Women in American Culture." *The Massachusetts Review* 27:4 (1975) 698–715.

Gristwood, Sarah. *Arbella: England's Lost Queen*. Boston: Houghton Mifflin, 2005.

Gwynne, S. C. *Empire of the Summer Moon: Quanah Parker and the Rise and Fall of the Comanches, the Most Powerful Indian Tribe in American History*. New York: Scribner, 2011.

Haile, Edward Wright, ed. *Jamestown Narratives: Eyewitness Accounts of the Virginia Colony, The First Decade: 1607–1617*. Champlain, VA: RoundHouse, 1998.

Hammond, Geordan. *John Wesley in America: Restoring Primitive Christianity*. Oxford, UK: Oxford University Press, 2014.

Hamor, Ralph. "A True Discourse of the present estate of Virginia." In *Jamestown Narratives*, edited by Edward Wright Haile, 792–856. Champlain, VA: RoundHouse, 1998.

Harrison, Peter. *The Bible, Protestantism, and the Rise of Natural Science*. Cambridge, UK: Cambridge University Press, 1998.

Harvey, Jennifer. *Whiteness and Morality: Pursuing Racial Justice through Reparations and Sovereignty*. New York: Palgrave Macmillan, 2007.

Hatch, Charles E., Jr. *The First Seventeen Years: Virginia, 1607–1624*. Baltimore, MD: Clearfield, 1994.

Hawk, L. Daniel. "*Avatar* in Three Dimensions." *Ashland Theological Journal* 42 (2010) 1–10.

———. "Indigenous Helpers and Invader Homelands." In *Joshua and Judges*, edited by Athalya Brenner and Gale A. Yee, 109–22. Texts@Contexts. Minneapolis: Fortress, 2013.

Hefling, Charles C., and Cynthia L. Shattuck. *Oxford Guide to the Book of Common Prayer*. New York: Oxford University Press, 2006.

"Henricus Historical Park." http://www.henricus.org/history/james-river.asp.

Honour, Hugh. *The New Golden Land: European Images of America from the Discoveries to the Present Time*. New York: Pantheon, 1975.

Horn, James. *A Land as God Made It: Jamestown and the Birth of America*. New York: Basic, 2005.

Howard, Harold P. *Sacajawea*. Norman, OK: University of Oklahoma Press, 1971.

Huetteman, Emmarie. "Lawmakers Press N.F.L. on Name of Redskins." *New York Times*, February 10, 2014.

———. "Senator Urges Redskins Change." *New York Times*, May 1, 2014.

Hulme, Peter. "Polytropic Man: Tropes of Sexuality and Mobility in Early Colonial Discourse." In *Europe and Its Others*, edited by Francis Barker, Peter Hulme, Margaret Iversen, and Diana Loxley, vol. 2, 17–32. 2 vols. Essex, UK: University of Essex Press, 1985.

Jahoda, Gloria. *The Trail of Tears: The Story of the American Indian Removals 1813–1855*. New York: Wing, 1975.

Janetski, Joel C. *Indians in Yellowstone National Park*. Rev. ed. Salt Lake City: University of Utah Press, 2002.

Jefferson, Thomas. *Notes on the State of Virginia* (1787). Edited by William Peden. Chapel Hill, NC: University of North Carolina Press, 1995.

Jenkins, William Warren. "Three Centuries in the Development of the Pocahontas Story in American Literature, 1608–1908." PhD diss. University of Tennessee, 1977.

Katzenstein, Josh. "Time to sideline Washington's race-based team name?" *Detroit News*, Septempter 21, 2013.

Kelso, William M. *Jamestown: The Buried Truth*. Charlottesville, VA: University of Virginia Press, 2006.

King, C. Richard, and Charles Fruehling Springwood, eds. *Team Spirits: The Native American Mascots Controversy*. Lincoln, NE: University of Nebraska Press, 2001.

Kingsbury, Susan Myra, ed. *The Records of The Virginia Company of London*. Vols. 1, 3. Washington, DC: United States Government Printing Office, 1933.

Kolodny, Annette. *The Lay of the Land: Metaphor as Experience and History in American Life and Letters*. Chapel Hill, NC: University of North Carolina Press, 1975.

Krause, Bernie. *The Great Animal Orchestra: Finding the Origins of Music in the World's Wild Places*. New York: Little, Brown, 2012.

Kukla, Jon. *A Wilderness So Immense: The Louisiana Purchase and the Destiny of America*. New York: Anchor, 2003.

Kupperman, Karen Ordahl. *The Jamestown Project*. Cambridge, MA: Belknap Press of Harvard University Press, 2007.

L'Amour, Louis. *How the West Was Won*. New York: Bantam, 1963.

Lange, Karen E. *1607: A New Look at Jamestown*. Washington, DC: National Geographic, 2007.

Lawson, Marie. *Pocahontas and Captain John Smith: The Story of the Virginia Colony*. New York: Random House, 1950.

LeBeau, Patrick Russell. *Rethinking Michigan Indian History*. East Lansing, MI: Michigan State University Press, 2005.

Lemay, Leo. *Did Pocahontas Save Captain John Smith?* Athens, GA: University of Georgia Press, 1992.

Levine, Stuart, and Nancy Oestreich Lurie, eds. *The American Indian Today*. Baltimore: Penguin, 1968.

Lewis, Susan K. "Pocahontas Revealed: Images of a Legend." http://www.pbs.org/wgbh/nova/pocahontas/lege-nf.html.

Limerick, Patricia N. *The Legacy of Conquest: The Unbroken Past of the American West*. New York: W. W. Norton, 1987.

Limon, Jerzy. *The Masque of Stuart Culture*. Newark, NJ: University of Delaware Press, 1990.

Lindley, David, ed. *The Court Masque*. Manchester, UK: Manchester University Press, 1984.

Little, Bryan. *The Story of Bristol: From the Middle Ages to Today*. Bristol, UK: Longdunn, 1991.

Littleton, William H. "Alexander Whitaker (1585–1617) 'The Apostle of Virginia.'" *Historical Magazine*, Protestant Episcopal Church 29 (1960) 325–48.

Lyytinen, Maria. "The Pocahontas Myth and Its Deconstruction in Monique Mojica's Play Princess Pocahontas and the Blue Spots." In *Native American Performance and Representation,* edited by S. E. Wilmer, 78–94. Tucson, AZ: University of Arizona Press, 2011.

Mancall, Peter C. *Hakluyt's Promise: An Elizabethan's Obsession for an English America.* New Haven, CT: Yale University Press, 2007.

Mann, Charles C. "America, Found & Lost." *National Geographic* 211:5 (May 2007) 32–53.

———. *1491: New Revelations of the Americas Before Columbus.* New York: Alfred A. Knopf, 2005.

———. *1493: Uncovering the New World Columbus Created.* New York: Alfred A. Knopf, 2011.

Marshall, John. *The Life of George Washington.* Vol. 1, 1804. Boston: Elibron Classics, 2001.

McCartney, Martha. "Thomas Savage." *Encyclopedia Virginia.* http://www. encyclopediavirginia.org/Savage_Thomas_ca_1595-before_September_1633#start_ entry.

McClintock, Anne. *Imperial Leather: Race, Gender and Sexuality in the Colonial Context.* New York: Routledge, 1995.

McKenzie, Robert Tracy. *The First Thanksgiving: What the Real Story Tells Us About Loving God and Learning from History.* Downers Grove, IL: InterVarsity, 2013.

McLuhan, T. C., comp. *Touch the Earth: A Self-Portrait of Indian Existence.* New York: Promontory, 1971.

Meagher, John C. *Method and Meaning in Jonson's Masques.* Notre Dame, IN: University of Notre Dame Press, 1966.

Miller, David Humphreys. *Custer's Fall: The Native American Side of the Story.* New York: Meridian, 1992.

Miller, Perry. *Errand into the Wilderness.* New York: Harper Torchbooks, 1964.

Moorehead, Alan. *The Fatal Impact: The Invasion of the South Pacific, 1767–1840.* New York: Harper and Row, 1987.

Morison, Samuel Eliot. *The Oxford History of the American People.* New York: Oxford University Press, 1965.

Morris, Edmund. *The Rise of Theodore Roosevelt.* New York: Coward, McCann and Geoghegan, 1979.

Nichols, David A. *Lincoln and the Indians: Civil War Policy and Politics.* St. Paul: Minnesota Historical Society, 2012.

Niebuhr, Gustav. *Lincoln's Bishop: A President, a Priest, and the Fate of 300 Dakota Sioux Warriors.* New York: HarperOne, 2014.

Niebuhr, Reinhold. *The Irony of American History.* Chicago: University of Chicago Press, 2008.

Nobles, Gregory H. *American Frontiers: Cultural Encounters and Continental Conquest.* New York: Hill and Wang, 1997.

Oehler, C. M. *The Great Sioux Uprising.* New York: Da Capo, 1997.

Olmstead, Earl P. *David Zeisberger: A Life Among the Indians.* Kent, OH: Kent State University Press, 1997.

Orgel, Stephen. *Ben Jonson: The Complete Masques.* New Haven, CT: Yale University Press, 1969.

Packer, J. I., and Gary A. Parrett. *Grounded in the Gospel: Building Believers the Old-Fashioned Way.* Grand Rapids: Baker, 2010.

Pennington, Edgar Legare. *The Church of England in Colonial Virginia*. Story and Pageant Series 55. Hartford, CT: Church Missions, 1937.

Percy, George. "A Relation." In *Jamestown Narratives*, edited by Edward Wright Haile, 497–519. Champlain, VA: RoundHouse, 1998.

"Pocahontas Descendant Genealogy Resource CD." http://GenealogyCDs.com.

Porter, Harry Culverwell. "Alexander Whitaker: Cambridge Apostle to Virginia." *William and Mary Quarterly*. Third Series. 14:3 (July, 1957) 317–43.

Price, David A. *Love and Hate in Jamestown: John Smith, Pocahontas, and the Heart of a New Nation*. New York: Alfred A. Knopf, 2003.

Purchas, Samuel. *Purchas, His Pilgrimes*. Glasgow, UK: 1906.

Rasmussen, William M. S., and Robert S. Tilton. *Pocahontas: Her Life and Legend*. Richmond, VA: Virginia Historical Society, 1994.

"REV Richard Buck." http://kubuildingtech.org/familytree/PS02_274.HTML.

Richardson, Don. *Peace Child: An Unforgettable Story of Primitive Jungle Treachery in the 20th Century*. 4th ed. Ventura, CA: Regal, 2005.

Robertson, Karen. "Pocahontas at the Masque." *Signs: Journal of Women in Culture and Society* 21:3 (1996) 551–83.

Rolfe, John. "A True Relation of the State of Virginia." In *Jamestown Narratives*, edited by Edward Wright Haile, 865–77. Champlain, VA: RoundHouse, 1998.

Roosevelt, Theodore. *Memories of the American Frontier*. N.p.: Westvaco, 1977.

Rountree, Helen C. "Pocahontas: The Hostage Who Became Famous." In Theda Perdue, ed., *Sifters: Native American Women's Lives*, 14–28. New York: Oxford University Press, 2001.

———. *Pocahontas, Powhatan, Opechancanough: Three Indian Lives Changed by Jamestown*. Charlottesville, VA: University of Virginia Press, 2005.

———. *The Powhatan Indians of Virginia: Their Traditional Culture*. Norman, OK: University of Oklahoma Press, 1989.

Rountree, Helen C., and E. Randolph Turner III. *Before and After Jamestown: Virginia's Powhatans and Their Predecessors*. Gainesville, FL: University Press of Florida, 2002.

Rowlands, Alison. "The Conditions of Life for the Masses." In *Early Modern Europe: An Oxford History*, edited by Euan Cameron, 31–62. Oxford, UK: Oxford University Press, 1999.

Rowlett, Lori. "Disney's Pocahontas and Joshua's Rahab in Postcolonial Perspective." In *Culture, Entertainment and the Bible*, edited by George Aichele, 66–75. *Journal for the Study of the Old Testament* Supplement Series 309. Sheffield, UK: Sheffield Academic, 2000.

Rynkiewich, Michael. "Mission in an Age of Imperialism." Unpublished manuscript, January, 2014.

Scarboro, D. Dewey. *The Establisher: The Story of Sir Thomas Dale*. Fayetteville, NC: Old Mountain, 2005.

Schlissel, Lillian. *Women's Diaries of the Westward Journey*. New York: Schocken, 1984.

Shakespeare, William. *The Tempest*. Edited by Jonathan Bate and Eric Rasmussen; introduction by Jonathan Bate. New York: The Modern Library, 2008.

Smith, John. "A True Relation of such occurrences and accidents of note as hath hap'ned in Virginia since the first planting of that colony which is now resident in the south part thereof, till the last return from thence" (1608). In *Jamestown Narratives*, edited by Edward Wright Haile, 142–82. Champlain, VA: RoundHouse, 1998.

———. "The General History of Virginia, New England, and the Summer Isles: The Fourth Book (selections)." In *Jamestown Narratives*, edited by Edward Wright Haile, 857–64. Champlain, VA: RoundHouse, 1998.

———. "The General History: The Third Book—The proceedings and accidents of the English colony in Virginia, extracted from the authors following by William Simons, Doctor of Divinity" (1624). In *Jamestown Narratives*, edited by Edward Wright Haile, 215–347. Champlain, VA: RoundHouse, 1998.

Snyder, Howard A. *Concept and Commitment: A History of Spring Arbor University*. Spring Arbor, MI: Spring Arbor University, 2008.

———. *"Live While you Preach": The Autobiography of Methodist Revivalist and Abolitionist John Wesley Redfield (1810–1863)*. Pietist and Wesleyan Series 17. Lanham, MD: Scarecrow, 2006.

———. *Models of the Kingdom*. Nashville: Abingdon, 1991; Eugene, OR: Wipf and Stock, 2001.

———. *Populist Saints: B. T. and Ellen Roberts and the First Free Methodists*. Grand Rapids: Eerdmans, 2006.

———. *Signs of the Spirit: How God Reshapes the Church*. Grand Rapids: Zondervan, 1989.

Snyder, Howard A., with Joel Scandrett. *Salvation Means Creation Healed: The Ecology of Sin and Grace: Overcoming the Divorce between Earth and Heaven*. Eugene, OR: Cascade, 2011.

Sparks, Jared. *Lives of Alexander Wilson and Captain John Smith*. Boston: Hilliard, Gray, 1839.

Spelman, Henry. "Relation of Virginia, 1609." In *Jamestown Narratives*, edited by Edward Wright Haile, 481–95. Champlain, VA: RoundHouse, 1998.

Steele, Ian K., and Nancy L. Rhoden, eds. *The Human Tradition in Colonial America*. Wilmington, DE: Scholarly Resources, 1999.

Stevens, Laura M. *The Poor Indians: British Missionaries, Native Americans, and Colonial Sensibility*. Philadelphia: University or Pennsylvania Press, 2004.

Strachey, William. "A True Reportory of the wrack and redemption of Sir Thomas Gates." In *Jamestown Narratives*, edited by Edward Wright Haile, 381–43. Champlain, VA: RoundHouse, 1998.

———. "The History of Travel into Virginia Britannia." In *Jamestown Narratives*, edited by Edward Wright Haile, 563–689. Champlain, VA: RoundHouse, 1998.

Symonds, William. "A Sermon Preached at White-Chappel, in the Presence of Many Honourable and Worshipfull, the Adventurers and Planters of Virginia. 25 April, 1609." https://docs.google.com/a/wipfandstock.com/file/d/0B-5-JeCa2Z7heDA2VzlyV3hzUzg/edit.

Thomasma, Kenneth. *The Truth about Sacajawea*. Jackson, WY: Grandview, 1997.

Thrush, Coll. *Native Seattle: Histories from the Crossing-Over Place*. Seattle: University of Washington Press, 2007.

Tilton, Robert S. *Pocahontas: The Evolution of an American Narrative*. New York: Cambridge University Press, 1994.

Tougas, Shelley. *Little Rock Girl 1957: How a Photograph Changed the Fight for Integration*. North Mankato, MN: Compass Point, 2012.

Townsend, Camilla. *Pocahontas and the Powhatan Dilemma*. New York: Hill and Wang, 2004.

BIBLIOGRAPHY

Tudor, W. E. *The Early History of Roscommon County*. Roscommon, MI: W. E. Tudor, 2011.

Twiss, Richard. *One Church, Many Tribes*. Ventura, CA: Regal, 2000.

Van de Water, Frederic F. *Glory-Hunter: A Life of General Custer*. Lincoln, NE: University of Nebraska Press, 1934, 1988.

Vaughan, Alden T. *American Genesis: Captain John Smith and the Founding of Virginia*. New York: HarperCollins, 1975.

Volf, Miroslav. *Exclusion and Embrace: A Theological Exploration of Identity, Otherness, and Reconciliation*. Nashville: Abingdon, 1996.

Wachutka, Genevieve. "Myth Making: Appropriation of Pocahontas in Hart Crane's The Bridge." http://digital.lib.lehigh.edu/trial/pocahontas/essays.php?id=10.

Wallace, Anthony F. C. *The Long, Bitter Trail: Andrew Jackson and the Indians*. New York: Hill and Wang, 1993.

Warrior, Robert. "Canaanites, Cowboys, and Indians." *Christianity and Crisis* 49 (September 11, 1989) 261–65. Online: https://www.google.com/?gws_rd=ssl#q=warrior+canaanites+cowboys.

"*Washington Post* Demands Change: Redskin Name 'Racial Slur.'" http://www.breitbart.com/sports/2013/09/14/post-redskins/.

Watson, Alan. *Jamestown: The Voyage of English*. London: Artesian, 2007.

Weatherford, Jack. *Indian Givers: How the Indians of the Americas Transformed the World*. New York: Fawcett Columbine, 1988.

———. *Native Roots: How the Indians Enriched America*. New York: Fawcett, 1991.

Weems, John Edward. *Death Song: The Last of the Indian Wars*. New York: Indian Head, 1976.

Wert, Jeffrey D. *Custer: The Controversial Life of George Armstrong Custer*. New York: Simon and Schuster, 1996.

West, Thomas. "A Short Relation." In *Jamestown Narratives*, edited by Edward Wright Haile, 527–32. Champlain, VA: RoundHouse, 1998.

Whipple, Henry Benjamin. *Lights and Shadows of a Long Episcopate*. New York: Macmillan, 1902.

Whitaker, Alexander. *Good News from Virginia*. In *Jamestown Narratives*, edited by Edward Wright Haile, 697–745. Champlain, VA: RoundHouse, 1998.

———. Letter to William Crashaw, August 9, 1911. Personal Papers, G. D. Collection, 1824–1889, Accession 41008, Misc. Reel 5314, Frames 80–81. Archives, The Library of Virginia, Richmond, Virginia.

———. Will, 1617. Accession 37568, Personal Papers Collection, The Library of Virginia, Richmond, Virginia.

Whitaker, William. "The Mediator of the Covenant Described in His Person, Nature, and Offices." http://www.apuritansmind.com/the-christian-walk/christ-the-mediator-by-dr-william-whitaker/.

Wildman, Terry M. *Sign Language: A Look at the Historic and Prophetic Landscape of America*. Maricopa, AZ: Great Thunder, 2011.

Wilson, James. *The Earth Shall Weep: A History of Native America*. New York: Grove, 1998.

Winchester, Simon. *The Men Who United the States: America's Explorers, Inventors, Eccentrics, and Mavericks, and the Creation of One Nation, Indivisible*. New York: HarperCollins, 2013.

BIBLIOGRAPHY

Wingfield, Edward Maria. "A Discourse of Virginia per Edward Maria Wingfield" (1608). In *Jamestown Narratives*, edited by Edward Wright Haile, 183–201. Champlain, VA: RoundHouse, 1998.

Woodard, Colin. *American Nations: A History of the Eleven Rival Regional Cultures of North America*. New York: Penguin, 2011.

Woodberry, Robert D. "The Missionary Roots of Liberal Democracy." *American Political Science Review* 106:2 (May 2012) 244–74.

Woodley, Randy S. *Shalom and the Community of Creation: An Indigenous Vision*. Grand Rapids: Eerdmans, 2012.

Woodward, Grace Steele. *Pocahontas*. The Civilization of the American Indian 93. Norman, OK: University of Oklahoma Press, 1969.

Woodward, Hobson. *A Brave Vessel: The True Tale of the Castaways Who Rescued Jamestown*. New York: Penguin, 2009.

Woolley, Benjamin. *Savage Kingdom: The True Story of Jamestown, 1607, and the Settlement of America*. New York: HarperCollins, 2007.

Wright, Louis B. *Religion and Empire: The Alliance between Piety and Commerce in English Expansion 1558–1625*. New York: Octagon, 1965.

Wright, Louis B., ed. *The Elizabethans' America: A Collection of Early Reports by Englishmen on the New World*. Cambridge, MA: Harvard University Press, 1966.

Yardley, J. H. R. *Before the Mayflower*. New York: Doubleday, Doran & Co., 1931.

Yong, Amos, and Barbara Brown Zikmund, eds. *Remembering Jamestown: Hard Questions about Christian Mission*. Eugene, OR: Pickwick, 2010.

Young, Philip. "The Mother of Us All: Pocahontas Reconsidered." *Kenyon Review* 24.3 (1962). 391–415. Republished in *Portraits of American Women: From Settlement to the Present*, edited by G. J. Barker-Benfield and Catherine Clinton, 13–33. New York: St. Martin's, 1991.

General Index

Abraham, Hebrew patriarch, 95,
  144–46
  call of, 146
Abrahamic covenant, 95, 144–45
Abrams, Ann Uhry, 89
Africa, 160, 183
  slaves from, 210, 214
African Americans, ix
Africans, ix
agriculture, 160, 220
  ecology of, 5
  Powhatan, 5, 36
  Virginia colonists', 80
  See also tobacco
Algonquin (Algonkian), 9
aliens, 148, 226
  as movie theme, 226
allegory, 122
America, 116
  as exotic, 159
  as virgin, 159, 215
  democracy in, 116
  God's blessing, 226
  significance of name, 209
  See also Central America; North
    America; South America; United
    States of America
American Dream, 155, 222–23
  and imperialism, 222
  as national metanarrative, 222–23
  elitist, 222
  waking from, 222
American Empire, xvii
American Revolution, 8

Americans, as divinely chosen race or
  people, 164, 199, 212
  as new race, 199
Amonute (Pocahontas), 3, 96, 103
"ancient planters" (earliest Virginia
  settlers), 80, 152, 147
Anderson, James, 75
Andrews, Lancelot, 100
Andrist, Ralph, 193, 194–96
angels, 164, 201–6
Anglican Church, xviii, 137–40,
  142–50
  clergy, 142–44, 226
  See also Church of England
Anne of Denmark, Queen of England,
  95, 119, 120, 122, 126, 167
Apaches, 198
Apostles' Creed, 100, 102, 104, 210
Appalachian Mountains, 71, 187, 212
Appomattocks, 15
Archer, Gabriel, 13–15
archetypes, 150, 181
Argall, Samuel, 52, 59–62, 72–75, 116,
  117, 132, 134
Ariel (character in *The Tempest*), 167
Arikara, 12
Ashland Theological Seminary, xvii
Assiniboin, 12
Atlantic coast, 71, 213–14
Atlantic Ocean, 52, 132, 146, 188, 197
atonement, 164, 210–11, 223–26
  and reparation, 223–26
  Pocahontas's death as, 164
Austria, 19
Avatar (movie), 177–78, 226